*Best wes
Pauline Hayton
March 6, 2019
Marco Island,*

Still Pedaling

by
Pauline Hayton

Still Pedaling

Copyright © 2015 by Pauline Hayton

First edition 2015
All rights reserved
ISBN: 978-0-9835863-6-4

No part of this book may be reproduced or transmitted in any form or by any means, graphic, electronic, or mechanical, including photocopying, recording, taping, or by any information storage retrieval system, without the written consent of the publisher.

For information address:
Pauline Hayton
3446 13th Ave S.W.
Naples, FL 34117 USA

Dedicated to people who are healing hurts and striving to find purpose in life.

Books by Pauline Hayton:

A Corporal's War
Naga Queen
Myanmar: In My Father's Footsteps
Chasing Brenda
If You Love Me, Kill Me
Extreme Delight and Other Stories
The Unfriendly Bee

Royalties from the sales of my books go to support remote Mount Kisha English School, Magulong Village, Manipur, India.

Praise for *Still Pedaling*

Once again Pauline Hayton has penned an amazing tale. In fact, she is quickly becoming one of my favorite authors.

In *Still Pedaling,* Hayton takes the reader on a journey which encompasses the entirety of her life. It is a brutally open and honest look at her – from childhood until the almost-present day. And having finished the book, I find myself wishing that I had lived near her because she is an amazing woman with an unbreakable spirit and a gargantuan-sized zest for life. I think the two of us would have been fast friends…

Yes, *Still Pedaling* is an autobiography – yet, it reads as easily as one's favorite fictional novel.

To say that she's a fighter who has overcome the odds and adversities of her life is an understatement. She is, without a doubt, a shining beacon of hope to all – whether they have struggled with the same, or similar, challenges she has faced or not. And somehow, through it all, Hayton always managed to take time to help others – to make a difference in their lives. I'm certain that those whose lives she's affected would readily agree that she's an amazing woman…

In summary, *Still Pedaling* is a five-star 'must read' book. A true 'feel good' reminder that life is what you make of it – no matter what your personal situation.— *Charline Ratcliff, Author, The Curse of Nefertiti*

Grit, gusto and spiritual grace animate a vibrant memoir

It's not often that one encounters an autobiography written by a non-celebrity that has the likelihood of reaching a wide audience, but Pauline Hayton has written such a book, revealing a life lived with immense challenges, plenty of setbacks, risky decisions and an evolution of goals and values.

Still Pedaling is Pauline's sixth book. Its effectiveness comes from the author's brutal honesty about embarrassing episodes and ailments; her considerable skills in selection, organization and style;

and her fully realized presence as a vivid, imperfect, unsinkable personality. Readers can put the variety of her experiences and the ways in which she created and maximized her opportunities in life to their own healing use. — *Phil Jason, Ph.D., United States Naval Academy professor emeritus of English, is a poet, critic and freelance writer with 20 books to his credit, including several studies of war literature and a creative writing text.*

Still Pedaling

Life is like riding a bicycle. You must learn to ride your own bicycle because no one else can do it for you. At first you wobble, fall off, get back on and wobble again, until, like magic, you get the hang of it. Once you learn how to ride, you've learned for life.

Your bike may come with an uncomfortable seat. Don't let that spoil your fun. You need to do more than complain about it, or feel angry or sad or indifferent. You need to change your seat to one that's comfortable to get maximum enjoyment during your ride. At times, the pedaling may be hard, especially when you're going uphill on a hot, muggy day with sweat stinging your eyes. But when you reach the brow of the hill, it's free-wheeling all the way down, with a welcome, cooling wind blowing in your hair and face. Just be alert and keep your hand on the brake in case something unexpected occurs. It usually does somewhere along the way when you're not paying attention.

Your bike may get a puncture, an event that halts your progress until the puncture is fixed. At other times, you may skid on a patch of gravel and fall in the dirt with the accompanying cuts and bruises, dirtied clothes and maybe even embarrassment. Cry if you need to, then pick yourself up, dust yourself down, clean your wounds with a spit-covered handkerchief, and get back on that darned bike. The road stretches before you, inviting, yet daunting, because it looks too far to the nearest town, if you can see a town. Just keep pedaling.

Remember, life is like riding a bicycle; you have to keep pedaling to arrive somewhere, and if you stop pedaling, you'll lose your balance and fall off.

ONE

I was a monster as a child. I have it on good authority from relatives who knew me at that time. I doubt I was born a monster, me with my sparkling blue eyes and an immediate sweet smile. My father doted on me, probably making up for missing my older sister Joan growing up. When he returned from four years in India and Burma during WWII, he had a lot of catching up to do, reacquainting himself with my mother and my sister. I was born approximately twelve months after his troop ship docked in Liverpool. Relatives tell me I was such a pain in the neck as a child, people heaved a sigh of relief when my parents took me home after an afternoon's visit. I wasn't quiet, and I freely spoke my mind, even as a young child. If someone bought me a present and I didn't like it, I'd say so. Looking back on that now, I blush with embarrassment at my big mouth.

My working-class parents lived in an industrial town in northeast England, in a street of grimy two-up and two-down row houses devoid of bathrooms. Toilets were outside, at the end of the small, paved yard, separated from our neighbors by a six-foot-high brick wall. We had a bath once a week, whether we needed one or not. Dad took the aluminum bath down from the nail where it hung on the yard wall and brought it into the kitchen. Mum filled it with water from the gas geyser—our only source of hot water, unless a pan of water was heated on the stove. We normally performed daily ablutions and hair washing at the kitchen sink or, alternately, we expertly washed our whole bodies from a small dish of warm water, starting at the head and working our way down to (in my case) dirty knees and feet.

Apart from our weekly bath at home, my friends and I would often walk to the slipper baths, a mile away in the town center. Our group, usually between five and eight of us, paid a few pennies on arrival. The boys went one way, and we went the other into the female section. The fully tiled cubicles contained a huge white tub with claw feet. We could sit in them with water up to our chins. The attendants kept them spotless and the copper faucets and pipes gleamed under the lights. We sat two or three to a tub. One of us would bring bubble bath and sponges. Laughing and screaming with delight, we tossed the sponges back and forth over the partition wall to our friends on the other side, until our allotted time was up. Much more fun than having a bath at home.

The view from our living room window and front door was of a twelve-foot high corrugated iron fence topped with barbed wire that surrounded Cleveland Bridge Engineering Works. All other thirty-two houses on the street had the same view.

I have fond memories of growing up in Thorrold Terrace. Everyone knew everyone. We kids played games together in the street. Both adults and children, skipped for hours, taking turns jumping rope.

Pauline with Joan and Snowy the cat in Thorrold Terrace

We played alleys

(marbles) in the gutter and searched for spiders under window ledges to put in jam-jars. I picked up a spider by its leg one day. The leg came away from the rest of the spider which ran up my arm. I've been scared of spiders ever since.

It wasn't only the children who played together, the adults did too. Mr. Blake, who lived with his family in Thorrold Terrace, was a valuable asset to the residents because he owned an old tour bus. We held Beetle drives and pork pie and pea suppers in our homes to raise money for the residents' annual outing to the seaside in Mr. Blake's coach. Beetle was a dice game. The number you threw on the dice allowed you to add to a drawing of a beetle. The first person to complete the beetle won the game.

In 1953, we were the only people in the street to have a television set. Learning to play the piano and piano practice was never an issue because the piano was jettisoned to make way for television viewing. The day of Queen Elizabeth II's coronation, our tiny living room was jam-packed with half the street avidly watching the coronation on our black and white, twelve-inch-screen television.

Much of life was lived outside our tiny homes. People sat on kitchen chairs on the sidewalk outside their front doors, breast-feeding, knitting, squeezing boils, perming hair and shelling peas while gossiping with passers-by. Monday was laundry day. By the time clothes and bedding were dry, they would be covered in sooty spots from industrial pollution and coal fires.

The coalman didn't deliver coal on laundry days, but when he did bring his horse and cart down the back alley, I skipped and jumped with excitement, eager for his gentle Shire horse to reach my house.

I'd shout, "Mum, I need a crust! I need a crust!"

She would pick up a couple along with her purse to pay the coalman.

As the coalman threw a sack or two of coal into the coalhouse, I held out my hand, palm upward, offering the towering Clydesdale a crust of bread. I loved the feel of his soft velvety lips brushing my skin as he took the offered crust.

In the evenings, we occasionally heard drunks returning home, slurring surly threats to spouses or singing their heads off or laughing raucously as they passed our living room window. Sometimes they argued loudly enough for my dad to go out and chase them on their way. One night, a Scottish woman, returning home from a night out with her husband, had an epileptic fit on our doorstep. As much as my parents tried to protect me from the sight by pushing me indoors, I stood and watched with a placid curiosity. So that's what having a fit looked like. Another day, incensed by her fourteen-year-old son's insolence toward her, our neighbor, Mrs. H. chased him down the street in her underwear, corsets and knickers revealed for the world to see. Brandishing a hairbrush, she shouted, "Come here, you little bastard! I'm going to beat your brains out!"

We were used to her sweet language, but running around outside in her underwear was a first.

I always felt my mother wasn't happy being cast back into the role of housewife and mother after her stint working in the Malleable Steelworks during the war. She was torn by her need for more than domestic bliss and society's expectation that she was exactly where she belonged. This showed itself in various ways.

When I was four years old and crying in the back alley where I had been playing sword fights with a young neighbor boy, Mother hurried out of the house, grabbed my arm, and shook me hard. "What's the matter now?"

"Robby stuck me in the eye with his sword!" I wailed.

She dragged me to Robby's house to tell his mother what he had done. Indignant that her son had blackened the good family name, Robby's mother proceeded to give him a thrashing to prove to my mother that she was a good parent who kept her children in check.

Contrite that her anger had caused the poor lad's beating, Mum reached out to still Robby's mother's arm. "Stop! Please stop. It was an accident. He didn't mean to hurt her."

Then she promptly dragged me off to the eye infirmary where my eyeball was stitched.

She wasn't always so impatient with me. She was also caring and creative, such as the time she made me a fancy dress costume. Off we went to the party with me dressed as a salad made from green crepe paper, complete with crepe paper sliced boiled egg, tomato, and spring onion. So here were the two sides of mother, clever, creative, and caring as a loving mother should be, but beneath all that was her repressed dissatisfaction and later, her repressed grief.

By today's standards, Thorrold Terrace could be considered a slum. It didn't feel that way, even when, at high tide, the drains backed up and stinky sewage bubbled out onto the street. Thankfully, our high front doorstep avoided the disaster of bobbing turds flooding the house, such as happened to low-step residents who unwittingly opened their doors, unaware of the danger lurking outside. As soon as possible after such an event, the air filled with the clinking of aluminum buckets as the women threw water and bleach over the mess to swill it away. Next came the rhythmic scratching sounds of numerous yard-brush bristles removing the filth from the cobbled road and concrete sidewalk, to make it safe for kids to play again.

Apart from the bobbing turds, most working-class people, in the north of England, lived in similar housing. Every week, housewives washed their windows, scrubbed their doorsteps, and swilled dirt from the footpaths outside their homes. We didn't feel deprived or particularly poor. Dad owned a cobbler's last and repaired our shoes. He made a good job of being the family cobbler. I received new clothes for Easter and other holidays. I had plenty to eat. We had neighbors, lots of friends, and extended family around us. If someone was sick, a neighbor cooked them a meal, sat with them, or called the doctor. If a family was hungry because the breadwinner had gambled or drank away his wages, someone always had potatoes, eggs, bread, milk, and tea to spare, even during rationing, which did not end until 1954.

When I was four years old, we started taking vacations at Robin Hood's Bay, a small North Yorkshire fishing village that clung to the side of steep cliffs. We rented one of the quaint cottages, with red pan-tile roofs. Built in the 1800s, these cottages sat at the bottom of the steep bank, along winding, narrow lanes, suitable only for foot traffic. Usually, one of Mum's sisters, Aunt Minnie and her family, joined us. We arrived in a steam train on a railway line that no longer exists. Colorful tubs and hanging baskets, overflowing with fuchsias, lobelia, pansies, alyssum, and begonias, decorated the station. The air reverberated with the humming of bees orgasmic among the nectar rich flowers.

Once settled into our cottage, we played cricket on the beach. I learned to ride horses by spending all my money on horse rides up and down the beach. At low tide, we spent hours on the seaweed-covered rock scars that stretched out to sea, sticking fingers in rock pools, playing with tiny fish and sea anemones. With long, hooked poles, the adults poked underneath the rock scars pulling out crabs and lobsters for the pot. Not to be outdone, we children picked winkles (sea snails) off the rocks, filling buckets with the sea snails to boil for a tasty treat. Years later, my daughter Jackie, and in turn her children, experienced the same delight that I found puttering around on the rocks. Now I live in America, one of my must-dos when in England is a visit to Robin Hood's Bay. It's possibly my most favorite place in the whole world.

Mum and Dad occasionally took Joan and me on weekend camping trips to The Lake District in Dad's motorcycle and sidecar. One time we got rained out of the campsite. In lashing rain, Mum perched behind Dad on the one-hundred-mile ride home. Joan and I stayed cozy inside the sidecar. At journey's end, Dad drove as carefully as he could along the street, but still caused a wake in the flood water. The filthy mess gushed over our neighbors' low steps and leaked into their homes. You can guess the neighbors had a few sharp words to say about that.

One cold January day, Dad went freshwater fishing, only to return that evening, frozen in place on the motorcycle. Unable to dismount, he honked his horn until Mum went outside. I could hear her calling him all the stupid nincompoops under the sun. Then she banged on a neighbor's door to ask his help in getting Dad off the motorcycle and into the house. Dad couldn't stop laughing at the ridiculousness of the fix he was in.

After running a hot bath for him, she told me, "Your stupid father fell in the river, in this weather. And instead of coming home to get dry, he continued fishing until it was too dark to fish!" She stuck her head through the kitchen door so dad could hear. "I didn't know I'd married such an idiot!"

It wasn't too long afterwards that Dad sold his motorcycle and replaced it with a Ford Popular.

Growing up, I was aware of my guardian angel watching over me. Running into traffic without looking, no problem. I'd be perfectly safe. Fearless, that was me. After not getting my own way over something, at eight years of age, I packed a shopping bag with toothbrush, clean knickers, and a chocolate bar and marched off into the wide blue yonder—well, it would have been the wide blue yonder if we hadn't lived in an industrialized town with dirty polluted air. Dad came looking for me and found me two miles from home. He grabbed me under the armpit, and with my toes barely touching the ground, frog marched me back to the house where I received a spanking. Just as well he found me. I wouldn't have returned of my own accord, too stubborn, according to my mother. I prefer being described as determined.

It would appear that my guardian angel was asleep on the job at times. But if it weren't for my willfulness when I was younger and ignoring my intuition when I was older, I could have lived a much easier life.

I have never once regretted growing up as I did or where I did. Spoiled by my father, I was full of confidence. My sister's life was not so sweet. Nine-years-older Joan had to go to bed early with me, otherwise I refused to go to sleep. She was also made to take me out with her to keep me out of my parents' hair. She hated having to drag me along with her and her friends. I don't blame her. Who would want to drag a nine-years-younger sister around, especially a horrible, precocious brat like me? I cringe when I think of how I used to be, demanding a shilling from Joan to go out and leave her and her boyfriend alone.

Still, my early life gave me a strong core. Unfortunately for me, this sense of permanence and stability would not last.

TWO

My mother became pregnant around my ninth birthday. We eagerly looked forward to this addition to the family. But it was not to be. When Mum started in labor, Dad took her to the hospital then returned home. Men weren't encouraged to attend births in those days. Sometime later, I walked with him to the red public telephone box at the end of the street so he could phone the maternity hospital. He looked grim on exiting the telephone box.

"What is it, Dad? A girl?" I asked, excited. "Have I got a sister or a brother?"

He ignored my questions until we were almost at the house. "The baby died."

I was stunned into silence. Then sadness came. No little sister or brother for me.

My mother was kept in hospital for two weeks after the birth, which was the norm then. What a brutal experience for her. The hospital kept her in a ward where other mothers were cooing over and breast-feeding their babies, while Mum sat empty-handed. How cruel and thoughtless could the medical profession be? After she returned home, a heavy pall hung over our home. I never heard another word said about my lost baby sister.

Mum started work at a tailoring factory, making coats for Dannimac clothing company, possibly as a means to get over her loss. Around that time, Joan announced that she and her boyfriend Herby wanted to get married in a hurry. No, she wasn't pregnant. Herby had reached that special age of twenty-one when he would be called up to do his two years National Service. Rumor had it that he could be posted to Cyprus. They wanted to be married before he left so Herby could claim a marriage allowance and married quarters.

October wedding over, I was down two sisters, one to marriage and one to death. At nine years of age, I became a latchkey kid, a state of affairs that lasted six years. Mum would call me as she left for work. Breakfast was usually fried bread, dipped in tea, cooked by my own fair hand. Then I'd leave for school, returning home to an empty house, unless Dad wasn't working a double shift on Middlesbrough docks. Because I was strong and independent and coped well with the latchkey situation, nobody thought I was feeling the loss of my sisters. Both Mum and Dad closed ranks and buried their feelings about losing the baby by working hard and improving our lifestyle. I felt cast adrift.

The focus was on ensuring I passed the eleven-plus examinations. All children had to sit the exam at eleven years of age. Knowing that this exam decided a child's future prospects, my parents encouraged me to do well in school. Passing the eleven-plus exam would allow me to attend grammar school, which, at that time, was the only way open to obtaining a degree at University. Passing it would also open up opportunities in the job market when the time came. Being a clever girl, I passed the eleven plus without a problem. It helped that I attended Derwent Street Junior School, a grimy, working-class school with dedicated teachers. In my class of thirty-three children, eleven passed the exam and five almost passed to be given another shot at it when they were thirteen. The rest were destined for secondary modern schools, where they would be educated for office, shop, and factory work. If you were a boy, and if you were lucky, you had the opportunity on leaving school to apply for an apprenticeship to be a tradesman, or failing that you could become a laborer.

My parents supported my interests in roller skating, and later, swimming. Mum sometimes looked exhausted as she watched me compete in swimming galas after her hard day's work. I knew she was doing her motherly duty and would much rather have been at home with her feet up, watching television.

By the time I was fourteen, I felt superfluous to Mum and Dad's relationship. They would come home from work and share their day's events with one another. I was rarely included in any kind of conversation. I left my parents to their own devices and gained what support I could from my friends and their parents. I didn't get angry or sad about it. I knew how the situation had come about. The still birth of my younger sister and the marriage of my older sister had changed the family dynamics.

Many a time my parents dragged me out with them on a Sunday afternoon drive into the nearby North Yorkshire Moors National Park. I argued to be allowed to remain at home with my friends. But no, I had to go with my parents. It wasn't that they wanted to spend time with me. They just wanted to be sure I wasn't getting into mischief while they were out for the day. I had been known to put Bill Haley's record "Rock Around the Clock" on the radiogram (a piece of furniture combining a radio and record player) and have it blasting with the bass booming so loudly, my mother could hear it when she got off the bus from work a quarter of a mile away. She would run from the bus stop, and arriving home out of breath, dash into the house, turn off the radiogram and scold me for inflicting such a racket on the neighbors. Anyway, as soon as we arrived in the countryside, they would set up deckchairs and start reading the Sunday papers. I was left to my own devices. Half the time, I ignored the beautiful surroundings to remain in the back seat of the car, sulking.

When I was fourteen, we moved to better-quality local authority housing. The three-bedroom house was surrounded by a myriad of similar homes, on a public housing estate. It had gardens front and rear, and hallelujah, an indoor bathroom! The move meant I lost the friends I had grown up with, but I already saw little of them. At eleven years of age, we all went to different types of secondary schools, and as a grammar schoolgirl, I always had two hours homework every night. There were no teenagers in my new neighborhood, so I was on my own apart from a few grammar-school friends whom I rarely saw outside of school, except for Elizabeth. She was my swimming partner, and we trained together several nights a week.

Our gym teacher was a snob. She was almost obsequious to the middle-class girls in my class, but she lorded it over the few working-class girls. I was a docker's (longshoreman's) daughter and the best swimmer in our class. It pained her to have to deal with this, yet she took all the kudos for having a winning swimmer to boast about. When I won the diving competition to become schoolgirl diving champion of Middlesbrough, she kept my trophy for the school display cabinet, and I quit swimming. I had proven to her and myself that working-class was the best. I had nothing else to prove.

In the 1950s, society's mores expected girls to remain virgins before marriage or be labeled as tarts, yet it was okay for guys to play the field. I hated the dual standard. The start of the swinging 60s, free love, Carnaby Street, and hippies changed all that. With my rebellious nature, I was intent on losing my virginity. I chose a guy who was proficient with the girls. He eagerly complied with my proposition, even though I was under the legal age limit. At fourteen, I progressed to a man twice my age. He was called Big John because he was tall, and he was a brawler. He worked at the small carnival in Saltburn, a seaside town half an hour away by train. People didn't cross him in his home town. At fifteen, I became pregnant. Expulsion from grammar school followed, although I didn't feel that to be a loss because I didn't think I was receiving an education to enable me to think, only rote learning to pass exams to go to college.

To say my parents were upset was an understatement. They did their best. Despite their anger and distaste, they met with John, my baby's father, who made all the assurances in the world that he would marry me. He didn't, of course. He left me in the lurch when I was six months pregnant. I was furious that he dumped me like that. But mainly my pride was hurt, and I got over it and had my lovely daughter. Despite pressure from my parents when I was pregnant, including my mother throwing a cup of hot tea in my face, I would not have an abortion or give up my child for adoption. Because I felt no disgrace, I was mostly oblivious to my parents' embarrassment and shame about me having a child out of wedlock. But they lifted their chins, squared their shoulders to face the neighbors, and stood by me. Of course, self-centered me took it all for granted, maybe because I would never turn my back on one of my own.

Fresh out of the maternity hospital, I held my two-week-old daughter Jackie in my arms, totally smitten by her. I promised to cherish and love her forever, knowing she would love me in return. Who needed her father? He no longer existed for us. He ran away, abandoned us, and I didn't care. It was me and Jackie against the world. My dad, proud grandfather that he was, took lots of photographs of his new granddaughter, anger about my pregnancy and my ruined life gone, thanks to my daughter's charm. My parents fell in love with her as soon as they laid eyes on her. Did they ever feel relieved that I was stubborn enough and strong enough to resist their demands to get rid of my child?

I still felt very much alone. The few friends I had were not mothers, and what little I had had in common with them could not keep us friends. Having my daughter completely changed my life. I was not free to do as I liked, and things that used to be important were important no longer. I had no regrets. My daughter was my anchor, and I loved her dearly. I was no longer adrift. My life had purpose. I appreciated my swimming partner Elizabeth's parents, good Christian people, inviting me to their house for tea to show they did not reject me or judge me for being an unmarried mother, which was still considered scandalous at that time.

With no school to attend, I walked the streets and parks, pushing Jackie in her pram for hours. One evening, I went swimming at the local public pool and met Alan. He flirted with me, made sure I knew he found me attractive. The attraction was mutual. I liked his auburn curly hair, ready laugh and London accent. Emotionally needy, I was flattered that he was interested in me. Anyway, shortly after my seventeenth birthday, I became pregnant for the second time. To avoid bringing more shame on my parents, we went to live in London, where he had a sister. Of course, there were arguments with my parents about leaving home.

Dad would say, "Why can't you learn from my mistakes?"

"Because I have to learn from my own," was my answer.

Giving up on me, Dad took Jackie and me to the bus station, not believing I was really leaving, until the bus pulled out of the stand.

Alan and I found a grubby, furnished apartment in Fulham, a mainly working-class borough in London filled with shabby Victorian terraced houses. At the end of the street was a daily market where I did most of my food shopping. Our apartment was situated at the top of three flights of stairs in a tall, narrow house. I scrubbed and scrubbed the apartment until I deemed it clean enough for a crawling baby. We lived happily for some months with Alan going out to work in his sister's business. Then Alan received a letter. I watched the color drain from his face as he read it.

I touched his arm. "What is it?"

"Nothing."

"No, it's something. Tell me."

His face showed many expressions one after the other, changing like a chameleon—sorrow, guilt, anxiety, resignation.

"Tell me!"

Alan handed me the letter and sat looking at the floor, waiting.

The letter was from his wife. *Wife?* Telling him to return home for the sake of their children. I suspected his sister had contacted her. I crumpled the letter even as I crumpled inside. We sat in silence for what seemed a long time.

"Do you want to go home to them?" I asked.

"No."

"I won't hate you if you do."

"No, this is where I want to be. The marriage was over long before I met you. We just stayed together for the sake of the kids."

I insisted he pay child support for his three children, even though it left us with barely enough to get by. The court had awarded child support for Jackie, but I never received a penny from her father, ever. It was important to me that Alan took care of his responsibilities. Eventually tiring of the financial struggle, Alan left me when I was seven months pregnant to return home to his wife and children. Talk about *Déjà vu*.

I applied for welfare, but the agency did not believe I was on my own, because, wouldn't you know it, when they sent someone to the apartment to interview me to confirm my situation, Alan, in his guilt, was in the apartment doing one last thing to help me before catching the coach home to Middlesbrough. He was fixing the ancient cast-iron stove so that Jackie and I and the new baby would be warm during the winter months. Not believing I was alone, the welfare department paid me a reduced amount of benefit and told me to appeal their decision if I didn't like it. Of course, I appealed. I had no choice. After paying the rent, I could scarcely feed Jackie with the money that was left. Jackie and I had one free pint of milk per day, provided by Britain's welfare system for pregnant women and children under five, and I tried to fill my empty, grumbling belly with cheap, windfall apples.

At the maternity clinic for my check up, the nurse weighed me.

"What's this?" she said. "You're supposed to be gaining two pounds a week at this stage in your pregnancy, and you're losing two! That's not good. You're not being silly, trying to keep your weight down, are you?"

I burst into tears. "I've no money to buy food."

"What!" she exclaimed, putting my chart to one side. "You have no food?"

She hurried me to the social worker's office. Hearing my story, the social worker was appalled and disgusted that I had been left in such dire straits in my condition by the welfare system that was meant to protect me. She dipped into the petty cash box and took me shopping for bread, cans of soup, eggs, and ham to make sandwiches.

"I'm going to contact the welfare department about your appeal. That could take some time, so I want to arrange foster care for Jackie. You're going to need it sooner or later when you go into hospital to have your baby."

My British stiff upper lip dissolved. My chin quivered, and my shoulders relaxed. At last, someone was taking care of me. As to Jackie going to foster parents, I reluctantly agreed, not sure how I would cope without my darling daughter, my anchor, to give me strength.

The very next day, the social worker took us to meet Hugh, a truck driver, and his wife Sheila, a warm-hearted couple in their mid-twenties, who lived nearby. They had been trying to have a baby for several years without success, owing to Sheila's miscarriages.

"You can visit Jackie as often as you want," Sheila told me.

And I did.

One evening, I started scrubbing the linoleum floor in my apartment. I was still scrubbing two hours later when my landlady knocked on the door.

"Pauline, you've been scrubbing the floor for ages. Are you all right?"

"Yes, I'm fine."

"You'll be in labor tomorrow. You mark my words. All this cleaning . . .you're preparing the nest."

She was right. My labor pains began around 10:30 in the morning. During the two-mile walk to the maternity hospital, whenever I had a strong pain, I had to stop and lean against a wall or a street light to catch my breath. Not a soul noticed I was having difficulty, or if they did, they ignored my plight. It was during this walk I developed the creed I lived by for many years:

I've got me and I can cope.

At the hospital, I told the nurses it wouldn't be long. They examined me and tucked me up in bed, telling me there was plenty of time. They left the room. A grunt and a yell a few minutes later brought them running to the birth of my second daughter.

"Why didn't you press the button for help?" the nurse chided.

"Why would I be thinking of you at a time like this?" I said.

My baby was going to have her father's hazel eyes. I left the hospital three days later and hurried to Owen and Sheila's to introduce the new baby to her sister. Over a cup of tea, Sheila asked if she and Owen could adopt Jackie.

I was horrified. "Oh no, not Jackie! I can't part with her. No, I can't do that!"

"What about your new baby, Pauline? It's been hard enough with one child. How will you cope with two?"

"I'm not giving my children away! No! No! I'm taking Jackie, and we're going home."

I couldn't get away from their house fast enough. Back at my apartment, I played with Jackie then breast fed my new daughter, and next day I registered her birth, giving her the name Kathleen. Like Jackie's birth certificate, the space for the father's name remained empty. All the while, Sheila's words reverberated in my mind. Then I received a letter from my parents telling me I could return home, but only if I gave my newborn daughter away for adoption. Pondering all the possibilities, about what life would be like for my children if I kept them both, about how life would be if I allowed Owen and Sheila to adopt Kathleen, I held Kathleen close. As she nestled into my neck, I savored her sweet baby smell, brushed my lips against her cheek, and looked around the pokey, shabby apartment. I would probably never be able to give my children anything better than this.

I went to see Sheila and Owen. "You can adopt Kathleen when I've breast-fed her for six weeks," I told the overjoyed couple. "Promise to let her know I gave her to you because I love her and want her to have a better life than she would ever have with me."

The deed done, my heart a shriveled nugget of lead, I returned to my parents' home with Jackie, shortly before my eighteenth birthday.

THREE

As soon as I returned home, my mother began to plan my life. "What you need is a nice office job and to mix with nice people. There's some being advertized in the jobs vacant section," she said, handing me the newspaper.

"Office jobs don't pay enough. I need money to put Jackie in the nursery and money for my lodge," I said.

"Why do you need a nursery for Jackie? I gave up work to look after her."

"I didn't ask you to do that."

She reached for the back of a chair to hold her up. My making my own arrangements for my life must have felt like a slap in the face.

I went to check out the nursery. Wrapped in plastic aprons, laughing toddlers dipped their hands in brightly-colored poster paint and dabbed them on sheets of paper. At another table, assistants were helping children make animals and figurines from Plasticine. Still others made simple words from alphabet letters. Mossman Terrace nursery in action. The warm, family atmosphere was perfect, and I arranged for Jackie's admittance. Recalling the tea in my face and the shaking I got when my eye was injured, I did not want my mother bringing up my daughter.

Then I looked for a job that would pay me enough to cover the cost of the nursery and pay my parents for our board and lodge. Mum wanted me to find office work, a decent job, a job better than she had

had in the factory. She wanted me to do better. After all, what was all their effort and sacrifice for as I was growing up? Unfortunately, the pay for an eighteen-year-old doing office work came nowhere near providing sufficient income for my basic financial needs. Instead, I found a job with the United Bus Service as a bus conductor collecting the fares. I could start as soon as I became eighteen. With my parents agreeing to help care for Jackie when I worked the late shift, I was all set. And as long as I worked some overtime, I would have some cash to spare.

After two weeks working at United, I spotted an attractive young woman, with shoulder-length, strawberry-blonde hair, sitting by herself in the canteen. I went over.

"Are you new?"

"Yes. It's my first day," she said. Her name was Lee.

I nodded toward a table where my driver and some friends were having breakfast. "Come and join us."

Lee and I were very different. She had striking good looks and an outgoing personality that came from being an army brat. Her father had been an officer in the British Army and was frequently posted to different bases. In those circumstances, you had to be able to make friends quickly or be lonely. I was brunette and not so attractive. I also was not so outgoing and did not have Lee's social skills. However, I was fun and had a terrific sense of humor. Our talents worked well together, and we went on many double dates.

Lee and I became known as the terrible twins. We had a rule not to become romantically or sexually involved with the men where we worked. The unexpected consequences of this were the wild fantasies our male co-workers developed about us. I daresay it didn't help that we sometimes arrived for our 4:30 a.m. shifts still in our night-clubbing clothes.

"Hi Ron," we'd call to the bus inspector overseeing the first shifts of the day, while removing our dangly earrings as we dashed up the stairs to the locker room. "Be down in a tick." In the locker room, sensible shoes replaced silver sandals, figure-hiding dust-coats, pulled from lockers, covered our cocktail dresses. Without a wink of sleep, we began our shifts. The bus inspector shook his head and smiled, possibly envious of the lifestyle he imagined us having. I had a lot of fun at this time in my life and shall be eternally grateful to my parents for helping with child care, thus allowing me to have some high-spirited, fun experiences.

Mum and Dad at Redcar beach with Lee

Lee's parents moved to a town thirty miles away. She didn't want to go with them, and my parents allowed her to move into our house. She lived with us for two years, until her mother died, then she left to care for her ailing father.

I returned to London for Kathleen's adoption hearing. I didn't have to go. But I wanted to. It was almost more than I could bear, saying a permanent farewell to my daughter. I met Sheila and Owen outside the court on a sunny April day. The trees sported bright green buds indicating winter's grey cold had passed. But it hadn't passed. It still had a grip on the heart of the old parent and the hearts of the new. Sheila and Owens faces were stiff, ashen, fearful that I would change my mind. With uncertain smiles, they gave me photographs of Kathleen, now renamed Joanne, and promised to tell her how much I loved her.

We climbed the steps into the court building. I couldn't stop crying throughout the hearing. At one point, I was sobbing so hard the female magistrate asked, "Miss Wickman, are you sure you want to give your child up for adoption? If you want to change your mind, this is your last chance."

"Of course I don't want to give my daughter up for adoption!"

Sheila and Owen gasped in horror.

Choking on my words, I continued, "I love her. I'm doing it because it's the right thing to do for her." I sat down, used my sleeve to wipe away snot and tears after failing to find a hankie in my pockets.

The magistrate's composure almost gave way under the onslaught of my emotional tsunami. She took a few deep breaths and much to Sheila and Owen's relief, quickly granted the adoption. I left the court feeling as if I had ripped out my heart and trampled it in the dirt. Despite my heartbreak, throughout the following years, I sustained myself with the belief that Kathleen-now-Joanne would come back into my life. I had absolutely no doubt.

The friendship I had with Lee was solid. We would never fall out over a man. Occasionally, I would date a man who had previously dated Lee and vice versa. But no man would ever be worth denting our relationship over. Patrick came to work on the United Buses. With his tall, muscular build, black hair and pale blue eyes, he was very attractive. Lee and I had a playful rivalry about spending time with such a handsome man. After a late shift, the three of us would go ten pin bowling. Other times we would go to the cinema. One evening, I went alone with Patrick to the movies. It was summertime. For me that meant hay fever. Tired from working overtime and taking anti- histamine medication, I fell asleep in the movie theater, with my head on Patrick's shoulder. He never let me forget how unromantic I'd been, snoring in his ear. Lee laughed, saying it would improve her chances with him.

While working on the United Buses, I occasionally crossed paths with Ken who worked as a bus driver for United in Redcar depot eight miles away. I was attracted to this confident, dark-haired, handsome man with a slow, sensuous smile to melt the ladies' hearts, and a physique to rival the best Chippendale dancers. Although he was thirteen years older than I was, we hit it off and occasionally met to go to the movies, or stroll on the beach. I liked that he was a character, very much his own man. Ignoring all the rules, Ken drove his bus with his pet monkey sitting on his shoulder, and no bus inspector ever said a word.

After a year working for United, I was ready for a change. I quit my job. Within twenty-four hours, I'd found work as a nightclub waitress. I had no experience, but thought it would be fun. At that time, the northeast of England was the main center, outside of London, for the nightclub scene. The 1960s economy in the UK was booming. Ordinary guys with trades such as welder, boiler maker, plumber, and electrician were making a lot of money. Being mainly shift-workers in the local heavy industries, nightclubs were the obvious places for these men to go for their entertainment. I was soon rubbing shoulders with some of the big names in showbiz— Tom Jones, Gerry Dorsey, who found fame after a name change to Engelbert Humperdinck, and numerous other famous entertainers.

I met some men who turned out to be unsavory characters. I was too naïve to realize this, being flattered that one of them wanted to date me and take me out in his red Jaguar car. One frosty, January night, he called to take me out.

"I want to make a detour to see someone first," he said.

We pulled up outside a house. "Come inside. It's too cold to wait in the car."

We climbed the stairs to an apartment, where I followed him inside. Seven men I had met as acquaintances during earlier dates with this man were standing round the room. It only took a second and an adrenaline jolt to realize I was in trouble. The leering, hostile way they looked at me, the way my body quivered and bristled sensing danger, they were a pack of wolves ready to tear down their prey, and I was that prey. I leapt for the door. Hands pulled my fingers from the door handle. I twisted and turned to escape. Seven pairs of hands picked me up and flung me on the bed.

I kicked and screamed, "Get off me! Leave me alone! No!"

Hands held down my legs and arms. Hands pulled down my pantyhose and lifted my skirt. I grabbed my pantyhose to keep it from being pulled down. Fingers pried my hand loose.

"Don't do this! Don't do it!" I cried.

From the way they looked at me, I knew I had ceased to be a human being to them. There was to be no escape. I was going to be raped no matter what.

I resigned myself to my fate, lying still and quiet, tears soaking my hair while they each climbed on top of me. Taking turns, they grunted and thrust into me while the others laughed or cheered on each man's performance. Some relished their power in the situation. Others, less eager to participate in my violation, only pretended. Mentally, I removed myself from the activities in the room, transported myself to a tropical island with palm trees, white beaches, and turquoise seas.

Then it was over. I dressed in silence with trembling fingers, unable to comprehend that this man thought so little of me, he brought me to this ambush for his entertainment.

"Oh, come on, it wasn't that bad, was it?" my date said.

I said nothing. Not then and not on the drive home.

I got out of the car.

My date wound down the window. "Come on. Give me a smile."

"Piss off! Don't ever come near me again!" I hissed.

I washed and washed myself, attempting to cleanse away the clinging loathsomeness of the deed. Defiled and betrayed, I raged and hated inside, yet made no report to the police. In those days, the fact that I had had two illegitimate children before I was eighteen automatically branded me a slut, and the belief was that sluts could not be rape victims. I would not allow my dirty laundry to be aired for the world to see and in the process humiliate my parents all over again. And for what? By swearing that I had been willing, the men would get off scot free. I would not waste my time. Reporting the crime to the police was not an option.

In the weeks that followed, my mind struggled to find a place of equilibrium. I was taking driving lessons at the time. My driving instructor George and I had had a rocky start. He had been hostile and suspicious because prior to choosing him as my instructor, I had tried out three other driving instructors and their vehicles.

"Why are you being so hostile?" I challenged him after our first lesson together.

"I'm wondering what you're up to, trying out so many instructors."

"I didn't like driving their types of car. So, you're going to have to live with it," I said, "because I like this car. I'm comfortable in it, and this is the one I want to learn to drive in. You're stuck with me as your pupil."

With the air cleared, we hit it off, cracking jokes together and generally liking each other very much. One evening, after the rape, he called at the house, catching me in the middle of my ironing, with my hair in rollers.

"You've got a driving lesson. Did you forget?"

I had. "Be with you in a sec."

I pulled out my rollers, ran a comb through my hair, and off we went. George was concerned about my mental state. He suspected I was preoccupied because I was pregnant.

"No, I'm not pregnant," I said.

The new availability of the birth control pill made it so much easier to avoid pregnancy, but only if you were married. Sexually active single women were still compelled to take a risk. I didn't really understand why I was so ditzy during that period. Had my mind been working overtime to wipe out the memory and the pain of being raped? If it was, it was successful. The event soon disappeared from my conscious mind. What also disappeared was my self-centeredness. Being responsible for and caring for my daughter had been my first step to unselfishness. Being raped by people who knew me was a second step, a step that completely destroyed, within my subconscious, any value I had of myself as a human being. Deep within, I carried the belief that I did not matter. I was a nobody. The rape reinforced the lack-of-worth feelings that developed in my early teen years from my parents' emotional neglect. Responding to all of that, I became seriously promiscuous.

The fun continued with Lee and me double-dating and going to nightclubs. All of this was done with very little money. One night, I wanted to see the show at the Fiesta nightclub, which was about six miles away. Lee was working. I had enough money to travel there by bus, buy a couple of drinks, and that was it. However, I went prepared. I didn't accept lifts home from anyone, only people I had come to know. This particular night there was no ride home for me, and I didn't have the money for a taxi. I retrieved my small duffle-bag from the check-in girl and left. Before long I was making my merry way home, roller skating along the road in the early hours of the morning.

A taxi driver slowed and drove alongside me. "Love, you've given me the best laugh I've had in a long time. Where do you live? I'll give you a ride home for free."

Next night, I was fired from my job as a nightclub waitress after spilling beer all over a man's lap. He felt bad for me, and we ended up dating for a while. I soon found another job with Northern Dairies, delivering milk to people's doorsteps. Spring was on its way. The cold of winter had gone, except, of course, for the snowfalls on my first week on the job. I enjoyed the physical work. I started loading my electric milk float at 5:30 a.m. and was usually finished six hours later. That left me plenty of time to catch up on my sleep and spend time with Jackie.

I was having sexual flings left, right, and center, acting out my attackers' view of me as a nobody. Of course, I became pregnant again. My heart sank. I couldn't do this to Mum and Dad again. I didn't want to have the baby. The father did not want me to have it either. He was a well-off businessman, and he arranged an illegal abortion for me. He drove me to a small house in town. It was neat and clean. The woman who was going to perform the act was in her forties, plump, pleasant, and attractive. She wore the Dusty Springfield heavy eye makeup in vogue at the time.

"Don't worry, love. I've helped quite a few women in my time. You're in good hands."

She took me upstairs, and I lay on the bed with my skirt pulled up and my panties pulled down. To perform the abortion, she slid a knitting needle into my vagina and jabbed until my waters broke. The deed done, I broke out into a cold sweat, nauseated. The baby's father paid the woman and drove me home. I never saw him again.

A day or two later, I felt terrible. My whole body ached, and I definitely had a temperature. It was a glorious hot, August day, and I could not stop shivering. I dressed in a polo-necked sweater and suede coat and caught the bus to the doctor's surgery. Patients didn't need appointments. You simply waited your turn. I started to writhe and groan in agony. My pain had no impact on the other patients in the waiting room. They stubbornly set their jaws, crossed their arms, and stared straight ahead. The message was clear. I would have to wait my turn. I almost giggled at the picture of them sitting there with their stiff faces. When I finally reached the doctor, he called an ambulance to take me to hospital straight from the surgery. I had septicemia from the abortion.

"If you hadn't come to see me today," he told me, "you would have died tomorrow."

At the hospital, doctors saved my life with massive doses of antibiotics. With the hospital only telling her that I had blood poisoning, and determined to find out what had happened to me, Mum demanded, "How did you get blood poisoning?"

Once, when I had been playing darts with Jackie's father, I had thrown a dart that stuck in his hand. He had developed blood poisoning that sent streaks of red up his arm.

"I don't know," I lied. "I must have cut myself on something."

I carry no guilt or shame about having an abortion. Marriage to the father was out of the question. I refused to heap more shame on my parents by having another child, and I certainly could never have gone through the emotional pain of giving away another baby for adoption. My heart had already been ripped from my chest. And because I felt absolutely that Joanne would come back into my life, I did not want her thinking something was wrong with her that I gave her away, yet I kept the children I had both before and after her. No, the best decision was to abort.

Later that year, promiscuousness left behind, I met a man who, without even trying, broke through my protective barricade. He wasn't tall and handsome. He was short and thin, but his wit and craziness made me laugh. He was fun. Broke but fun, and his name was John S. Driving me home from the nightclub, he took a short cut over a ploughed field in his wreck of a car he called Bessie. I couldn't stop laughing as we bounced over the rough earth. I hadn't felt so light and carefree in a long time. When I kissed him goodnight and entered the house, I felt I was walking on air. I had heard of the expression, but now I was actually experiencing it.

My next date with John had me bawling my eyes out because I couldn't go, and as he had tickets for a show, Lee went with him instead, while I stayed at home nursing chickenpox caught from Jackie. Our fledgling romance blossomed after this precarious start. He worked as a bus driver on the corporation bus service, so I quit my job to work with him. Bus drivers and bus conductors worked on a rota so that in each thirteen-week cycle, a bus driver would work with a conductor for a week before moving to the next person on the rota. People were always willing to swap shifts, so I worked with John most of the time. I also went to the family planning clinic and passed myself off as a married woman in order to obtain birth control.

The job was a lot of fun with much camaraderie. Most of my work companions had a sense of humor. One day I went upstairs to collect fares. There was only one passenger, a man, sitting right at the back of the upper deck. *I smell a rat,* I thought as I made my way toward him. Sure enough, he was exposing himself. I gave him his ticket and as I turned to go, I nodded at his penis and said, "If I were you, I'd put it away. It's not worth showing off."

On the Dennis model buses, the conductor could stand near the driver and talk with him. We laughed when I told him what had happened. The passenger got off at the next stop and, as he did so, my driver wiggled his little finger at him, and we burst into paroxysms of laughter.

One of the drivers I worked with, Antonio, was Italian and had been a prisoner of war in a nearby prison camp. He had fallen in love with an English girl, and instead of returning to Italy, he had married her and remained in England.

Sometimes, an occasional driver was hostile, accusing me of taking a job from a man who had a family to keep. I always replied that I had a family to keep too, because my child's father chose not to support us. That always shut them up.

The relationship with John became serious. My heart fluttered whenever he was near. However, he was married, but separated from his wife. He had three children that he paid child support for, which was why he was always broke. In those days, obtaining a divorce was difficult. Usually, one person had to be at fault such as being caught committing adultery. Later, the law changed so that a divorce could be obtained after two years separation, with nobody needing to be in the wrong.

Before I met John, Lee, Jackie and I had gone on a package vacation to Calella de la Costa in Spain. I fell in love with the Spanish way of life and the Mediterranean food. I met a young Spaniard called Juan and had been corresponding with him as a pen pal. Our first vacation had been such fun, lots of guys, lots of Bacardi and coke, and interesting tours, a completely different experience from life in England. We liked Spain so much that Lee and I had already booked our second vacation in Spain before John came into my life. Spain was calling, and I dreamed about going to live there.

Me, Jackie and Juan, Minorca, Spain 1967

Off we went on vacation. Juan was doing his national service, and as he had informed me that wages in the Spanish army were pathetic, I took plenty of money to take him out. Leaving Lee on her own in Calella for a few days, I flew with Jackie to Minorca where Juan was stationed. Juan wasn't as hard up as expected. Apparently, he was a bit of a card sharp. He booked us into a hotel room with one big bed for all three of us. I hesitated at the threshold.

"Juan, I'm in love with someone in England. Nothing can happen between us." Fortunately, Juan accepted the situation and behaved like a gentleman during our stay.

Sitting in a café by the beach, I said, "Juan, I love Spain. I want to come and live here."

"For me, it is the best country. If you and John come to live in Calella, I promise to help you find a place to live."

I glowed with hope and excitement at the possibility of making my dream come true.

I returned home to John's ecstatic welcome. Sitting on the sofa, I eagerly shared my holiday snaps, including photographs of Jackie and Juan playing together on the beach, photos of the three of us in a café taken by the waiter. Joy at having me home again switched to suspicion, a block of ice wedged between us. John believed I had been unfaithful with Juan and nothing would convince him otherwise. Next thing I knew, John had booked a last-minute vacation in Spain and off he went. When he returned, his collection of snapshots included pictures of an attractive brunette. I could tell by her glowing expression that she and John had had a holiday romance. So this was John's revenge for my supposed infidelity. My feelings for him took a hit, but we moved past it. Well, maybe not completely, but I understood his reaction better when I remembered he and his wife were separated because she cheated on him.

Life in Spain beckoned. John was willing to try it too. Preparation included learning Spanish at evening classes. A few months before my planned departure, Dad sold me his ancient, jumbo-sized luxury car for a few pounds. Things were falling into place. John, skilled in mechanics, made whatever repairs were needed. Departure was set for April 1st, April Fool's Day. Then John got cold feet and backed out.

"If you don't want to go, I can't make you," I said. "But I'm still going. I'll look you up if I ever come back to Middlesbrough."

The night before leaving, I kissed him goodnight, no hard feelings. People were free to do as they pleased. I didn't own them, and they certainly didn't have to do things to please me. I would miss him though. I did love him, but not enough to be corralled by him.

Next morning, I found John on our doorstep with his passport and suitcase.

FOUR

With the car parked in the ferry, we headed out on deck and breathed deeply of the ozone-rich air. Sea breezes whipped our carefully combed hair into a mass of tangles as we took our last look at English shores. Excitement rippled in our bellies when, deep below deck, the ship's giant engines kicked into life. Churning water, the ferry left harbor to plough the twenty-three miles to Calais through a moderate swell. The White Cliffs of Dover faded from

John and Jackie on the sea ferry to Calais 1968

sight. On the other side of the English Channel, France and the second leg of our journey waited. We soaked up the sunshine, the fair weather and calm seas taken as a good omen, and grinned at one another in delight.

We left Calais docks with some trepidation. Accidents were common for British motorists adjusting to the European system of driving on the opposite side of the road to Britain. Calais's industrial port and town were similar to our home town, but neater and cleaner. To escape the urban bustle, we hurried south, along the main road into France's lush countryside, heading toward Paris. We took care to negotiate the turning circles correctly. It wouldn't do to be ticketed for a traffic violation at the start of our new life. For mile after mile, sycamore and poplar trees lined the straight roads, casting shadows that shaded our eyes from the bright sunlight. Green fields sprouting potatoes, cabbage and onions spread out to the horizon behind trees and hedgerows. After two hours, we stopped in a village that was trapped in time. Elderly Frenchmen in black berets sipped cognac or coffee at roadside cafes, while reading the newspaper or watching an intensely played game of boules on a nearby stretch of flat, sandy ground. Plump, middle-aged housewives passed by, carrying baskets filled with groceries and golden sticks of bread. Using my schoolgirl French, I placed an order with the impatient waiter. He must have had his own interpretation of my faltering vocabulary because we ended up filling our grumbling stomachs with goat cheese, bread, olives and a large bowl of carrot soup—not at all what I'd ordered. Time to move on. We bought bottles of pear juice and a kilo of apples to take with us. Barely a hundred yards from the bistro, a scraping noise beneath the car of metal on tarmac brought us to a halt. Fear and disappointment twisted my innards. I felt like a prisoner on the run whose dash for freedom had been brought to an abrupt end. Without the car, everything would fall apart. It contained all I owned—my books, Jackie's toys and our luggage. If we had to travel to Spain by coach or train, we would lose everything except our suitcases.

"John, what is it?"

"Don't know, but I'll soon find out."

With that he was under the car. He reemerged a few minutes later.

"Exhaust fell off. I need some wire."

Looking along the street, we made out a hardware shop. We all traipsed inside. As I flicked through my pocket French dictionary for the appropriate words, John, on seeing the wire he wanted, picked it up, showed it to the shopkeeper and made a painless purchase. In no time at all, he had the exhaust securely attached to the car.

"It will last forever," he reassured me.

And off we went.

Four-year-old Jackie coped well with the 1,500-mile drive. We stopped often to see the sights, stroll in parks, or dine in bistros. Three nights we stayed at inexpensive hotels. By the time we arrived in Calella, Jackie was fond of salami sandwiches.

Calella, formerly a fishing village, was a popular tourist town. In the summer, strolling tourists clogged the narrow streets in the old part of town, but at this time of year, locals could move freely and swiftly go about their business be it shopping or socializing in the many bars and cafes, where the main activity was putting the world to rights. I soon learned to walk in the shade whenever I could during the scorching summer months when the long, golden beach was so hot, walking on the sand burned your feet. The fields where Juan and I had picked strawberries only two years before were now a hive of activity. With builders erecting hotels and apartments for even more tourists to visit, squealing drills and the roar of diesel machinery filled the air, disturbing the relaxed, friendly ambiance of the nearby bars and restaurants.

Juan, true to his word, found us accommodation on the upper floor of his middle-aged Aunt Maria's house that provided a large room for sleeping and a bathroom. Maria lived on the ground floor with her sister and mother. The street was full of old terraced houses most of which had been modernized to include garages on the ground floor now that most people had vehicles. Some houses were still in the painful throes of demolition and reconstruction.

We had no work visas, so we could only look for casual work, and that was hard to find because we had arrived far too early for vacation season. With money running low, we lived on sticks of French bread and jam. The French bread did not keep our stomachs filled for long, so I asked the baker to make us one loaf of whole wheat bread per day, which staved off our hunger for many hours. We went for long walks to pick wild figs and prickly pears to supplement our diet. One time, Juan speared an octopus for me to cook. We sure needed strong teeth to chew on that rubbery devil.

When Maria realized our stay was to be six months, she turned a rustic storage room off the courtyard into a make-shift kitchen, installing some kitchen chairs and an old oak table, covered with an oil cloth. On another counter top, was a two-ring cooker that ran on bottled gas. We obtained water from the faucet in the courtyard, and I washed the dirty dishes in a bucket. Meals were simple—liver, fish, chicken and omelets, all cooked with mounds of garlic and onions in the frying pan, accompanied by bread, salad, and fresh fruit. Very healthy. During mealtimes, numerous lizards entertained us by scampering on the beams overhead. Some days, Jackie and I spent hours watching the ant trail crossing the courtyard to climb the lemon tree growing in the center. Sometimes, she played with the baby rabbits Maria bought at the market and kept in hutches in the courtyard. We watched them grow bigger, and then they disappeared one by one.

"Where did the rabbit go, Mummy?" Jackie asked every time one vanished.

I hadn't the heart to tell her, "Into Maria's cooking pot."

With Juan's help, John found a job as a waiter at a beach bar. Working outdoors, under continual sunshine, John's dull complexion and mousy hair gave way to an attractive, tanned face, and sun-streaked tawny mane. The times I visited the bar and watched John work, I could see his self-confidence grow. In this fun-filled, carefree environment, his personality sparkled, thriving from female vacationers' flirtations with him. I didn't worry, not even when single, tipsy, female tourists called their most favorite waiter in the world to their table, or stroked his leg or held his hand for too long. Our commitment to one another was solid.

Then one night, John didn't come home. The following morning, as Jackie and I were leaving for market, I caught him throwing the travel rug from the car into the tub of washing water. He reeked of guilt. It was written all over him, his eyes, his expression, his actions. He refused to say where he'd been, wouldn't look at me, disappeared into the shower to wash away the stench of sex, and I knew. He had cheated on me, made love to another woman in my car. Nauseated, numb, and once again, betrayed, I went through the motions, continued my daily tasks. It was all I could do not to vomit while frying garlic and onions for our meals. Not a morsel of food passed my lips for five days, the nausea knot in my stomach making me ill. The weight fell off me. He showed concern. So what! Before we left England, snuggled together on the sofa, we discussed what a big deal it was for me to take the socially unacceptable step of living with him as his wife when we were not married. I had put my trust in John, believed his words when he said we would be together forever.

Numbness receded to be replaced by unbearable pain. Tears flowed like waterfalls. My body felt bludgeoned. I would put Jackie to bed and read her a bedtime story from pages shaking so much I could hardly see the words. It was no good, I had to go and see for myself. I washed my face and left the house. Many times I turned back, not sure I could face the truth. It would be like allowing them to throw a custard pie in my face, only it would not be funny. At the beach bar, I sat down and ordered a drink.

John almost tripped over his feet when he saw me. "What are you doing here? Why don't you go home?"

"I had to come and see with my own eyes."

"You're imagining things."

"No, John, I'm not."

"Don't make a scene," he said, depositing my drink in front of me.

Over my *cuba libre*, I checked out the women in the bar. One caught my eye. From the seductive glances she was sending John's way, it was clearly the vivacious blonde, dripping in gold. From her accent, she sounded Dutch. John's attempts at trying not to appear head over heels in love with her while I was present, clinched it. The scraping of a chair at my table distracted me. Looking up, I found the owner of the bar joining me. Leering at me, he took my hand and stroked my arm.

"John tells me you are not really his wife. I have always wanted you. Now I know you are not married, well . . ."

Horrified, I pulled my arm away. Not only had John let me down by cheating, he'd told the bar owner we weren't married. Unprotected by my "husband", John's boss treated me as a slut, fair game to be propositioned and groped.

"Don't ever touch me again," I said, running from the bar, fearing I would vomit.

Returning home, I drank red wine until I passed out. It would be my nightly solace while John spent his nights with the Dutch woman until she returned to Holland. Even after she left, he stayed out drinking with Juan. He didn't want to make love to me, didn't want to be unfaithful to her. Just stick the knife in John, why don't you, and give it a twist while you're at it?

I found a job on Pineda Beach, selling boat tickets from a small kiosk for boat trips along the Costa Brava. One day, Jackie was not feeling well, and Maria offered to care for her while I went to work. Making the arrangements with Maria caused me to miss my train. The next train would not arrive for one and a half hours. I set off walking the six miles to Pineda, along the path that ran alongside the railway tracks. I was still striding out an hour later when a man stepped from behind a patch of tall grass a few feet ahead of me. He was dressed as a waiter in white shirt and black pants.

He grabbed my arm and tried to force me to go with him to a stand of trees farther from the path. No way was I going with him. I was not going to go through rape number two, not for anyone.

"Get lost!" I told him in my best evening-class Spanish, struggling to escape his grasp. When that didn't work I used all the swear words I could think of, taught to us by Juan and his friends. I twisted, pushed and kicked. He held onto me, uttering not one word, all the time trying to force me off the path. I dug in my heels. He pulled out a handgun and jammed it in my ribs. This didn't intimidate me one iota. In fact, I became even more enraged. The struggle continued—him trying to force me towards the trees, me stubbornly resisting and becoming more and more determined that he was not going to have his way.

A part of me, the logical part, was standing to one side of the battle of wills, asking me in exasperation, *What do you think you're doing? You have a young child in your care in a foreign country. What will happen to her if you are shot and killed?* But I was so incensed by this . . . upstart. I could not allow myself to be raped again.

I don't know how long the struggle continued, probably only minutes, although it seemed like hours. Eventually, the man gave up and ran away. Expecting to be shot in the back, I held my breath, stood motionless, heart pounding like a pile-driver. Nothing. I plucked up the courage to look back. Black birds burst from nearby bushes, startling me. I froze in fear, my breathing rapid and shallow, unable to take my eyes off the bushes in case he was hiding there. Nothing. The fluttering of a passing yellow butterfly freed me from my terror trance. Through my tears, I surveyed the sandy path, trees, bushes and long grass. Nothing but a quiet, peaceful scene.

He had gone.

My knees almost buckled when I tried to walk on. My legs shook. I could so easily have been killed, and then what would have happened to Jackie? All day long I brooded about the morning's events, and on returning to Calella, I dropped by Juan's local bar to tell him what had happened.

"Pauline, you are very pretty," he said, "but not so pretty that someone would try to rape you at gun point."

He doesn't believe me! I was shaking as if he had thrown ice-water in my face. A lump formed in my throat. Unshed tears. Unexpressed despair. My chin trembled.

"Pauline, saying these things will not bring John back to you."

I showed him the bruise where the attacker had pressed the gun barrel into my ribs, and still he doubted my story.

As an afterthought, he added, "You know, if this is true, you cannot report it to the police. You are working without a work permit. It would be unwise to draw attention to yourself."

Of course, he was right about that.

I drew what satisfaction I could from the fact I *had* stopped the attacker from raping me, that I *had* survived intact, and that my daughter still had her mother to love and protect her.

Let down by my friend Juan and thinking John would be happier if I was not around, I decided to return home. I searched everywhere for our passports, until John admitted to hiding them so I could not leave him. Did that mean he really did love me? No. This was his attempt at damage control. He did not want word of how he had treated me to reach our home town.

And in all that, I only wanted him to be happy and move on if that was what he needed to do. Where was I in all this? Nowhere, a nobody. I was of no importance, that much was clear, even to myself.

Stuck with continuing the façade of living with John, I focused on enjoying my work and my daughter who came with me to the kiosk every day. After two months without uttering a word of Spanish, she sprang to life. Catalan flowed fluently from her tongue! With her blonde hair and freckles, Jackie was a novelty. Local small-business people adored her. Each day, after the tourists had bought their tickets and sailed off along the coast, the man from the nearby café, the fruit-seller or the stationmaster would come to the kiosk and encourage her to speak.

"*Ola, Rubia,*" they greeted her.

Speaking slowly to me and enunciating each word so that I would understand, they asked to take Jackie to the café, or the fruit stall or some errand they had to make. Jackie disappeared all the time. I never worried. The times I did check up on her, I usually found her determinedly pulling the knob on the pinball machine in the café, rigged by the owner so she could play for free. She would be so engrossed in pulling the ball shooter to get the machine to make clanging noises, her half-eaten pastry often lay forgotten on her plate. Other times, I would find her helping out at the fruit stall. Her Nordic appearance and fluency in Catalan, made her a novelty that encouraged shoppers to stop and buy fruit just to hear her speak. I didn't mind her exploitation. I could see Jackie was happy playing shop. Normally, Spanish housewives pawed and picked their way through the produce, being particular about their choices. But when Jackie was there, they encouraged her to pick out peaches or tomatoes or onions for them. Her pay was all the fresh fruit she could eat and the pleasure of helping. Occasionally, when the station master went home for his lunch, he took her with him to have lunch and play with his small children. Everybody around the kiosk acted as her parents, returning her when they thought it was time. One kind man spent hours helping me improve my Spanish language skills by talking slowly to me in Spanish. I felt very much at home by the kiosk on Pineda beach, surrounded by love and affection. It was hard returning to Calella, where I spent the evenings alone, getting drunk on copious amounts of red wine once Jackie was sleep.

Then I met Frank Murtha, an elderly American, living in Spain. His philosophy was, "Why live like a pauper in New York when I can live like a king in Spain?" We shared the same birthday, only Frank was fifty years older than I was. He had never married. Too cynical for that. We had long discussions over coffee about interesting articles he read in *The International Herald Tribune*, ranging from newly discovered fossils to politics. He enjoyed having someone to speak to in English, and I enjoyed his company, not to mention his dry humor. His Spanish-language skills were limited, but that was not the reason he always said "grassy ass" instead of *gracias* when he needed to thank a Spaniard. We continued writing to one another after I left Spain. He would send me newspaper clippings to discuss in our letters, and I would do the same.

Frank Murtha, Calella, Spain. 1968

The time was coming to leave Spain. Our tourist visas would soon expire. I could barely hold back my tears. I didn't want to go back to England. John wanted me to go to London with him where he had an aunt who would help us start a new life there. Not wanting to continue the façade of living with John, I had applied for nanny's jobs found in *The International Herald Tribune*. I was offered an interview in London for a job as a nanny in Cleveland, Ohio. In a hurry to make the interview, we sped through France to catch the Calais-Dover ferry. The car broke down. I would not make the interview. I called the American to tell him. It was all I could do not to beat my breast. I was already grieving at having to leave Spain, and now I was losing my opportunity of a new life. Not wanting to return home with another failure under my belt, I stayed with John. In London, I would be able to do temp work or part-time work as a comptometer operator, training my parents had paid for. Temp work was difficult to find in my home town. In London, I should be able to earn enough and have the flexibility needed to care for Jackie.

John's aunt was not welcoming to me. Whatever I did to help—cleaning, cooking meals while she was at work—was never good enough. John, she was pleased with, but with me she was downright unpleasant. It was queen-bee syndrome. She could not endure another female in the house. Even her own daughter had been driven out when she was seventeen.

Unable to find decent, affordable accommodation and wanting to remove Jackie from this horrid situation, I took her to my parents to be cared for until I could find a place in London we could call home. With Jackie safe, John and I moved into a bed and breakfast hotel at Kings Cross, which was run by Graham, an easy-going Welshman. We lived there for eight months. Scouring the newspapers for jobs, I found one for John with National Cash Registers. He had mechanical aptitude and sailed through the test and interview. I found work three days a week as a comptometer operator, totaling invoices for a company that owned numerous hotels. The office was near Piccadilly Circus and at lunchtime we went to the basement of one of the company's hotels for our lunch. On the four days I didn't work there, I helped serve breakfast in Graham's bed and breakfast hotel and cleaned bedrooms. My third job was as a barmaid three nights per week. In my spare time, I searched for an affordable flat.

Six months after our return from Spain, John said he had to go away for a few days. He was being very secretive. When he left, I doubted he would return. It was time for some serious consideration. Where was my life going? Nowhere. What about my daughter? I was letting her down, and I missed her, but I didn't want to return to Middlesbrough. Then one day, when I was leaving the office to go for lunch with the girls, I found John leaning against a wall, on the far side of the narrow lane, waiting for me.

"Go on, I'll catch up with you," I told my friends.

John greeted me with a big smile. He was affectionate, eager to see me after five days away. He took my arm, and guided me to a coffee shop on the corner. With coffee and sandwiches ordered, he took hold of my hand across the table. I don't know what I was feeling at the time. Confused? Last time we were together, he was secretive, distant. Now, here he was so happy to see me.

"I've been to Holland," he said.

I remained silent and expressionless in the face of more betrayal and deceit.

"I've been to see Anke, the woman I . . . met in Calella, to see if our relationship could go further."

I really wasn't interested. "And?"

"It was only a holiday romance for her. Now I know it's over and has no future, I want it to be me and you again. I want to give all my love to you."

Really! You know what you can do with your love.

"I've been thinking about my future too, while you've been away," I said, "and I've decided it's not with you. I'm going back to Middlesbrough to the one person who has loved me unconditionally since she was born."

I felt strong and sure. John was on his own to do as he wished. Me? I was going home.

FIVE

It felt good to be in my home town. People waved greetings across the street or from a passing bus, something that never happened in London where, apart from my work colleagues and friends in the hotel, I was anonymous and invisible.

I settled in with my parents and applied for welfare. I didn't want to work until I was sure Jackie had recovered from her insecurities from the unsettling moves and separation from me. The first thing to do was apply for subsidized local authority housing for us. Then it was attending evening classes at Kirby College, an adult education college, to catch up on the qualifications I had failed to get as a result of being expelled from school. I had ability, and didn't find studying to be particularly difficult, and besides, I would need some qualifications for when I started job hunting.

In town, I bumped into Bill Collett, a bus driver I used to work with. He'd always had a soft spot for me. He told me most of the drivers I'd worked with had left the corporation buses to work for Beeline, a long-distance coaching company. "You'll find us most evenings in the bar in the Park Hotel, unless we're away overnight. Come and see us. You look as if you could do with a good laugh."

The Park Hotel was a short walk from Kirby College where I took my evening classes. I began to stop by the pub on my way home, where I drank inexpensive lime and soda. The guys welcomed me into their fold as one of the gang. Evenings filled with laughter in the Park Hotel became the highlight of my week. Sometimes, Dave, a driver with Beeline who had to pass my house to get home, gave me a ride home. He became a close friend and felt like the brother I never had. More often than not, I walked the almost two miles home. In those days, it was generally safe to walk the streets alone late at night.

One night, I was walking home, my route taking me along a deserted, tree-lined avenue in a middle-class area. At the end of the avenue was an isolated lane, which led to a bridge that crossed over the railway line. From there, it was only a five-minute walk to my parents' house. I often walked the route and never felt anxious.

That warm summer's night, the full moon was shining. I was content, filled with the laughter of the previous few hours. Life was going well. From out of nowhere, a stern voice ordered, "Go the long way home."

I stumbled in surprise then said out loud, "Okay," not questioning it even though going the long way home would add forty minutes to my journey. Maybe I was so relaxed I was almost in a trance.

I arrived home around midnight and went to bed. The next morning, as I swam and played with Jackie at the public swimming pool, friends asked me if I'd heard the news.

"What news?" I asked.

"A girl was attacked on the railway bridge last night."

I was shocked then filled with gratitude for the guardian angel who had been watching over me the night before.

At the age of twenty-four, I was offered a local authority apartment, five minutes' walk from my parents' home. It came at a good time. After two and a half years of living with my parents, I was on the verge of outstaying my welcome. Grinning, I strolled round the light and airy, spacious apartment. It was above a butcher's shop in a strip mall. It was also in need of some serious TLC. Nevertheless, I was delighted. This was my very own place. Not my parents' house. Not a furnished rental property. This was an unfurnished place with lots of space for me and Jackie to spread out in.

It was going to take a lot of hard work to make it pleasant to live in, but I didn't have to move in immediately. I could continue staying with Mum and Dad until it was up to scratch. My first thoughts were of what color paint to buy. Then I had to learn to paint.

I made lists of the materials I would need, then set to, scraping off six layers of wallpaper.

Living on welfare leaves you with very little spare cash. I was poor. But I had been saving up for this day for several years. It cost more to buy colored paint instead of white, but I wanted, no, needed, color in my house. Color lifted my spirits, helped me feel vibrant and alive.

After painting five ceilings in one day, I was exhausted and my neck and shoulders ached. The following day, I returned to inspect the previous day's work. Appalled and shocked, I ran from room to room then slumped to the floor and sobbed my heart out. Tears of despair rolled down my cheeks as I stared aghast at the newly painted ceilings. All my hard work had been for nothing. The new coat of paint had bubbled and peeled. Then I began swearing.

When I calmed down, I scoured the decorating books. No answers there. I called my mother. She came to see.

"I would say the ceilings had whitewash on them, and you can't paint over whitewash, it's a mix of lime and water," she said.

"Whitewash in this day and age!" I raged.

I took a day off and strolled round the park in the sunshine to gather myself for the chore that lay ahead. Next day, I began washing paint and whitewash off all the ceilings to prepare them for primer and another coat of paint. Stubborn and determined, my mother had always said of me. She didn't know the half of it.

Weeks later, ceilings and walls in pristine condition, we moved in. With a chit from the welfare department, I obtained some used furniture free of charge from a charity—three beds, chests of drawers, wardrobes for the bedrooms, and a sofa for Jackie's play room. I already had my deceased grandmother's oak dining table and chairs, her linens, and some pots, pans, and cutlery that Mum and

Dad had stored in their house. My parents gave me their old sofa and sideboard. Some of the furniture was not very pretty, but we had enough for our needs, and it was better than sitting on milk crates.

SIX

Jackie, by then eight years old, loved our new home, and her school was directly across the street. She could call to me from the school fence. Shortly before we moved in, Jackie arrived at the apartment carrying a Sylvester cat look-alike.

"Look, Mum, this cat needs a home."

"It may well need one, but not here. Anyway, it probably has a home already, and its owners are looking for it. Now take it out."

Neither the cat nor Jackie was listening. The black cat with white paws and chest moved in before we did. And she was pregnant. We called her Tibby and prepared a nest of torn papers for her in the kitchen. Tibby didn't take the hint. Overnight, she took the papers upstairs to the airing cupboard and made a nest to her own liking. We arrived one day to find she had delivered two black kittens.

How on earth was I going to feed us all on my paltry income? Easy. Growling Stomach and Hunger Pains became my middle names. But emotionally, Jackie needed her pet and that was all that mattered. When one of the kittens died, we kept the survivor. So now it was only two extra mouths to feed.

With winter approaching, I went to see my bank manager to ask for a loan.

"My apartment only has a coal fire in the living room. That won't keep us warm in the winter. I want to buy a gas fire to warm the living room and a gas boiler to heat the water, which will cost less than using the electric water heater," I said. "I also want an overnight electric storage heater to place in the entrance hall. Its heat will rise to warm the bedrooms in winter."

He checked the papers in front of him, information about my savings account, and looked over the figures I had prepared.

"Miss Wickman, I'm impressed," he said. "I've never given a loan before to someone on welfare, but I'm giving one to you. I can see how over the years you have saved from your low income, and I have no doubt you will repay your loan."

Outside the bank, I jumped into the air and clicked my heels. Saved! The large eight-foot by four-foot, metal-framed windows in the living room and my bedroom would not keep the cold out in the winter, and I hadn't relished spending long lonely nights shivering in the cold.

I switched to day classes. Moving out of my parents' home meant I had no one to watch Jackie when I was at evening classes. The teachers told me I was clever enough to go on to college if I wanted to. It was something to consider at a later date. I was grateful that the welfare system was providing me with the opportunity to be home for my daughter and to study for educational qualifications, but living on the poverty line was difficult. A few years after we moved into our apartment, inflation was raging at twenty-five percent a year. Before receiving my annual cost-of-living raise in welfare income, I was twenty-five percent below the poverty line, and more often than not, had more week than money. Not having food for me to eat before pay day was common, and if I ever had none for Jackie, I sent her to visit my parents. Sometimes, I went too. Pride would not allow me to tell them how I was struggling to make ends meet. Besides, I wasn't sure how much sympathy I would get. Mum had told me stories of her parents' difficulties trying to feed their large family when she was growing up in the depression. I was so poor, I cut worn-thin sheets and towels down the center. Then I placed the less worn side edges to the center and stitched them in place with the sewing machine I had invested in to make our clothes. I was grateful for the sewing skills I'd learned from my mother when I was a teenager. Many of Jackie's clothes I made from clothing bought in rummage sales. At the market, I bought remnants for pennies and made patchwork curtains and bedspread, with a pink and white color scheme, for Jackie's bedroom. I made curtains from discounted fabric for living rooms and bedrooms. My biggest project was making a winter coat for myself when I attended a tailoring class to obtain a City and Guilds qualification in tailoring.

Apart from family, my bus driver friend Dave was my only visitor. I was always pleased to see him even though he mainly needed a friend to listen to his romantic ups and downs. Still, he helped us decorate our Christmas tree, which didn't stay upright for long with the cats considering it one of their toys. I gave up when I came home and found the tree on the floor surrounded with colorful glass from smashed baubles. Dave also occasionally babysat for me. I had bought a guitar and went to weekly lessons. I figured having to practice every day would help me develop the self-discipline necessary for when I went to college. I learned to play well technically, but my heart was not in the music and after starting college, I gradually stopped playing. I lost my scrabble partner when Dave found the love of his life, and his visits tailed off.

Welfare recipients at that time were allowed to earn the grand sum of two pounds per week. I took a Saturday morning job at Welfords Bakery, doing comptometer work, totaling bills, invoices, and anything else that was required. One day, I was walking the three miles home from work, (to save money, I walked everywhere, except in inclement weather) when the tooting of a car horn got my attention, and a mini-car that had seen better days pulled up alongside me. The driver wound down his window.

"Pauline, is that you?"

I bent down and looked in.

"Ken! What are you doing here?" I said, pleased to see an old friend. "You're a long way from home."

"Just going to work, in Welfords."

"You work in Welfords? So do I. In the office, part-time on Saturdays."

"Where are you going?"

"Home."

"Hop in. I'll give you a lift. I've plenty of time before my shift starts."

Ken was a long-distance semi-trailer driver, delivering Welfords' baked goods to shops on the other side of the country. He started work at 4:00 in the afternoon and drove through the night. Ken dropped me at my apartment.

"Do you get out much?" he asked.

"No. I'm a single parent, Ken. Too hard up and no baby sitters."

"How about going out with me at the weekend, you and Jackie?"

"I'd love it," I said. No playing hard to get for me.

"See you then."

Dave came over a few days later. Over a game of scrabble, he told me I was perkier.

"Oh, I met an old friend the other day, Ken Archer."

"Ken Archer? I know him," Dave said. "He used to work for United Buses out of Redcar depot same as me."

I began dating Ken. I felt safe with him. He was confident and kind and included Jackie in our outings, except for the occasional times Mum and Dad babysat for me. A playful rivalry developed between Dave and Ken. They both lived in the seaside town of Redcar and their paths often crossed. They would joke with one another.

"You going to see Pauline tonight?" one of them would say.

"Yes."

"In that case, I'll stay away. I know you wouldn't stand a chance if I was around."

Fortunately, Ken knew that Dave was a friend only, even when he came to see me more often after his girlfriend broke his heart by going off to Australia with someone else.

One night, a noise I didn't recognize startled me from sleep. Relieved that Jackie was staying at my parents, I crept downstairs to tackle the burglars. Lying on the hall floor beneath the letter box, I found boxes of cakes and fruit pies. Giggling, I ran to the living room window and opened it.

"Hey, handsome! You with the black hair!"

Ken looked up and smiled.

"Do you want a coffee?" I asked.

He locked his tractor trailer door and bounded up the stairs to my apartment. So at 3:30 a.m., I piled the boxes on the counter top and put the kettle on.

I nodded toward the food. "Rations?" I asked with a big smile.

"Thought they'd come in useful. They're rejects. Marks and Spencer rejects a full tray even if only one pie has a damaged lattice top. They'll only be sold to the pig farmers. You may as well have some."

I nodded sure that Ken had brought the food parcels because he remembered my reaction when he took me out for dinner at a fancy restaurant. I couldn't enjoy the meal no matter how much I tried. It pained me to think the money he spent on that one meal was almost two weeks food allowance for me and Jackie.

I gave him a key so that he could come in and put the baked goods in the kitchen instead of through the letterbox. The next time he brought pies, a swish-swish sound I didn't recognize woke me up. Heart thumping loudly, I sneaked downstairs only to discover Ken. The swishing noise was caused by his nylon overalls when his thighs rubbed together as he walked.

One day, Ken took Jackie and me for a drive into the countryside. On a narrow country lane, he swerved, stopped the car, and ran back to pick up a hedgehog in the road and take it to safety. That was when friendship turned to love.

A few months later, Ken and I went to see the movie *A Clockwork Orange,* which contains a rape scene. Leaving the cinema, people were laughing about the movie. I felt out of synchronicity with everyone else. I was disturbed, unsettled, as if someone had slipped me a roofie and violated me while I was unconscious. Something wasn't right, but what? The feeling continued for weeks then months, affecting my relationship with Ken. My doctor gave me tranquilizers, but they didn't help. I slipped into a depression. Concerned, Ken lent me his mynah bird. It certainly lit up my life. Whenever I walked into the room, it gave a loud wolf-whistle, which made me laugh. Mynah birds are good imitators and this one was no exception. It kept making a noise that at first I had difficulty deciphering. Then I laughed out loud. The bird was imitating Ken's struggling car battery slowly bringing Ken's engine to life on a cold winter's morning.

Dad called in to bring his electric drill so I could put up some shelves. He also wanted to see Ken's mynah bird, which rose to the occasion by entertaining Dad with a selection of noises he had learned. Over a cup of coffee, Dad told me he and Mum were planning to go on a coach trip to Bournemouth on the south coast.

Poor Dad had no idea how out of tune he was with his wife.

"You know Mum wants to go abroad, don't you?"

Dad lifted his head, blinked his eyes several times. "No she doesn't. We have no desire to go abroad. Nothing wrong with Bournemouth."

"Dad! You walk around with your head up your Kyber Pass! Why do you think Mum has travel brochures all over the house for coach trips to Europe? Or hadn't you noticed?"

This was one of those rare occasions Dad was struck dumb.

"If you look at the clues, you'll see Mum wants to go farther afield than Bournemouth and the south coast."

Next thing, they were going on vacation to Belgium, and every vacation they took after that was somewhere on the continent.

My depression worsened. Memories of being raped five years earlier had returned to my conscious mind. I noticed no feelings attached to the event, merely an acknowledgement of the facts. Eventually, after eighteen months together, Ken told me he was seeing someone else. I didn't blame him. I'd become clingy and needy. I even begged him to marry me.

"Pauline, you have ambition. You want to go to college, get a well-paid job. I'm not ambitious enough to be the man for you."

Although heartbroken, I knew he was right. I kissed him on the cheek and sent him on his way. I was bereft. I started binge eating. The result? Thirty extra pounds.

I hadn't been seeing much of Dave, who was busy dating, trying to find someone special. But when his mother died, he visited frequently, and we cried on each other's shoulders.

As if I didn't have enough misery, the coalminers went on strike. With winter approaching, England was on a three-day working week to try and conserve fuel supplies. There were frequent power cuts. That winter, I spent many a lonely night, sitting by a hurricane lamp loaned to me by my parents, reading with Tibby curled up on my lap, trying to keep warm. Thank goodness I had a gas fire to warm the living room. The electric storage heater, however, could not work without power, and the rest of the apartment was freezing. I had few blankets and piled our coats on Jackie's bed to keep her warm, while I shivered under the few covers on my bed. Sometimes, I was so cold, I crept into Jackie's bed to snuggle up to her for warmth. I was also glad that Tibby had out determined me to become a member of our household. She increased her attentions toward me, sensing my wretchedness, the darkness in my mind engulfing me as much, if not more, than the dark shadows in the corners of the room. With my depression worsening, I returned to my doctor.

"I feel suicidal," I told him. "I can barely get out of bed in the morning. Those tablets you gave me are not helping me at all."

He arranged an appointment with a psychiatrist. I wasn't too impressed with him. He should have been taking the tablets he prescribed for me. Maybe he was. Anyway, he switched me from tranquilizers to anti-depressants after hearing my symptoms.

I told him how I had to drop one of my college courses because I couldn't concentrate. How, when I walked home from college, I stood on the railway bridge, wondering if the next train would be the one I would jump in front of, but how I fought the urge because I didn't want my mother bringing up my daughter. I told him I felt as if an alien being had taken over my body, and that I hid away because even though I still looked like me, I was not me, and I didn't want anyone to think it was. I felt as if I'd fallen into a deep dark well, and was stuck at the bottom, unable to climb out.

His response was to tell me to keep taking the tablets.

The pills helped eventually, when I reached the maximum dose. Whenever I tried to reduce the dose, the suicidal feelings returned. The medication was helping me to cope with the symptoms of depression so I could get on with my life, but they were doing nothing to heal the cause. I was naturally optimistic and resilient. Feeling this way was not normal for me. There had to be a cause that needed to be ferreted out and dealt with.

I struggled on, doing my best to protect Jackie from my problems. Fortunately, she had lots of friends, who often played in our apartment and slept over. Being a single parent, our apartment was the place for kids to hang out so as to keep out of their own parents' hair.

The entrance to our apartment was between two shop doorways. As Jackie was coming home one day, Harold, the butcher downstairs, was on the doorstep, smoking a cigarette. "Do you like meat?" he asked her.

"I don't know. We don't eat much meat," she said.

Hmm. Why is Harold talking to children? Do I need to watch him?

A few days later, Harold stopped me as I was going out. He was in his doorway, blue striped apron stained with blood and bald head gleaming with sweat from the heat given off by his large copper boilers. He was rolling a cigarette. His horn-rimmed glasses were so greasy and dirty, I don't know how he realized I was there.

"Your daughter says you don't eat much meat. Is that right?"

"Yes, that's right. I don't have the money to buy meat. We eat lots of eggs and cheese and beans."

"So it's not because you're vegetarian or anything, then."

"No, just hard up."

"Maybe we can help each other out," Harold said.

I took a step back from this rotund, sweating man in his late fifties. "What do you mean?"

He spoke as if offering me a business proposition, but I detected a hint of pleading in his voice. "If I supplied you with some meat, sausage, bacon, ham, steak and kidney, would you invite me up for a cup of tea mid mornings when you're home?"

Seeing my hesitation, he continued, "You saw they changed this place from a retail shop to a small factory. I miss chatting to customers. It's lonely with only myself to talk to all day."

I felt extremely dubious, but also felt I could be misjudging him. "Okay," I said. "Let's see how it goes."

Fortunately, it went very well. Harold never made any indecent propositions to me, and we enjoyed our chats over tea. I also don't know how I could have put food on the table without his help in a period of raging inflation. He was a life-saver.

Later that spring, Graham in King's Cross, wrote to ask if I would run his hotel so he and his wife could take a vacation together, something they hadn't done in ten years. Of course, I jumped at the chance. Anything to earn some extra money. Jackie and I caught the coach to London and took care of business for Graham and his wife. I was glad I did because Graham died unexpectedly soon afterward.

Still struggling with depression, I completely lost any confidence I had in my psychiatrist when he asked if I was a lesbian. At that time, to save money, I had my short hair trimmed at a man's barber shop as he charged less than women's hairstylists, but my haircut was not manly. I also wore pants most of the time as I walked everywhere and wore comfortable walking shoes. It also saved me a fortune in pantyhose. How would I ever get well in this doctor's care?

Then, out of the blue, I received an unexpected visit from John. I knew straight away why he'd come. It was a repeat of his visit to Holland. He'd met a woman, and they were talking marriage. He had to see me one last time to see if sparks still flew between us. They didn't. I'd moved on, and once I've move on, I don't go back. An overnight stay, because he had driven a long way, and he was on his way home. He was obviously not impressed by my poor furnishings and lack of money, so it was goodbye and good riddance.

Soon after, in a raffle, I won a week's vacation in a caravan at Staithes, a picturesque fishing village on the north Yorkshire coast. It was a welcome break. I'd not been able to take Jackie on vacation since we moved into our apartment. Mum and Dad had taken her places, but the only thing I could afford was a free walk round the nearby public park and playground. Dad drove us to Staithes and gave me some money for food. We took Jill with us, one of Jackie's friends. She was also from a hard-up family. We had fun playing on the small beach and walking along the cliff top in the fresh sea air and eating fish and chips from the fish shop, a luxury for us.

Also that year I had another visitor. Frank Murtha wrote from Spain and asked if he could visit. Of course, I replied I'd be delighted to see him. He arrived in November. Bad time of year. He couldn't stop complaining that the cold weather was too much for him. He had braved the chilly English weather to offer me a deal—marriage. If I agreed, I would, as his wife, qualify for income from his American social security. Having noticed how little I had to live on, he said, "You won't have to be so poor anymore, and you will still get that income after I die."

I gave his proposition a lot of thought. It was *really* tempting to think of escaping our poverty-stricken existence. In the end, rather than uproot Jackie again to return to Spain as Frank's wife, I refused his offer. After he left to go back to Calella, I pondered his extraordinary suggestion. It was some years later, after Frank died of a heart attack, that I realized he was hoping I would marry him to take care of him. Being alone in Spain when he had his first heart attack, the Veterans Association had shipped him back to America for treatment. He had written to say that as soon as he was well enough to leave the New York hospital, he would find passage on a ship to Spain. The only thing on offer in America was to be taken in and cared for by a family as long as he gave them his social security allowance, and he wasn't prepared to do that. As soon as he was able, Frank sneaked out of the hospital and returned to Spain, only to die eighteen months later.

I was still studying, working toward qualifications that would get me into college to earn a degree, which seemed the best course of action. I would receive a student grant, which would be ten percent more than my current welfare income. Only problem was, I had no idea what I wanted to do with my life, so how was I supposed to choose which degree to study for?

The reference librarian found The Vocational Guidance Association in London, which had an excellent reputation for putting people on the right track. Using the small amount of money saved toward my winter fuel bills, I traveled to London on the overnight coach to face a busy day—vocational guidance test in the morning, interview regarding the preliminary results in the afternoon, and overnight coach home—a five hundred mile round trip. The suggestions offered in the interview did not appeal to me. In fact, they were downright disappointing. All the way home, I silently cursed at wasting my savings. Two weeks later, the written report arrived. It contained several suggestions—journalist, teacher in adult education, probation officer, psychologist, or social worker. I didn't fancy any of them. For days I rebuked myself for squandering my bill money. During my interview, I had been told that probation would probably be the best career for me. I had been angry and disappointed about that. My perception of probation work was of having to deal with insolent, cocky, fourteen-year-old lawbreakers who thought they knew it all. Did I really want to make a career of working with those people? No, I did not.

Once I'd calmed down, I checked out which colleges offered the courses I could take to obtain qualifications for each suggestion. Apart from studying to become a probation officer, all the other careers required a move to another town. No deal. Uprooting Jackie was not an option. The only thing left was a course at our local polytechnical college if I were to follow the vocational guidance assessment of me. A three-year Social Studies Bachelor of Science degree course, followed by a two-year probation and social work course would bring me to a probation career. I was pleasantly surprised to discover, on visiting the local probation office, that probation work was vastly different to what I had imagined it to be. It was interesting, diverse, and challenging. Maybe I hadn't wasted my money after all.

At twenty-eight years of age, I applied to Teesside Polytechnical College to be admitted as a mature student.

But there was still some cleaning up of the past to do before I started my new life. I had applied for maintenance, after Jackie was born eleven years earlier, and was awarded the grand sum of seventy-five pence a week. I never received a penny. I applied to the court for an increase and that's when Jackie's father came back into her life. She was delighted to be spending time with him. At school she had been taunted by other kids about not having a father. I had told her she did have a father only he didn't live with us. One day, the bullying became physical. Jackie stood at the school fence, calling to me in our apartment. I opened the window.

She was crying. "William hit me!"

"Jackie, go and hit him back. Right now! You tower above everyone else. Just hit him, and he won't mess with you again!" I yelled and shut the window.

When school finished, Jackie bounced into the house.

"So, did you hit him?"

She grinned. "Yes."

"Did it feel good?"

"Yes."

"Don't ever let anybody bully you again. Now you know how to stand up for yourself, you can do it again."

There was no more name calling or bullying at school after that.

Jackie bloomed. Meeting her father filled the empty space inside her. Like him she was tall, had blonde hair and freckles. This was where she came from. However, it became apparent that Jackie's father wanting to spend time with her was a ploy to try and rekindle a relationship with me. When he finally understood that it would never happen, he began missing his visits to Jackie, and soon they ceased altogether.

Jackie had opened her heart to him, and he had broken it as he had broken mine all those years before. "I hate him," she said. "I wouldn't spit on him if he was on fire on the footpath in front of me."

"Jackie, don't hate him. Your dad isn't a bad man. He's just an irresponsible man. If he was meant to be in your life, he would be. The only reason your dad and I got together was to have you. That was his sole purpose for coming into my life. His job is done."

I was never able to convince her to think more kindly of him.

The years between twenty-four and twenty-eight was one of the two darkest periods of my life. Dealing with suicidal depression and poverty required all my strength and determination, but it was the poverty that left the biggest emotional scars that I still carry to this day. Not having the money to take Jackie to the beach only seven miles away, not being able to take her to the public swimming pool, which was on our doorstep, not being able to indulge her teenage needs for electronics and fashion, not being able to take her to the movies or on vacation is still a knife in the heart, and lack of money for socializing left me lonely and isolated.

Living on welfare for such a long time was something I chose to do. Despite the struggle, improving my long-term situation through education was worth the effort. Discipline and budgeting skills kept me from a life of financial chaos, otherwise I'd have been one of those people whose electricity would be cut off for not paying the bills, or I would have been up to my eyeballs in debt, or thrown out of my apartment for not paying the rent.

At the time, because of my creed, "I've got me and I can cope," I failed to recognize the help that came my way to show me I was not facing the world on my own. Only later in life was I able to marvel at the amount of succor and support I received in my time of need: Ken's love and stability; butcher Harold providing us with much needed food; Dave's friendship; Graham asking me to run his hotel, allowing me to earn much needed extra cash; our cat Tibby, a companion, who helped me through my depression and loneliness and helped Jackie to feel loved; the vacation I won in a raffle; closure with both Jackie's father and John S.; and finally, vocational guidance that put me on the path of a satisfying career.

SEVEN

Twenty-eight and still not married. To my family I was on the shelf, I'd let life pass me by, meaning any opportunity I'd had to get married had been and gone. Both my mother and sister married when they were eighteen, and here I was, ten years older and still single. At first, the comments caused me to feel dissatisfied with my life, that something was lacking. Then I realized I was really very happy. Having been accepted by Teesside Polytechnic, I was moving toward my goals. I also met Alan through a singles club. We hit it off immediately. He was eight years older than I was, a bald, short, solidly-built man, who wore thick glasses, not exactly handsome, but energetic and not afraid to voice his opinion on political matters or call someone out whom he thought was a poser. Life became stimulating, filled with laughter and lively discussions. He was divorced with teenage children who lived with their mother, which meant he was comfortable with Jackie being around. He was also self-employed as a truck driver. More drivers in my life? What was it about me and drivers?

First day at the poly was an induction day where faculty members introduced themselves to the students. When Malcom Sweeting, the student counselor, spoke, I sat up and paid attention. Maybe he would be the person to help me find the root cause of my depression.

As soon as I settled into the academic routine, I made an appointment to see him. Counseling sessions took place in his cramped office. A tall man in his late fifties with a graying beard, more often than not Malcom wore a corduroy jacket with elbow patches. Piles of interesting psychotherapy books sat on his desk, which he would study between appointments with students. Malcom had been a lay preacher. In that occupation, he started developing his counseling skills. Although he was not a certified counselor, I have found few counselors who could match his proficiency, patience, acceptance, and ability.

We finally uncovered the cause of my depression during our tenth session. Malcom asked me to name the three most painful things that had happened to me.

I blithely listed three events—being raped, giving a child away for adoption, and feeling emotionally neglected by my parents.

"Tell me about the rape," Malcom said.

I laid out the facts of that night.

"Pauline, you are giving me facts. Tell me how you felt and how you feel now."

Long pause.

Reaching deep down inside, I dredged up my feelings. I didn't recognize my own voice. With tears streaming down my face, my body trembling, and a shaky voice that kept breaking with emotion, I recalled my anger, anguish, despair, feelings of betrayal, and my loss of self worth. My strong emotional response took me by surprise. I was an empty vessel with filthy grease clinging to my inner walls, and with one simple question, Malcom had reached in and scraped the debris away. I had no idea I had been so deeply affected by having been raped. I thought I was coping so well, but I was coping by keeping all knowledge of the event in my head, remaining completely oblivious to the pain in my heart.

Thus I became aware of the tremendous emotional pain I carried as a result of being raped. With awareness came liberation. I now knew what I was dealing with. No more floundering around in the dark like some lost soul. I had a goal to work toward—the healing of my pain, the healing of self, and Malcom would be my ally, my confidante and guide during my painful journey. With this realization, I was freed from the need to take antidepressant medication. From being in a situation where I required the maximum dosage just to function, I quit cold turkey with no ill effects whatsoever. Previously, when I tried reducing the dosage, I began feeling suicidal again. But not this time. I was no longer down that deep, dark well. I had hope.

Shortly after stopping the medication, I had my final appointment with the psychiatrist. He was appalled that I had stopped cold turkey instead of slowly reducing the dosage. However, I listened to my own inner guidance. All would be well. I didn't need medication any more.

Malcom's sessions included dream interpretation. He believed the subconscious offered insight and guidance through dreams. My earlier dreams were along the lines of being chased by secret agents in black suits, intent on hunting me down to kill me. Sometimes, I was chased along the streets of an industrial English town, sometimes along the streets of a Greek Mediterranean village, sometimes day, sometimes night. In every dream I was terrified, but somehow escaped by finding a dark corner to hide in, a disused warehouse, for example, usually surrounded by spider webs and spiders, which scared me every bit as much as my pursuers. As my healing journey progressed, I began having healing dreams such as finding a neglected horse covered in ticks and sores. In the dream, I washed the horse, pulled off the ticks and rubbed ointment on its sores. Malcom explained that I was the horse, and I was healing myself.

I received counseling from Malcom all through my three-year degree course. At one point, concerned about my possibly becoming too dependent on him, Malcom introduced me to a group therapist who was an expert in Transactional Analysis. The concepts used in T.A. were helpful, particularly the idea of Parent, Adult, and Child ego states, and Racket feelings (a feeling, such as anger or sadness or resentment, that becomes a subconscious habitual reaction to events in your life) and Strokes, which refers to the human need for attention. If we don't get attention for being good, we'll settle for negative attention by being naughty. The concepts made it easy to understand my life and my interactions with others. I taught the concepts to Jackie to show her how my depressed state had probably affected her. In later years, I took the tools T.A. gave me into my probation work. Clients found it an easy way to understand their situations, leading to change in attitude and family dynamics.

By participating in group-therapy, the reactions of others in the group showed me I had value as a person, that I was not worthless like the rapists had treated me. I learned to love and accept myself, warts and all. I did not have to be perfect or any other way to be loveable. I just had to be me. This knowledge enabled me to love and accept other people as they are with all their imperfections. I also learned let go of the fear of rejection and ask for help. I practiced that a lot in role playing.

During one group-therapy session, the therapist asked, "Can you forgive your attackers, Pauline?"

My heart hardened as concrete. "No. I'll never forgive them."

The idea of forgiving involved an element of my being superior to people who hurt me, and I didn't feel that way. However, I was able to hand them over to God, which freed me from having any particularly strong feelings about them. I was able to let go, knowing that no one escaped what they did. After dying, everyone must face up to their actions or lack of action in this life. There is a spiritual law of cause and effect. You can make up for your misdeeds by doing good, but you can't eradicate them. I rest easy knowing that all is seen and all is dealt with appropriately by a higher power.

After Jackie's father died, he appeared to her and then to me. Although we were unaware at the time that he had died, we later checked at the registrar's office of births and deaths. Telepathically, he asked me to forgive him. I told him I'd let go of any feelings I had about him and the difficulties he'd caused me by not meeting his obligations. He had to face the karma he'd created for himself, and my forgiving him had nothing to do with it. You reap what you sow.

The love and support I received in my therapy groups caused me to want to help others heal their pain as I had been helped. I would be able to do this in my probation work.

Alan and I were still dating. He would have liked a commitment, but I couldn't. I didn't love him enough to consider marriage. I was too focused on achieving my goals, even though life with Alan would never become boring. One winter, we volunteered with an organization that sought to help homeless men living in squalid conditions. We worked on a soup run, taking hot soup and sandwiches to homeless people in the area. Many were alcoholics, some turning to drink because they could not cope after their wives died. They were living in fetid, derelict houses, filled with the odor of feces and other filth. The warming food we brought on a cold winter's night, the few minutes companionship and conversation, and our recognition of them as our fellow human beings lifted their spirits, at least for a little while. I was grateful to and filled with admiration for Alan for sharing this experience for me.

One night, Alan and I were supposed to be going out to a show. He arrived with a blackened face and smelling of smoke. Having left the deep frying pan on the stove when he went to have his bath, he emerged from the bathroom, to find his house filled with smoke and the kitchen on fire. Fortunately, he put the fire out with an extinguisher. We spent the next couple of months washing the inside of his house and painting over the smoke damage. Another night, Alan fell asleep on my sofa. Opportunity knocked. Unable to resist and knowing I was dicing with death, I took my scissors and snipped off the long strands of hair he combed over his bald pate in a useless attempt to hide his baldness. A shiver of fear. How would he react? I'd really pushed my luck this time. When he woke up, I told him with some trepidation what I had done.

There was no explosion of anger, he merely said, "You thought it was pointless combing my hair over?"

"Yes," I said, "you're bald. It's okay to be bald. It's a part of you, and it doesn't bother me at all."

We had many a long discussion about what I was learning in sociology and economics. My efforts inspired Alan to become a mature student himself. As I was on the verge of completing my degree course, Alan embarked on a new life as a mature student at Harlech College, in Wales, studying for a degree in social history.

While a student at Teesside Polytechnic, I read some books about the teachings of Sathya Sai Baba, a highly revered spiritual teacher in India. Inspired by what he had to say, I developed a new creed to live my life by. According to my understanding of his teachings, all you had to do to live a spiritual life was fill the day with love and love your neighbor as you would wish to be loved.

I still practice this creed forty years later. It's not difficult. I go to the supermarket. If I see someone looking miserable or some senior alone, I'll start a conversation. More often than not, they enjoy the social exchange. Maybe I'll be the only person they'll talk to that day, apart from the checkout operator.

The studying, the caring for my daughter, and working part-time left me too exhausted to obtain good grades. Something had to go. The only thing I could do was quit my job. Mum didn't help with her constant, "Why don't you give up the struggle and find a nice office job?" She may have thought she was helping, but subconsciously, she was trying to sabotage my plans to obtain a degree, as her dreams of making something of her life had been thwarted by her parents.

In the end, I went to see a hypnotist. Despite all my efforts studying and revising, I was not retaining the information I needed to pass my final exams. Under hypnosis, the hypnotist programmed my subconscious. "You will recall everything you need to know to answer the exam questions. Everything you read you will retain in your mind, ready for the knowledge to come out during your exams."

It worked. I felt inspired when I read the questions and began scribbling down the answers to everything the examiners wanted. With a Bachelor of Science degree under my belt, I was ready to take on the two-year social work course.

EIGHT

The Home Office in London paid me a trainee's salary while I trained to become a probation officer. That increased my income by six pounds a week. Having learned to live on my student grant, I diligently saved that extra money during the two years of the course, knowing that it would be enough for a deposit to buy an inexpensive house when my course ended.

Several three-month residential placements were required during the course. My first placement was across country in Wales in a residential home for boys. The experience was fun. *Grease* was all the rage, and the boys were always dancing to the music. I'm not sure how valuable it was for learning to be a probation officer, but it was a pleasant break.

Four months after that I was sent to Liverpool, on placement with a private charitable social-work agency that helped poor families. One of the most important things I learned there was to have knowledge of what resources were available in the community that could help your clients. While I was away, Jackie and Tibby (Tibby's offspring had been killed by a car some months earlier) stayed with my mother. But, after a few weeks, Jackie wanted to live at home on her own with the cat. She was fourteen and a half years old. I was only halfway through my placement with six weeks still to go when I returned home to talk to her.

Two years earlier, she wouldn't wear the clothes I made for her. I also discovered she had given away to her friends most of her toys and her beautiful books that I had hoped she would pass on to her own children. I was heartbroken. The sacrifices I had made to provide her with those things had been for nothing. I sat her down at the kitchen table and went over our family budget. I pointed out that she had been receiving more than her fair share of the budget money for clothes and entertainment, while I had much less for myself.

"Does that seem right to you?" I asked.

"No."

"Things are going to change," I said. "From now on, I'm going to have my fair share of the money."

I had put her on a monthly clothing allowance from which she could buy her own clothes and shoes. If she splurged on expensive items, if she frittered the money away and did not put money to one side for a winter coat, well then, she would be cold.

Jackie had been shocked but rose to the occasion, surprising me with how well she managed her money. Now she wanted to live in her own home by herself. I told her I would agree if she showed the same discipline with a housekeeping allowance, and if her friend Jill's mother, who lived only four doors away, would allow Jill to sleep with her overnight.

My heart was in my throat at this experiment. I felt she was sensible enough, and I knew Mum and Dad would keep a close eye on her. She should be safe if she followed the rules I made about bedtime and what time to be in at night and who to allow in the house. However, if the plan fell apart and something bad happened to Jackie, I knew I could kiss my career goodbye.

"I trust you to be grown up and sensible," I told her.

Crossing my fingers and saying a prayer, I caught the train back to Liverpool, trying to reassure myself that it was only going to be for five weeks.

Fortunately, Jackie was sensible and stayed safe.

I loved the course work and my placement in the local probation office was an eye opener. Phil, my supervisor, had the same wicked sense of humor as I did. One day, he sent me on my first visit to the bridewell, the police cells beneath the court building, to interview defendants who had received prison sentences, in case they needed to have a relative informed or, if they had pets, make arrangements for their care.

"Knowing my luck, the prisoner will probably tell me to go fuck myself," I told Phil.

He stayed in the background as I approached my first prisoner and introduced myself.

"Go fuck yourself," he said, not happy at having received a ten year sentence.

I couldn't help myself. I burst out laughing. Not very professional.

My placement in the probation service opened up a new world for me. I felt surrounded by friends. I was included, indeed welcomed, at social events. Any lingering feelings I had of being lonely because something was wrong with me evaporated. I had arrived in a place that felt like home.

Shortly before I returned to college for my last term and final exams, I developed a nagging feeling I had an ailment that needed attention. Every three or four weeks, I went to my doctor to tell him something was wrong with me, but I couldn't explain any symptoms. My doctor was becoming exasperated. Maybe he thought I had some sort of crush on him. He gave me a full physical and a pap smear. The physical showed I was in good health. For some reason the pap smear could not be tested. I was told not to worry about it, and no one suggested performing another pap smear. I still couldn't shake the strong intuitive feeling that something was seriously wrong. Thankfully, my body's innate wisdom caused me to develop vaginal candidiasis. By now I felt unable to pester my doctor again. I went instead to the special clinic that would treat the fungal infection. The term "special clinic" was the euphemism given to the out-patient clinic that specialized in treating sexually transmitted diseases.

Another pap smear was performed. It came back positive for early stage cervical cancer.

"You need an operation at once," the doctor told me.

"It will have to wait, Doctor. I'm taking my social work exams over the next two weeks. I've worked hard for five years for this. No can do."

The doctor hesitated before setting the date for the earliest possible time after my exams were finished.

Shocked to discover I had a deadly disease at age thirty-two, I spent several days adjusting to the realization of my mortality in typical fashion, ranting and raving to God.

"I'm not ready to die yet. You'll just have to wait. There's too much to do, I have a daughter to bring up, a new career to start, a new life to build, so much of the world to see. So you've had it, God. You'll just have to do without me."

This episode really made me realize what was important in life. Not once did I say to God, not yet because I haven't owned this or that. I wanted to live because I wanted to experience more loving, more exploring, and more creating. It took me four days to come to terms with my situation. I was determined to live. I then had to tell my mother, who had already lost two sisters to cancer. I was strong now and prepared, able to comfort and reassure her that I would come through with flying colors. That did not include putting my arms round her. She was not a hugging person, at least with me.

I was the one needing an operation for cancer, studying for exams, in the middle of a house purchase to be followed by a house move, and starting a new job, all within the next four weeks, and I was the one comforting everybody else.

I took my exams, and knowing I'd done well, happily had my operation. Obviously, it was a success because I'm still here today. Within two days of leaving hospital, I was packing boxes and moving. Before I started my job, my sister Joan and her husband Herby took me on a trip to Gothenburg, Sweden to visit my cousin, Erika. I think Joan had been shocked that I, her invincible, precocious brat sister, had experienced cancer, and this was her way of saying she was glad I was alive.

Also traveling on the North Sea ferry was an Englishman named Hugh. He saw me on deck, alone, reading a good book, and enjoying the sunshine and a rare, calm North Sea crossing. He sat beside me and started a conversation. Turning my attention back to the book and ignoring him did not deter him. Before the twenty-four hour crossing was over, he had Joan and Herby under his spell and me agreeing to date him while I was in Gothenburg. At forty-three, Hugh was ten years older than I was. He was also recently divorced and the bitterness showed. His favorite song was Donna Summer's "I Will Survive". But he was also charming, fun, and I soaked up the attention he gave me. My last night in Gothenburg, I spent with Hugh. He prepared a champagne and caviar breakfast and laughed when I told him I preferred coffee, toast and marmalade. Before I returned to England, I'd fallen for him. With all the vacation time I had as a probation officer, I could visit Hugh, working for automaker Volvo, for five days every ten weeks. It had all been sudden and unexpected, but we were sure we wanted to marry.

Friday the thirteenth of July, South Bank probation office welcomed this spanking new officer. South Bank was a small town, three miles from Middlesbrough. It developed to house workers in the surrounding heavy industries of shipyard, steelworks, and the local chemical plants. Housing consisted of streets of terraced houses, much like the one I grew up in, local authority subdivisions, and larger private semi-detached homes. It was primarily a rough-and-ready blue-collar area. Cyril, the senior probation officer, had turned the probation office into a resource for the whole community by encouraging his team to offer help and support to residents as well as offenders. People could come to our office with all sorts of problems, knowing they would be helped or referred to the appropriate agency, following a phone call to give them a personal contact there. The probation service was valued in South Bank.

As I started my new career, moving us away from poverty, sixteen-year-old Jackie left school. After seeing me spend my evenings with my head in books studying, she had no desire to enter higher education. In our recession-hit country, few jobs were available, but, by her own initiative, she found a part-time job serving in a newsagent's shop. Fears and tears and resistance about leaving school and starting life as a young adult dissolved.

Our new home was not grand, a terraced house with three bedrooms and one and a half bathrooms. It needed a lot of work. After a day in the office, I spent my evenings scraping off wallpaper, sanding, painting, putting on new wallpaper and laying carpet to create a pleasant home environment.

Ten weeks into my new life, I met Peter.

We had mutual friends, including Eric, a probation-officer colleague. One evening, Eric and I went to a pub before going on to friend Benny's birthday party. I sat across the table from Peter. I couldn't make out his eyes behind his glasses, but he stood out from his friends, self-assured in a quiet way. I found him interesting. It wasn't an earth-shattering feeling, merely a muted acknowledgement, an almost subconscious connecting of energy. Nevertheless, it was there. I found him even more interesting after we left the pub to move on to Benny's house where the celebration continued. The lights were dim, the beat of disco music resounded throughout the place. I was dancing with Eric when the floor cleared and in pranced Peter doing the can-can in his underpants along with five other men kicking their legs to partygoers' cheers and whistles.

Later, at the drinks table, I was ladling the potent punch into my glass when Peter approached. I could tell he was under the influence. He looked down at me, not hard to do, I was only five-foot two.

"What's a pretty girl like you doing with this lot?"

"What do you think? I'm enjoying the party."

"Would you like to go out with me?" he asked, slurring his words.

"Why would I want to do that?"

"I'm only going to be around a few more weeks. I'm waiting for my visa to go and work in Israel. My pal's already gone, and I've no one to kick around with."

"Okay, I'll hang out with you. My boyfriend's working in Sweden. I get lonely too. It will be nice to have someone to do things with. But it can't go anywhere. I'm involved with Hugh in Sweden."

We were both on the same page. We'd hang out together for a few weeks until he left the country. Instead, I gradually fell in love with him.

Our first date, I rushed home late from work, delayed doing a home interview for a court report. There had been a Yorkshire terrier in the house, an itchy Yorkshire terrier that would not stop scratching all the time I was there. I prayed I would not take any of his fleas home with me. No such luck. I spotted a black spec on my cream corduroy pants, slapped my hand down, missed it and watched it leap off into space. Shoot! Now I would have to treat Tibby for flea control! Then I remembered—Tibby had died two days after I met Peter. She just curled up and died. A choking lump formed in my throat. The pain of her loss was almost unbearable. She had been with us eight years. Jackie and I wept uncontrollably at the unfairness of it. Jackie had gathered up Tibby's stiff-as-a-board corpse and taken it to bed with her, until I gently insisted we needed to bury Tibby in Gran and Granddad's garden. That had been only two days before.

Peter and I ate dinner in a cozy country pub with low, oak-beamed ceilings and an eclectic collection of fox-hunting memorabilia.

"I think we should lay some ground rules for our relationship," I said.

"We're having a relationship?"

I acknowledged his dry wit with a nod and continued. "I just want to make it absolutely clear this is about short-term companionship, so there'll be no complications."

"No worries. I'll be leaving as soon as my visa comes through."

It was a good deal for the two of us. Peter was a local man. At thirty-three years of age he had never married or even been in love. During the previous seven years, he had worked abroad as an electrician on various construction projects, such as building natural-gas pumping stations and oil installations in Togo, Iran, Oman, Saudi Arabia and Algeria. He was now waiting for a visa so he could work in Israel on a military airfield.

Dinner over, we returned to my house for a cup of coffee. I switched on the living room light.

"Tibby!" I called. Excited, I turned to Peter. "Did you see her? Tibby's ghost! She ran across the floor and through the closed kitchen door!"

Peter looked at me as if I had a tile loose. He was surely thinking what the hell had he got himself into.

Peter sauntered into the kitchen while I made coffee. "You saw your dead cat?"

"Yes, isn't it wonderful? She's still with us! I'm so happy! Wait till I tell Jackie!"

Now he was sure I was strange.

We sat on the sofa, and as I had not yet bought a coffee table, placed our coffee mugs on the floor and continued talking. Peter picked his mug up to take a drink. He pointed to a black speck doing the breast stroke in his coffee.

"Do I pay extra for this?"

Mortified, I stumbled through an explanation of my home visit for a court-report interview with a flea-ridden dog in the house.

I expected the craziness to frighten him off. Not so. We arranged to meet again, and we saw each other regularly. Six weeks later, Peter confessed he loved me. I was confused. I loved both Hugh and Peter. Peter's steadfastness tipped the scales in his favor. I wanted stability. We were alike. I liked his sense of humor. He liked to travel. He accepted me as I was. I bade farewell to Hugh. It wasn't too difficult. I knew he was cheating on me while he was in Sweden. He was recently divorced and raw, still needing to reassure himself nothing was wrong with him.

Peter proposed. The day after his proposal and my acceptance, he received a call. His visa had arrived. His response?

"Shit! Why didn't you call me earlier? I'm getting married now and can't go."

That response set the tone for half of our marriage, which was full of banter and light-hearted dismissal. If it ever changed to being ultra lovey-dovey, I would know in an instant that he was being unfaithful. The other half, the negative half, developed later.

Peter and me at Niagara Falls 1981

Peter wanted to know how I came to choose him instead of Hugh.

Not being a diplomat, I told him, "I made a list of pros and cons for both you and Hugh. You both had the same number of pros, but Hugh had more cons, particularly after he told me he would smooth over my rough edges to make it easier for me to mix in his social circles. I happen to believe I'm good enough as I am, and I'm done with men who don't think I am good enough."

I'd always been considered a bit of a black sheep, or at least unconventional enough to frequently spring surprises on family by coming up with wild ideas. It was common for my family to comment, exasperated, "What on earth is she up to now?"

Joan discovered our engagement announcement in the newspaper. "My goodness! Look, Herby! Pauline's finally done it. There's an announcement for Pauline's engagement in the paper . . . to Peter."

"Peter! Who the hell's Peter?" Herby asked.

That was how quickly our romance developed, only a few weeks and we were engaged. To celebrate, we went out for dinner in the Dragonara Hotel's top-notch restaurant.

"So, when shall we get married?" Peter said.

I wasn't one to mess about once I'd made a decision. "Tomorrow."

Peter turned to the couple dining behind him. "Excuse me, what date did you get married?"

We married on March 29th, the nearest Saturday to the couple's wedding day. Peter wanted a white wedding with all the trimmings. "It will be the only wedding I'll go to as a groom," he said. He had to pay for it from his savings. I had no money, and Mum and Dad weren't prepared to pay for it as I'd been living on my own for many years.

Even though he'd stopped practicing his faith years before, Peter wanted a church wedding. We visited the parish priest and didn't make a good impression.

"If you don't attend church services or practice your faith, why do you want to get married in church?" the priest asked.

"You put on a better show than the registry office," Peter said.

Bang goes your church wedding, Peter.

Despite Peter's wise-ass answer, the priest persevered, and we organized a date. Maybe he was hoping to make a convert out of me. We had to attend several sessions with the priest to discuss my marrying into the Catholic faith. Peter, who disliked Catholic priests, especially after being taught by sadistic Jesuits at school, was his usual bolshie self in a situation where fear-filled, angry memories were being reawakened. Still, we got through everything and made it to the wedding ceremony by the skin of our teeth.

I later heard from a probation colleague who was very involved with that church that the priest had said, "Your colleague is a lovely person, but him! The marriage won't last."

The night before the wedding, I was still sewing clothes for the honeymoon. I stood on a chair while Peter pinned up the hems on my skirts. Everything was fine. We kissed deeply before he went home, and exhausted I fell into my bed. Two hours later, I was wide awake, staring into blackness, too jittery to sleep. In fact, I packed a bag to run away. I sneaked down stairs so as not to wake Jackie. Coming out of the kitchen, I found her in the living room, standing over my bag with her arms crossed.

"Where do you think you're going?"

"I'm off. I can't go through with it. I'm not marriage material," I said, my panicked voice squeaky and several octaves higher than usual.

My filled-with-dread guts were churning in flight mode. I needed to escape.

She led me to the sofa. "Sit down," she said, pushing me to sit. She went to the front and back doors, made sure they were locked, and she had the keys. "You're not going anywhere. I'll call Gran and Granddad to stand guard if I have to."

"I'm scared, Jackie. My relationships with men just don't work."

Jackie sat beside me, put her arm round my shoulder, shook me gently. "Mum, Peter's okay. You'll be all right, or he'll have me to deal with. Let's have a cup of coffee and calm down. It'll be daylight soon."

NINE

Honeymoon on the Greek island of Rhodes over, I returned to work. Now he was married, Peter was not going to work abroad anymore. His brother, Richard, an electrical supervisor on a construction project at the local chemical plant, gave Peter a job.

Being a probation officer suited me down to the ground. I worked in a structured environment, but was allowed a good measure of autonomy. I loved the job. Five probation officers and a senior probation officer worked in South Bank's small office. We also had three secretaries on our team who ensured our court reports arrived in court on time, and our files were kept up to date.

Adjusting to married life's give and take was difficult. We had both been single a long time. Peter had left home when he was twenty, and apart from working abroad, his life had been spent living in lodgings. He had a picture in his mind of what family life should be like, with everyone sitting down to dinner together. He tried to force Jackie and me into that mold and became frustrated in the process, because it wasn't going to happen. At sixteen, Jackie was busy with her own social life, and I was happy to let her get on with it. Peter had difficulty adjusting to the way things were rather than how he wanted them to be.

Peter was laid off when the contract at the chemical plant ended after six months. With England in a recession and the north of England one of the hardest hit areas, finding a job would have been the equivalent to finding a gold nugget. The situation was exacerbated by Peter discovering he had been blacklisted years earlier. He had no idea why. Being unemployed and dependent on me as the breadwinner was difficult, but not because he minded being a kept man. He was frustrated that even though he was highly skilled, employment eluded him. Peter had been used to earning good wages while working abroad, but because he had been working abroad for seven years, he did not have the contacts to help him find work in Britain's dire economic situation.

We had to adhere to a strict budget. He became depressed and his negative attitude came to the fore. I tried to be supportive and listen, but it didn't help. He picked on Jackie for the slightest thing. It was easier to do that than lash out at me. I hated that he was so critical of her for no good reason, but I also realized that he was reacting to his own frustrations and that basically he was a good man.

Jackie must have confided in my parents, who in turn became angry with me for allowing Peter to hurt her. As for me, I was also having a difficult time elsewhere. I entered the probation service filled with an eagerness to help people, only I hadn't reckoned with the bureaucracy of the service, which left me frustrated and stifled and unable to work to my highest ability and ideals. Then Jackie moved out to live with my parents. I was devastated, heartbroken that I had failed to protect her, and angry at Peter. Yet I could not give up on him. Neither could I forgive him for driving my daughter away.

During this time, indulging in some horseplay with Peter, I discovered I was not fully healed from being raped. The wounds were still raw. Peter grabbed me in a bear hug. I panicked, came close to being hysterical as I fought my way free of him. Feeling hurt and rejected, Peter took refuge into the kitchen. My reaction surprised and puzzled me. It took a while for my heart to stop pounding and for me to understand what had happened. The bear hug had rendered me powerless, reawakening the feelings I experienced during the rape attack. I went into the kitchen, put my arms round his waist from behind, and explained why I had reacted as I had. Just as well, as only a few weeks later, one of my attackers appeared on television being interviewed about a successful venture he'd started.

I leapt out of my chair, shouting, "I hate that man! Turn it off! Turn it off!" as I stormed from the room.

Obviously, I still had a ways to go to be healed.

With tension at home and tension building in me about the work situation, I eventually cracked. I woke up one morning and started crying and could not stop. I was having what is commonly called a nervous breakdown. It took nine weeks for me to recover enough to return to work.

Fortunately, a place of salvation was near at hand. The Greater World Christian Spiritualist Church was only three blocks from our house. One Sunday night, with both of us down in the dumps, with no money to go out, and being curious as to what happened there, I suggested we attend the service. The small church was a converted corner shop and only had space for a congregation of sixty.

We found a church full of people having lively conversations and laughing. No reverent silence or speaking in hushed tones. Ken Briggs, the president of the church, recognized us as new visitors and ushered us to seats in the back row. Minutes later, the medium entered and took her place on the rostrum. She was introduced to the congregation, and the divine service began with hymns, prayers, and an address (sermon) by the medium. This was followed by forty-five minutes of mediumship, when the medium passed on messages from people in the spirit world to their loved ones in the congregation.

Most of the messages seemed mundane to us, but with strong effects on the recipients. Some people smiled or laughed out loud, with the congregation laughing along with them, such as when one person received a witty message about stopping smoking from a father who had died of lung cancer.

"Don't think I can't see you when you sneak away to the garden shed for a smoke. You may fool Ada (his wife) but you don't fool me."

Some messages were sad or poignant. Approaching four people who had arrived late and who were dressed for a night on the town, the medium said, "I'm told this is your first time in a spiritualist church and that you didn't plan on being here tonight."

One of the visitors said, "We were on our way somewhere else, and somehow we ended up here."

"I know," the medium said. "Margaret is telling me she brought you here."

The four gasped, put hands to mouths, raked in handbags for tissues to dab their eyes.

"You lost two of your children in a house fire. Margaret is saying she's sorry she couldn't get them out. She tried. But, everyone is all right here. Your grandparents are taking care of Helen and Joe. It's time for you to let go of the guilt and know they're fine."

Tears of relief rolled down the visitors' cheeks. The whole congregation was close to tears along with them.

After the service, we stayed for tea and cookies.

Ken Briggs approached us. "First time here?"

"Yes. First time in any spiritualist church," Peter said.

"How did you find it?"

"It was interesting, moving. I'm not convinced about communicating with spirit . . .yet."

"Just accept what you can and leave what you can't," Ken said. "We're all at different stages of progress, and it's good to have a questioning mind."

He explained a basic premise of spiritualism that life continues after the transition called death, and that it's possible to communicate with the people who have passed into the spiritual dimension. "People don't change just because they've moved on. They're still the same as they were on earth—mean, humorous, sweet, thoughtful— the only difference is they no longer reside in their physical bodies."

It was easy for me to accept these concepts. At sixteen years of age, I went through a period of believing that once you're dead, you're dead. That was the end of it. No afterlife. Then, while giving birth to Jackie, I had an out-of-body experience, I was up by the ceiling, looking down, watching her being born from a perspective most mothers don't experience. Although out of my body, I was still very much myself in thought and personality. I knew then that the body was merely a vehicle for carrying the real me around in the physical world. The real me was more than just a physical entity, and I could exist without my body.

"The important thing to remember," Ken said, "is that in this lifetime we are spiritual beings, having a spiritual experience by expressing ourselves through a physical body."

Peter and I began to attend the friendly church on a regular basis. With our marriage strained, exacerbated by Peter's misery with his unemployed state, and me angry toward Peter for driving Jackie out to live with my parents because of his constant criticism, and my parents angry with me for staying with Peter with his destructive attitudes, we found comfort in the church. Our spirituality developed to a higher level, encouraged by even the most seemingly trivial messages we received. One message from my grandmother had a big impact.

The medium told me, "You were in the store buying wallpaper this morning, weren't you?"

"Yes," I answered.

"I know because your grandmother's telling me about it. She was with you. She's pleased you chose the paper with the yellow flowers," the medium said, "but she wishes you'd had kinder thoughts towards the store clerk."

My jaw sagged in shock. I *had* been thinking the store clerk was a jerk. He'd been useless. Now here was the medium telling me my grandmother knew what I was thinking and feeling. Oh, boy! That could be embarrassing. In no time at all, I cleaned up my "stinking thinking." I did not want to be having thoughts I would be ashamed of or embarrassed about my grandmother knowing. As per Sathya Sai Baba's teachings of filling the day with love, I trained myself to encourage loving, caring feelings rather than negative, angry, or sarcastic ones. I was also learning that thoughts are living things with a life and energy of their own. A thought is like a pebble dropped in a pond, sending out ripples that reach the outer edges. Send out lots of negative thoughts and the banks around the pond will erode as will a child who is continually shown she is not loved or is unimportant. Thoughts affect the people we come into contact with. I made a conscious decision to do my best to have only positive thoughts.

This attitude was helpful in my probation work with clients. It also helped in my relationship with Peter, who, damaged as a child, was emotionally inaccessible behind a protective fortress he had built around himself. He was hungry for loving attention, only he wasn't prepared to take the risk of letting people get close.

On telling my parents we were attending the spiritualist church, my mother responded with mockery as expected. "*Now* what have you got yourself into?"

She insisted on attending a service with us, wanting to see what we had gotten ourselves involved with. The medium delivered his last message to my mother. It was from some long gone relative. Then the medium said, "I don't know why I'm telling you this. You see spirit yourself."

My head swung round so fast I almost fell off my seat. My mouth dropped open.

After the service, I asked Mum, "What was that all about? Do you see spirit?"

Mum relied with a shy, "Yes."

"Tell me about it," I said.

Apparently, when someone in the family was seriously ill, Mum received visits from sisters or brothers, who had passed on. They told her she needed to go see whoever was ill. She had kept this under her hat, thinking she was some kind of freak, which explained why she was so keen to come to the church. I later discovered that numerous family members had occasional experiences of at least one of the forms of mediumship. When I saw Tibby's ghost in the living room that was mediumship known as clairvoyance. One day, my nephew, on arriving at the steel mill where he worked, heard a voice telling him to park far away from his usual parking place. This is called clairaudience. He listened to the warning and parked several spaces away. Sometime during his shift, a truck loaded with steel girders drove through the parking lot and some of the girders fell off onto the car parked in my nephew's place.

Around this time, my sister Joan told me about a conversation she had with her young granddaughters, where they told her about another life they had shared with her and the things they did together, only she wasn't Grandma then, she was their sister. Joan had the sense to listen and encourage their memories rather than shutting them down. As the girls grew older, the memories were left behind.

My whole family was having a spurt of spiritual growth.

Peter was still down in the dumps from being unemployed. I wanted him to have a car so at least he could visit his mother more easily. On my way to and from work, I passed a garage that sold used cars at prices we could afford. I dragged Peter to see them. Bob Parvin, the salesman, casually strolled from his office, more interested in rolling his cigarillo and licking the cigarette paper than pushing us into a sale.

He picked a flake of tobacco from his tongue. "Take your time. Look around. I don't sell cars to people. I only help people buy the cars they want. What price range are you looking at?" Bob led us to a large, daffodil yellow, wedge-shaped car and promised us a good deal. None of the vehicles impressed Peter, and we drove away empty-handed. Knowing how impulsive I am, Peter made me promise not to buy the car.

I promised. Then one day, it was as if an invisible hand turned my steering wheel into the dealership. I ended up in the garage, paying a deposit on the car. Peter was incredulous. Even I couldn't believe what I'd done.

When I called in the garage to pay the balance, Bob said, "You look terrible. Are you ill?"

"Well, you've got a cheek, insulting me now you have my money!" I said, laughing. "Anyway, I've got hay fever. Every summer, I feel like death warmed up."

"Maybe I can help." He pointed to a certificate on the wall behind his chair, which indicated he was certified as a spiritual healer by the National Federation of Spiritual Healers.

I checked out his certificate. "Why not? For the past seventeen years doctors have given me every treatment they have to offer, and look at me. I'm in a worse state than if I had the 'flu."

I sat on a chair and closed my eyes. Bob stood behind me and held his hands over my head for fifteen minutes. He moved to one side, and I opened my eyes.

"Did you feel anything?" he asked.

"No, not really."

Bob was not put out by my unresponsiveness. "If you find it helped, you can always come back."

I returned to the office. On my desk I lined up eye drops for itchy eyes, nose drops, and tissues for my runny nose, and lozenges for my post nasal drip sore throat. Then I got on with the business of writing reports. Two hours passed before it struck me that I hadn't wiped my nose in a long time. Usually, it was red and sore from continual wiping. More often than not, tissues would be stuck up my nostrils. My eyes weren't itching and needed no rubbing, and my sore throat had disappeared. That night, I had to make a major decision—should I take a chance on not taking my anti-histamine, or should I play safe? If I made the wrong decision, I would suffer terribly. I took a chance. I was fine for two days. Then hay fever symptoms returned, and I ran straight back to Bob.

Twice weekly visits were required during that hay-fever season to keep the misery at bay. But the following year (and all the years after that) I remained hay fever free. Bob had cured my affliction that had been so severe if I ever went for a walk in the countryside in the summer, I had to be carried home on the verge of collapse.

TEN

As Britain's recession grew, heavy industries were hardest hit, with as many as 30,000 men a year losing their jobs in the local steelworks. In the area served by my field office, the unemployment rate among men increased to fifty percent, and in some subdivisions, it was as high as ninety percent. One year, there was only one real job for the five thousand school leavers to fight over. But never fear, Maggie Thatcher and her Tory government were keeping the hoards off the streets with job programs and not-worth-a-spit training.

Fortunately for Peter, one of the four million unemployed, the probation service started a work-creation scheme for offenders and ex-prisoners called Cleveland Resolution, named after the nearby Cleveland Hills. I put Peter's name forward for an interview. Because of his experience as a supervisor while working abroad, he was given the job of supervising offenders on the scheme. His team built stiles, fences, planted trees, and maintained country bridle paths. His two years of unemployment had finally come to an end.

I had settled into my probation work and accepted the limitations of the organization's structure. Instead of clinging to my ideal of how I should be working to improve people's lives, I adjusted my thoughts to doing my best in the situation. I was happy, but our workloads were high. Because of the economic downturn and lack of work, young men living in my area felt they had no future. Their perception was that everyone else was having the good life while they were struggling to survive on the dole. Some were not prepared to accept the unfairness of it and turned to crime."

We needed two more probation officers in our office to meet the increased demand for our services, particularly for writing court reports. Something had to give. Michael and Nigel, two colleagues who started at the same time as I did, kept their files up-to-date by working in the office at weekends or taking files home to work on them in the evenings. I wouldn't do that. We signed contracts when we started the job. We were to work a certain number of hours per month for our salaries, and during those hours I gave the probation service and my clients my all, but I was not prepared to take work into my personal life. The deputy chief probation officer wanted to see me. My senior warned me it was about my files not being kept up to date.

My dad was a union secretary. Even though a moderate union secretary, he took no nonsense from the dockworkers' employers. So when the deputy chief probation officer came to my office to speak with me, being my father's daughter, I couldn't keep my mouth shut. It didn't take her long to start lambasting me, basically telling me I was incompetent, because I could not keep my files up to date.

"Let's just hold that thought about being incompetent," I said, "because in my opinion, it's management that's incompetent." I had to get things off my chest even though it was likely I would lose my job. I couldn't help it. I was too much like my father. "I don't know how you have the audacity to come here accusing me of falling down on the job. We have enough work in this office to employ two more probation officers. Where are they? Why aren't you providing them? We normally write between eight and ten court reports a month each. We're actually writing around seventeen reports per month, twenty-eight above normal for the number of people in this office. How am I supposed to keep my files up to date?"

"Let me ask you this," the deputy chief said. "How is it that Mike and Nigel are managing to keep their files up to date?"

"I'll tell you how. Mike comes into the office every Saturday and spends a day he is not being paid for to work on his files. Nigel takes his files home and works on them after his children have gone to bed. These are hours surplus to their contracts with the probation service. I won't do that. You can have me one hundred percent for the hours I'm paid, and I promise you that you do get one hundred percent, but I'm not working hours I am not paid for, especially when management is not doing its job of providing us with the resources we need."

She blinked rapidly then stared at me tight-lipped. Rousing herself, she picked her handbag off the floor and held it tightly on her knee. "I want you to keep timetables of your days' work, to see where your time is being spent. I'll talk to your senior about it." She left the office with little more to say. I doubt any subordinate had stood up to her before, and I fully expected a pink slip for my big mouth. While I waited for my dismissal, I comforted myself that I had been right in saying what I did. I was even more amazed when that dismissal didn't come. But we did get Russell, another, fresh-from-college probation officer in our office.

Peter and I continued attending the spiritualist church. I felt embarrassed because I often fell asleep during the service, at least, until a medium told me she could see spirits healing me as I slept. We joined psychic-development classes in the church. Our abilities to experience on a psychic level increased.

One day, when I was on office duty, a man in his fifties came to the probation office for help. He presented some problem that I recognized as not the real reason he was there. Then a black and white sheep dog materialized beside his chair. It looked so real, I doubted what I had witnessed. The dog was sitting, looking up at his master, and I realized the man was lonely and grieving for his dog.

"Have you any pets?" I asked.

"Had a dog for years. He died a couple of months ago. He was a good dog. Kept me active. We always went for long walks together."

"Bet you miss him, don't you?"

"Aye, that I do."

"Ever thought of getting another one?"

"Couldn't look after one properly now. My knees hurt, so I can't walk far. It was a blessing that he died. I'd have hated to let him down by not going on our walks."

"Some breeds of dog need a lot more exercise than others. You know the pound is full of little dogs that will die if they don't find a home."

The man looked up from staring at the carpet, a glimmer of hope in his eyes. Only a few days later he came to show me his new companion, a dachshund toy-poodle mix.

❖ ❖ ❖

During one church service, the medium told Peter that he had healing abilities. She encouraged him to participate in the church's healing services. We all have the ability to heal, only sometimes we put our energy into other things, such as earning money to raise our families, or practicing a musical instrument. So although healing ability is natural, I wanted Peter to go on training courses given by the National Federation of Spiritual Healers, a highly respected organization in Britain, to develop his abilities to the highest level. He did nothing.

A year or so later, when I was told that I too had healing ability, I didn't mess about. I booked us on every NFSH healing course available. They took place at Tekel's Park, Headquarters for the Theosophical Society, near Camberley, in the south of England. Despite my finding Peter's negativity irksome, our healing work brought us closer together. Peter never felt anything when he was healing, whereas I felt tingling in my hands, and when the tingling stopped, the healing was over. Feeling nothing, Peter had to take everything on trust that something good was taking place. At times, he would stop healing all together, thinking he was fooling himself. He really shouldn't have had any doubts about his ability to help both people and animals, because he often received wonderful proof.

Peter made good use of the hated yellow car to visit his mother, who was confined to a wheelchair, from having a stroke twenty-five years previously. She was in her late seventies and lived alone. On weekends, Peter would visit her and prepare her meals and provide some companionship.

During one visit, she told him she had seen a man at the end of her bed in the middle of the night. Peter bristled on hearing this and checked her apartment doors and windows to make sure they were secure. She had not been afraid of the man, neither had she felt threatened. At the time, she had a pain in her head that was preventing her from sleeping. The man had stroked her brow until the pain went away, all the while telling her in a soothing voice to go to sleep. With more details, Peter realized the man she was describing was his father as a young man. Peter's father had died at eighty-four years of age, shortly before I met Peter. We wondered why she would have this visit from her husband, but only two weeks later, she became ill and died. We felt Peter's father had been waiting close by because he knew that the end of her earthly life was near.

Shortly after the funeral, we moved to the outskirts of Middlesbrough to a new house, with a garden full of builder's rubble. We still continued to attend services in the church. After two years, the Cleveland Resolution work-scheme ended. Peter was again unemployed. However, the government had created another scheme that paid a small weekly allowance for two years to enable people to start their own businesses. Peter attended a business course at the Polytechnical College and applied for the allowance to start his own electrical business.

Peter and I settled into a marriage with loosely defined roles. My work was mainly sedentary, so at home, not being a domesticated person, I tended to do physical work such as cleaning the vehicles, gardening, painting, and decorating. Peter, on the other hand, did physical work all day long, so he did most of the cooking. After a hard day's work, it was common to find Peter throwing food together to produce some unique delicious dish that he could never replicate, while I released work-related stress, scalping the roses with my pruning shears.

At this time, I was not happy in my marriage. Peter was making very little money as he struggled to build his business, and each setback brought out his negativity, which sapped my energy. Peter tended to look for reasons why we couldn't do something. I looked for ways to make things happen. Chalk and cheese.

We were members of an organization called Junior Chamber, which helped professional members develop leadership skills. One day, a member came up with the idea of visiting our partner organization in Holland. He proposed making use of a scheme that provided money to cover the cost of first-time visitors to the European Parliament. Eight members could visit Holland cost-free by going in two cars and traveling via the European Parliament in Luxembourg.

First thing out of Peter's mouth was, "We can't do it."

I set my chin. Here we were, going through Peter's garbage routine again. "Why not?" I snapped.

"It will cost too much, and we don't have any money."

"We've just been told the grant from the European Parliament will cover everything."

"What if it doesn't?"

I rolled my eyes and said, "Well, you can do what you like. I'm going."

"You're going?"

"Watch me."

"In that case, if you're going, I'm going too."

With Christmas looming, Peter and I argued about my buying Christmas presents for family. "Listen," I would say. "I bought Christmas presents when I lived on welfare, why shouldn't I be able to buy them just because I married you? I do have a good job, you know."

Despite fighting back against Peter's negativity, it always spoilt my pleasure in such family events. I was becoming depressed. To boost my spirits, I pinned a large poster on our bedroom wall that said:

> A WONDERFUL CHANGE IS COMING
> INTO MY LIFE SOON.

I read it last thing at night before I turned out the light and first thing in the morning when I opened my eyes.

Jackie and Gordon on their wedding day

Three years after being bridesmaid at my wedding, I was the bride's mother when Jackie married her sweetheart Gordon. They had two young daughters, Donna four and Sarah two. I bought the girls a Texas Instrument toy computer for Christmas, ignoring Peter's negative onslaught about wasting money. Waking in the middle of the night to find him missing from our bed, I sneaked downstairs and found him on the living room floor, totally captivated with playing with their toy computer.

"Ah-ha! There you are."

He was sheepish at first, then he tried his crazy logic on me. "Well, someone has to check it's suitable for the girls and not a waste of money."

"Okay, what's the verdict?"

"It'll pass."

"Well, at least we know it's suitable for you," I said and returned to bed.

Around this time a friend of ours, Maurice, a salesman for an electrical wholesaler, came to visit. He was all of a dither, couldn't sit still, kept wringing his hands, fiddling with his rings, and stroking his neatly trimmed beard.

"I didn't know who else to come to," he said, breaking into a sweat and mopping his brow after coming into the warmth from the wintry weather outside.

He was in a predicament, he told us. Two years before, realizing he had a drinking problem, Maurice dealt with it by becoming a Muslim, because Muslims aren't allowed to drink alcohol. It had worked. He had stopped drinking, but he now had a new problem.

"The imam says it's time for me to marry. A good Muslim man must have a wife and family. They want me to marry a Pakistani woman, a doctor. I can't do it. I'm . . . I'm . . ."

"We know, Maurice," Peter said.

Maurice sat up straight. "What! What do you know?"

Peter glanced at me. "We know your secret. I knew two weeks after meeting you nineteen years ago."

Maurice almost passed out in horror. "How did you know?"

Peter smiled. "Maurice, you're fifty years old and have never married. You wear feminine rings. We just know—and it's all right."

There was a long silence while Maurice stroked his beard and digested Peter's words. "I can't marry her, Peter. I've never slept with a woman, ever. The idea of it makes me feel sick."

"No, you can't marry her. It wouldn't be fair to her," I said.

Tense, Maurice kept fidgeting, his eyes bounced around the room, looking anywhere but at us. "How do I tell them that I can't? What if they want to know why?"

I hated to see him so distressed. "Maurice, we accept you and love you as you are. If you can, you must tell the imam the truth about why you can't marry the woman. If they turn their backs on you, then that is their loss. Can you really go on living a lie to belong to that religion?"

I made a cup of tea, and he calmed down. We never did hear how it worked out with the imam, but having taken the first step with us, and finding us accepting of him, I hoped Maurice had the courage to let the world know who he really was rather than feel he had to live a lie.

Peter and I were still struggling to get along. To put an end to arguments about who should be doing more to keep the house clean, I employed a housekeeper one morning a week. Her name was Joan, a widow who needed the money. Six months later, Peter, who was at home doing paperwork in the spare bedroom-turned-office, found Joan crying in the kitchen.

"What's wrong, Joan?"

"Oh, Peter, I'm going into hospital the day after tomorrow. I've got breast cancer, and they're going to remove a lump from my breast."

At first, the shock of Joan's announcement took Peter's breath away. Then he offered her some healing. He sat Joan in a chair, stood behind her and balanced her energy fields.

As she left, Peter told her not to worry about her job. It would still be there for her when she eventually returned to full health. He was surprised when she turned up as usual the following Monday.

"Peter, I want to thank you," Joan said, tears springing to her eyes. "When I got to the hospital, they x-rayed my breast again and couldn't find anything. Nothing! I was sent home. No operation."

They danced a jig round the kitchen to celebrate, and Joan remained cancer free for as long as we knew her.

After we bought the car from Bob, we became friends with Bob and his wife Lyn. Once a month we had a meal in the other's house, Chinese in theirs, Indian in ours. We learned a great deal about healing from Bob's own personal experiences.

Somehow, one of my ex-clients heard of my healing activities, and he came to see me. My first thought on seeing him come into the office was that he had been in more trouble with the law. But it wasn't that.

"Mrs. Hayton, it's my wife Gill. She has multiple sclerosis. I've heard you can heal people. Will you do some healing on her?"

I nearly fell out of my seat with shock. I had thought I'd kept my healing activities quiet and separate from my work.

"How do you know about my healing?"

"A friend of mine goes to the spiritualist church, and you healed her during a healing service. She had a nasty rash, psoriasis, and when she got undressed for bed that night, the rash had gone, and it hasn't come back."

I agreed to treat his wife during my lunch breaks. Each session, the healing energy built up strongly in her living room. Often, her mother, who lived nearby, would sit in the room while healing took place, saying she benefited from the healing power just by sitting on the couch. I guess their cat felt the same way because she would run to curl up under the dining chair that Gill sat on during healing.

One day, when we were alone, I told her that every illness or disease appears for a reason. That reason could be to get you to change unhealthy living habits or change your way of thinking or to let go of anger or resentment. But it doesn't just appear out of the blue. All illness and disease is your friend, alerting you to the need for change in you, to point you in another, better, direction.

I asked her, "What purpose is your illness serving in your life?"

Gill's blue eyes opened wide at such an unusual question. "I don't know."

We hugged and Gill followed me to the front door as I was leaving.

She touched my arm. "I want my husband to feel needed."

It was my turn to be surprised. "Gill, before I come back, could you think of some other way to help him feel needed besides killing yourself through this disease?"

Having decided she could help her husband feel important and needed without allowing multiple sclerosis to destroy her, Gill began to recover and eventually gave up her disability allowance and returned to work.

A few weeks after that, a young man arrived at the office with his broken arm in a plaster cast. He should have reported to see his supervising officer the day before, but instead, came to see me so that I could stop the throbbing pain in his arm. I was becoming a little concerned at how clients were discovering my healing abilities. Nevertheless, I put my hands on his arm and the pain stopped.

"That's neat," he said. "You know, my Mum is a psychic medium. She's taught me a lot about the afterlife. And my dad's from India. He's taught me a lot about Eastern philosophies."

"How can you possibly reconcile your spiritual knowledge with your offending, which obviously caused distress to your victims?"

We had a long conversation about karma, the law of cause and effect, and how we are spirits with a body, on earth to have a spiritual experience within the restrictions of a material world.

"I can't reconcile it," he said, "so I'm not doing it any more. Once my probation is over, no one will have to deal with me again."

I had many such conversations with clients who hungered for a deeper meaning of their lives. I never initiated these discussions. I was not a probation officer to convert people to a spiritual belief system. That was a preacher's job. However, healing work can take many forms. One recurring role in my life was that of being a catalyst to enable people to reach their full potential by breaking free of their self-imposed restrictions. Working with probation clients was perfect for that. I always felt my job was to find the key that would open up a client's life to a happier, law-abiding existence. If that meant clients were searching spiritually, then I shared what little spiritual knowledge I had with them.

Talking about finding a key—I had a client, Tank, a twenty-four year old, six-foot-four, muscular man who was highly intelligent. His leather jacket gave him the air of a biker only without the motorcycle. Like most of my young male clients, on leaving school he faced at least ten years without being employed in a real job. They lived on paltry government allowances and low-paid job-creation schemes from leaving school to marrying and raising children. They would become a tossed-on-the-scrap-heap, unskilled generation. Anyway, Tank was well-known for his rebellious spirit.

He reported to see me one day and during our conversation announced, "I'm my own man. I'll always be free because I rebel against things."

"Really!" I said. "You believe that?"

He grinned beneath his bright green Mohican hairstyle. "Of course."

"You know you're mistaken." He was about to object, and I held up my hand to silence him. Now Tank had not done very well in his life, lots of petty thefts, some fights, but he was curious to hear what I had to say. "Tank, I am going to tell you something. Listen and learn. When you are rebelling, you're not free. You know why? Because someone else, by what they say, controls you. They decide what you will rebel against. A really free man comes up with his own thoughts. No need to rebel like being jerked on a leash. You've got intelligence. You've got a mind of your own. Do your own thinking. Remember, when you're rebelling, you're not free."

Tank sat there struck dumb, but the cogs in his mind were working overtime. Then he stood up, all six foot four of him towering over me, and said, "I'll see you next week, Mrs. H."

The following week he returned a free man, having thought about our discussion the week before. Tank never got into any further trouble worth mentioning, and he ditched his green Mohican hair cut. We had found the key that would lead him to a happier life.

The English probation service developed from charitable work with offenders. Our job description was basically to advise, assist, and befriend. On top of that, we had our responsibilities to the court for ensuring clients kept their promises to the court and stayed out of trouble when on parole. This was achieved mainly by befriending the clients. We encouraged them to mend their ways by taking them under our wings rather than by coercion. To this end, the service developed a scheme for orienteering in Dalby Forest. This entailed participating in a cross-country competition in which runners followed a course using map and compass. If we were experiencing difficulty in getting a client to trust us enough so that we could be a good influence on him, we applied to go orienteering. This enabled clients to see us less as probation officers and more as human beings.

I went orienteering with a couple of clients; they really gained a different perspective of me, especially when they had to push my backside up an almost vertical ten-foot log to climb a steep bank or wait while I caught my breath after lumbering through trees, bracken and mud. Competitive clients became impatient, eager to be off to find the next marker. They wanted to win. Others were more helpful and patient, urging me on and not to die on them as I struggled to keep up. Orienteering was a great tool for breaking down barriers. One of my clients, a young man in his twenties, lived in a high-rise building. He was arrested several times for rappelling down his building. This was his attempt to keep his spirit alive rather than allowing his unemployed state to drag him down. A day's orienteering with him revealed he had a lot of skills that could be used in an outward-bound school. I made enquiries on his behalf and found such a school on the other side of the country, in Wales, that would employ him as an instructor. On receiving the news, his happiness could not have been greater if he had won the lottery, which, in a way, he had.

ELEVEN

With my fortieth birthday looming, I made two decisions. One, I was not going to grow another year older without experiencing skiing, and I was going to do something about the stiffness I was experiencing in my ankles. My mother suffered with arthritis and had a knee replacement that was not as successful as she had hoped for. I was not going that route.

Peter absolutely did not want to try skiing. He would go only if I could guarantee Jamaica warmth and sunshine on the slopes. So off I went to Austria with a group of work colleagues. I did brilliantly. I know that because the ski instructor, a handsome young punk, kept raising his eyes to the bright blue skies, saying in his cute Austrian accent, "No problem." Trick skiing? Child's play. Showed off by whizzing down a slope at sixty miles an hour on my backside. The biggest challenge that first year was getting up after I had fallen. It took several days to accomplish this skill. Then I sprained my ankle. No more skiing. All that remained was indulging in the après ski gluhwein, which I did all day long, although dancing on the table was reserved for the evening performance.

Despite the challenges, skiing was so enjoyable I went three more times, before I emigrated.

Having made my skiing debut, it was time to do something about my arthritis. I rarely take prescribed drugs because, in my opinion, they treat symptoms and not causes of health problems. I scoured the classifieds in health magazines. A modest advertisement caught my eye. It was for a small, naturopathic clinic called Shalimar in Frinton-on-Sea, north of London. Indian naturopath, Kiki Sidwha, ran the clinic. I booked in for two weeks.

After a seven and a half hour drive, I knocked on the door of a large Edwardian house close to the town center and was greeted warmly by one of Kiki's assistants. I would not see Kiki until the following morning.

"Would you like to start your fast now?" she asked.

"Fast? What fast?"

"Everyone goes on a water-only fast at first."

What had I let myself in for? "If you don't mind, I'd like a meal tonight. I'm very hungry. I'll get my head into gear to start my fast in the morning."

I met other residents at breakfast. Some, like me, were sipping water. Others were tucking into vegetarian food. Patients warned us newcomers, naked beneath our house robes, ready for our interview with Kiki, of headaches and feeling nauseated, while we were fasting.

Apparently, feeling like hell would pass after our bodies had been cleared of toxins.

Waiting to be interviewed by Kiki Sidwha, I realized the man was world famous. One young woman was from France, another from America. Georgette, the French girl, entered his room before me. She let out a scream followed by a tirade in French. I couldn't understand her words, but she was definitely upset. The door opened. She charged out leaving a Maelstrom in her wake as she disappeared into the hall and up the stairs.

My turn next. I lowered my eyebrows to their normal position and entered Kiki's office.

"I want to make sure I don't develop arthritis like my mother," I said, in response to his questions. "Oh, and I'd like to lose weight."

"Let's see," he said. "Robe, off, off, off."

I looked at him amazed. He waved his hand for me to get on with it, and I dropped my robe. He walked round me, studying me intently. I felt like a painting in the Louvre, except I had thoughts and feelings and curiosity as to what would come next after Georgette's reaction.

"Robe on, on, on, on," Kiki said. "You will fast for seven days. Water only." My eyebrows hit my hairline for the second time that morning. "You will go on long walks every day and also sit in the sunshine to absorb the light. All good for health. Later, we will discuss the foods you should not eat to avoid developing arthritis. You know emotions too play a part in developing disease. Arthritis often comes from carrying resentment. You will meditate, practice yoga, and see the truth of this. You may go."

Puzzled by Georgette's reaction, I went looking for her. Striding out on our prescribed walk into town and along the seafront, I asked why she'd been so upset.

Her French accent sounded so sexy compared to my blunt Yorkshire delivery. She smiled apologetically. "I have calmed down now. For many years I am anorexic. I only recently started to recover, so when Kiki said I had to go on a four-day fast to start my treatment with him, I thought he had lost his mind—and told him so." She laughed. "It is okay now."

Being the new kids on the block, Georgette and I spent our days together, walking, sitting in the sunshine, sipping water while the other residents ate. The spotty skin on her face and back cleared up. The weight fell off me. I suffered no nasty side effects from the fast. I was the envy of those not so lucky.

Georgette returned home before me. Glowing with health, skin clear, she left Shalimar with big smiles. I was twelve pounds lighter when I left. Kiki warned me not to eat any dairy or wheat products for six months and then reintroduce them slowly into my diet. "Keep your thoughts happy and you should remain arthritis free," he said.

And, with the occasional taking of fish oil or oil of borage supplements, arthritis remained at bay.

❖ ❖ ❖

Peter and I had toiled for years to turn our garden, initially full of builder's rubble, into a beautiful flowering shrub garden. Every month of the year something of interest was on display—flowers, berries, shapes, leaf color. Once, we hired a rotator for the weekend. Of course, it poured down. Peter braved the weather and tilled the earth, his wet hair plastered to his forehead. He couldn't see much with the rain belting down on his glasses. The soil in the garden was red clay. We needed to mix in organic matter to improve it for growing plants. We went for walks in the woods, taking with us black plastic sacks and filled them with leaf mold that we liberally dug into the clay with seaweed fertilizer. We commandeered Peter's van that he bought for his electrical business and lined it with plastic. Then we drove fifteen miles to a riding school that was giving away horse manure for free. I can't help but smile when I remember the number of times we drove home with our heads out the windows and the van stinking to high heaven. Still, it was worth it. The rose garden outside our kitchen door was spectacular. Even boys around eight years old, passing on the footpath while I was outside pruning, would comment, "Lovely roses you've got there, Missus." The garden was our pride and joy, one of the few places where Peter and I worked harmoniously side by side.

We liked our neighbors, Jeff and Anna. Jeff worked on the North Sea oil rigs, two weeks on and two weeks off. Anna was from Malta. All her mannerisms were filled with Mediterranean flair, with arms flung here, there, and everywhere when she spoke. She was an excellent saleslady. If I ever saw her working in the ladies clothing department in Debenham's, she would usher me to racks of clothes and choose colors that made me look fabulous, colors that complimented my skin tone, colors that made my eyes sparkle. With her warm, broad smile, customers simply melted into the moment, and Anna made a sale.

While Jeff was away on his two-week stints on the oil rig, Anna often popped in for a glass of wine during the evenings. One day she arrived upset. Her father had died six months earlier and his affairs had not yet been finalized. He had been living with a woman, but had left his house to Anna's two teenage sons. Even though she had been provided for in his will, the woman had so far refused to leave the house. Anna asked me to read the tarot cards for her. I was a novice at tarot readings, but went ahead.

"All your problems will be resolved within six months," I told her.

Six months later, everything *was* resolved for Anna. An operation on her back went horribly wrong, and she died. She was forty, same as me. Having the operation had filled her with dread. In the days before she went into hospital, Anna put her affairs in order, returning borrowed items such as books and a scarf. She made sure all her bills and paperwork were up to date, completing these tasks with such fervor, it was as if she had a premonition.

Jeff was devastated, his life dark without Anna's *joie de vivre*. One of Anna's so called friends had already been to visit Jeff, supposedly to offer her condolences, but really to rake through Anna's beautiful clothes and grab what she could while Jeff was too numb to react. He asked me and Betty, another of her friends, to empty Anna's closet while people were taking refreshments after the funeral. He couldn't bear to see her things hanging up or her jewelry lying around any longer. He wanted it gone.

With guests mingling downstairs, rather than carry black plastic sacks through the house, Betty and I threw Anna's belongings from the en-suite bathroom window onto our drive, where Peter retrieved them and took them into our house. Betty and I thought packing Anna's clothes would be a tearful task, but we ended up laughing, recalling fond memories engendered when Anna had worn her flamboyant earrings and certain colorful pieces of clothing. We set aside Anna's valuable jewelry to leave in her sons' bedrooms. Peter and I went on suicide-watch mode, comforting and supporting Jeff as best we could. I missed Anna too. I had grown used to having her effervescent personality lifting me up after a hard day's work.

Returning from a visit to a prison, I passed Bob Parvin's new garage location and called in. As usual, we talked healing. As a car dealer, Bob came into contact with many people from all walks of life. He told me about one doctor with an injured knee who was a regular client for healing. Most of the medical profession had no idea how spiritual healing could help their patients, but Bob wasn't shy about telling them. Bob's doctor client was so impressed with his results from Bob's efforts, he encouraged Dr. B., a prominent orthopedic doctor in town, suffering from multiple sclerosis, to go to Bob for healing. Bob cured him of multiple sclerosis, but some months later, the doctor died of pneumonia. At the time, Bob's healing of Dr. B. created waves in the medical community.

As I continued to my office, I was struck with the thought that two years earlier Dr. B. had operated on Anna's back, and according to Bob, had been diagnosed only two weeks afterward with multiple sclerosis. Anna had died from meningitis after the operation. I loved Anna and was still furious about her dying at forty years of age. I always believed the surgeon had nicked her spinal cord, causing the infection. I had no proof, only a gut feeling, and here was Bob telling me this tale. If the doctor was operating when he was in the early stages of multiple sclerosis, his hands may not have been as steady as they should have been. A surge of anger had me gripping the steering wheel so tightly, my knuckles turned white. Then I remembered the surgeon had died anyway, despite being cured of multiple sclerosis. Bob believed that Dr. B. had been brought into Bob's life to receive healing to show the medical profession just what spiritual healing can achieve. And that had happened. The fact that Dr. B. had died only a few months after being declared in complete remission from multiple sclerosis meant it was his time to leave this world. The moral of this story was that Anna's death had meaning too, even if I couldn't figure out what that meaning was.

We had been without a housekeeper for almost a year since Joan moved away to live with her son. Anna's friend Betty took her place. Betty, known as Big Bette because of her statuesque build, was struggling financially and emotionally after separating from her husband. She also suffered from low self esteem because of his numerous infidelities. One day, we suggested she might like to come with us to the spiritualist church in Gresham Road. With luck she

Big Bette, friend and former president of Greater World Christian Spiritualist Church, Middlesbrough, England

would receive a message that would help her. Big Bette did receive a message, a wonderful healing message from her mother who had died a few years earlier. After that, Betty regularly attended the services.

    We watched in awe and with great pleasure, seeing her confidence and self esteem grow in leaps and bounds as her spiritual understanding increased. Two years later, she was elected president of the church, a position she held for many years. While president, she worked diligently to raise funds and make improvements to the building. She strived to increase membership of the church, especially increasing the ratio of younger people who came to the services and classes. She was fulfilled and in her element, a confident leader who had found her niche.

    Then she took her philandering husband back, believing his promises that he had changed. It didn't take long for her to realize he hadn't, that he mainly wanted her services as cook/housekeeper with benefits. She became ill with non-Hodgkin's lymphoma. Using her spiritual knowledge, Big Bette amazed her doctors by teaching them that her cancer was a form of energy. As such she would visualize the cancer taking certain shapes, sizes, and colors. She then used her imagination to bring in other forms of energy to transform the cancer. She was successfully treating herself and doing well, until she realized that instead of being supportive in her quest to live, her selfish husband was cheating again. Her health took a nosedive. Disappointed and hurt, she gave up on life. With the spiritual knowledge Big Bette had gained, she had no fear of dying. She knew that life continued after death, and she would share that life with her mother who would be there to greet her.

Membership of the spiritualist church had helped Big Bette to understand that disease is energy. Attending the church brought us into contact with people who understood spiritual matters. We were grateful for that when Jackie and Gordon moved to a larger house. Four-year-old Donna started going to her parents in the middle of the night, wanting to sleep in their bed rather than her own.

When she blurted out one night, "The man can have my bed. I don't want to sleep in it anymore," we realized there was a spirit presence in the house. As Peter and I were inexperienced, we asked Betty Gunn, a medium at the church, to come to our aid.

She went into Donna's bedroom, where she made contact with a man in spirit, an unsavory character who spent his last years lying in bed sipping whiskey. As she worked to send him to the light to complete his passing, she relayed information to us. His wife had died thirteen years earlier and had been waiting patiently for him to let go of his earthly pleasures. He wasn't eager to join his wife. In fact, he was downright insulting toward her, saying such things as, "I'm not going with that old bag!" With effort, persistence, and strength of will, Betty made the man move on, and Donna experienced no further problems.

TWELVE

I like a challenge and my probation colleagues were happy to give them to me. When people well-known to the probation service required reports because of yet another offence, the general consensus during team meetings was "give them to Pauline." I didn't mind. My colleagues saw that I had a knack for making clients feel better. If clients arrived at the office in a foul mood, or angry or distressed and their own supervising officer was unavailable, they were directed to my door. Thirty minutes in my office, and they usually left feeling much calmer, happier and more positive.

One of my clients arrived unexpectedly at my office. Mike was an intelligent man, with a gravelly voice, broken nose, tattoos, and the muscular build of a laborer. He was on probation for petty theft after his wife walked out on him and their two young sons, leaving him facing eviction because she had not paid the rent for months.

At 5:00 p.m. on a Friday, I was alone in the building. Mike was distraught, but couldn't bring himself to tell me what was troubling him. He admitted he was so ashamed of what he had done that he had tried to hang himself that afternoon. That got my attention.

"Okay, here's what I am going to do, Mike. I am going to lock the front door to the office so that you can't leave, because I'm not having you disappear in the state you're in. Next, I'm going to put the kettle on to make us a cup of coffee. Then I'm going to phone my husband to warn him I'll be late home. Then we're going to talk. Is that all right with you?"

He nodded.

Returning to my office with coffee, I phoned my husband in front of Mike. "I have a client in the office with a big problem. I could be late home tonight. If we can't solve the problem, we could be here all weekend. I'm just letting you know, I won't be home until we've sorted this out."

After confirming that I was not in any danger, Peter was satisfied. He understood how I worked.

Hearing this and seeing my commitment to him, Mike eventually opened up. He had done a terrible thing, and I told him so. Knowing how strapped Mike was for cash, a known criminal had paid him to break someone's leg with a baseball bat. However, the fact that he felt such remorse that he tried to hang himself, showed me that all was not lost, that he was basically a decent man. After talking with him for ninety minutes, I felt he would stay safe. I unlocked the office door and allowed him to leave with a promise that he would come to see me first thing Monday morning.

Monday morning, he turned up at the office a new man, in good spirits as if a huge weight had been removed from his shoulders.

Another of my clients, Scottish John was a short man in his fifties, with jet black hair, and no stranger to the probation service. When drunk, he often called in the office, belligerent and angry. Some years earlier he had served three years in prison for stabbing his wife, who fortunately survived the attack. He had a serious drink problem. Struggling with life, he committed some minor offence and asked to be placed on probation for his sins. He was homeless, drinking heavily, and certainly needed some help. The magistrates agreed. All my colleagues, tired of this nuisance client, voted that I should be John's probation officer. I didn't know a lot about the man, but liked him. He was sober, charming, polite, and pleasant at his first appointment. He was also hungry for someone to be interested in him, someone to care. After that first meeting, John willingly spent hours in my office, where I grew to know him well.

We came up with a list of things for him to achieve to have a more stable life. Finding accommodation was top priority. Not a homeless hostel, John insisted, but his own apartment. With his record, that was easier said than done. He would do his best to quit drinking, and I would teach him to read and write.

Much of John's rage, which ran riot when he was drunk, came from the emotional pain he carried from his childhood. John was born in Scotland, into a strict pastor's household. His brothers and sisters grew up to lead successful lives, but John, despite his good level of intelligence, was unable to learn to read and write. Therefore, he did not do well in school. In fact, he was labeled a stupid idiot by teachers, family, and friends. The fact that he was illiterate was a shame he carried all his life. He wept bitterly during long counseling sessions, eventually coming to understand he had nothing to be ashamed of. The school system had failed *him* for not realizing he was deaf. Getting a hearing aid was added to our to-do list while he was on probation.

Realizing that excessive drinking was his way of numbing his emotional pain, John was filled with guilt and remorse for the bad things he had done. Through his tears he told me he was heartbroken that his children wanted nothing to do with him. He was tired of being put down. All his life people had been putting him down. We had long talks about the afterlife. What would happen to him when he died? He was sure he would go to hell. When he tried to cut down on his drinking, he suffered with DTs (delirium tremens). He would see devils and goblins crawling up his chest, pulling on his clothes and hair to drag him to hell. I shared with him all the spiritual knowledge I was learning at Gresham Road Spiritualist Church.

"You know, John, the God I have come to know is a God of love."

"That's why he'll have nothing to do wi' me. He's turned his back on me," John said.

"John, because you are trying to be better than you have been, God loves you more. He wants you in the fold, safe from your fears."

I had been training to be a hypnotherapist and asked John if I could hypnotize him during his next appointment. He was willing. John really did want to lead a better life.

Because John was deaf, I had to raise my voice so he could hear me. "You are now a non-drinker, John. Drinking alcohol has no purpose in your life. You are filling your life with goodness. You now live an alcohol-free life. You are a sober non-drinker."

Forty minutes of sober, happy life intoned suggestions later, John left the office. I went on my coffee break to be greeted by my colleagues intoning, "We are all non-drinkers. Alcohol has no part in our lives."

When the laughter died down, Nigel asked, "When is your next session with John? We thought we'd line our clients up outside your office door so they could be hypnotized too."

John was on probation for two years. As his order was coming to an end, he committed another minor offence. The magistrate granted his wish of a further two- year order. John had been mainly living with various drinking buddies. I had approached numerous housing associations to take a chance on renting him a small apartment, with no luck. Then my senior gave me the name of a housing manager who owed him a favor. The manager was reluctant to consider John as a tenant (to put it mildly) but I convinced him that John would be a good tenant if given the chance. I could arrange for John's rent to be paid directly to the housing association before John received his disability benefits, so there would never be any rent arrears to be concerned about. John also kept himself clean and would keep his home clean.

Owing to his homelessness and chronic asthma, John was given priority on the housing list. Some weeks later, he had an apartment. I found furniture and household items through the probation service's community service department, and he moved in. John reported like clockwork to the office, where I continued to teach him to read and provided him with easy reading books so he could practice at home. With determination, he progressed to reading the newspaper. His drinking had lessened considerably. Now that he had a kitchen, he spent his meager income on preparing food for his homeless, alcoholic friends who were not taking care of themselves.

We still had long discussions about the afterlife. Being unable to forgive himself, John was fearful of ending up in hell.

With a reduction in my workload and my clients free of crises, and our tenth wedding anniversary fast approaching, it was time to meet Peter's brother, Norman, who lived in South Africa. So off we went. I had been feeling that Peter and I would soon be going to live abroad. I had no idea where. All I knew was that it would be a warm, sunny place. During this visit, we would check out South Africa as a place to live.

Norman and Maureen and their adult children welcomed us warmly. We were the only people from Norman's side of the family to visit them since they immigrated to South Africa. At numerous barbeques we met Norman and Maureen's friends, including a Scotsman called John, who, with his short stature and jet-black hair, looked very much like my Scottish probation client John.

Over grilled steaks and South African wine, Norman announced a wonderful surprise for us. "I've arranged for us to visit the Kruger National Park."

I jumped up and down with excitement. "We weren't expecting that!"

"When I called to make the booking, the clerk told me I had to book a year ahead. That was a shock. So I wheedled, begged and charmed, and told him my brother was coming on his first visit to South Africa, and I hadn't seen him in over ten years . . . and so on. He relented and found us a camp we could stay in for four nights. We go on Monday."

Peter and I high-fived.

Maureen sat up front with Norman. Peter and I sat in the back seat of the Mercedes. I'd been impressed that Norman owned a luxury car. He'd done well for himself in South Africa, where he worked as a manager of an opencast coalmine, much better than if he had stayed in England. Like most white people, Norman and Maureen had a comfortable lifestyle. Their black housekeeper, who had been with them thirty years, had helped raise Maureen's three children. They all treated with her with the affection of a family member. Once we realized we held opposing viewpoints to Norman and Maureen regarding apartheid, we avoided such discussions. It was more important to make our visit memorable and pleasurable. Intent on proving that not all black people lived in poverty and squalor and not all white people lived high on the hog, Norman drove us to Soweto Township to show us Minnie Mandela's luxury home, amongst others. Then he drove us to an area of Johannesburg where poor white people lived. Satisfied he had proven his point, the matter was not mentioned again.

Norman drove to the Kruger National Park along modern highways, through scenic countryside with rich red soil and escarpments covered in straw-like dry-season vegetation.

"We get a better chance of seeing animals at the watering holes when it's the dry season," Maureen said.

We stopped for a quick lunch at a gas station and roadside café. I used the outside restroom. When I came out, I was amazed to find Maureen horrified I had mistakenly used the BLACKS ONLY toilet. I had to bite my tongue, I was so angry at such rules.

Norman smoothed the tension away by telling us, "We have to arrive before they shut the Park gates, and once inside, where speed limits are dead slow, we have to reach our camp before they close the camp gates."

"We're going to be locked in at night?"

"To protect us from lions."

Oh, boy, what have we let ourselves in for?

We were delighted to find our accommodation at the camp was in a self-contained thatched hut, with one bedroom, veranda, shower and toilet. Norman and Maureen had the hut next door.

That night we dined in the camp restaurant and tried amarula liqueur for the first time. "Made from the berries of the amarula tree," Norman said. "Baboons and elephants often get drunk when they eat the berries that ferment in the animals' stomachs."

I felt like a memsahib on safari, sipping my drink and listening to lions roaring. For the first time in my life, I was thankful we were fenced in.

At breakfast the next morning, another visitor told us where there was a lion kill beside the road. "Well worth a visit," he said.

Norman found the kill encircled by cars. "Keep the car windows up, although I don't think we'll have any problem with them," he said, nodding in the pride's direction. "Too full to move. But a lion can smash a car window with its paw." Comatose lions with bulging bellies surrounded the baby giraffe's carcass. Waiting vultures jostled for position in the trees. We watched for a while, but as there was little activity from the dosing lions, we drove away to see hippopotamuses in a river pool, a leopard trotting along the road ahead of us, dung beetles rolling dung across the road, tortoises toddling along, giraffes and kudus hiding among the trees and a bull elephant on the road ahead that brought Norman to an immediate stop.

"What's wrong?" Peter asked.

Maureen answered. "We had a run-in with a bull elephant one time. It was very scary. Slowly, back away," she told her husband.

The elephant studied us, shook his head and lifted his trunk. Norman kept reversing. Then the elephant disappeared into the bush. A few steps and the huge animal vanished.

Over the next few days, the giraffe carcass began to reek. Even with the car windows closed, the stink of putrefaction invaded the vehicle. We held our noses, plugged nostrils with Vicks, but still could not escape the stench of rotting flesh. Huge numbers of heaving maggots caused the carcass to move. Stuffed lions, and now satisfied vultures, stayed with the giraffe until the bones were bare.

Returning to Johannesburg, we learned that Nelson Mandela had been released from prison. It was a great occasion for the country, an indication that South Africa was moving forward. But, concern about instability in the country after Mandela's release had Norman and Maureen talking of possibly moving to Canada, and we decided that South Africa would not be the place where we were going to live.

We returned home in time to attend the Sunday service at Gresham Road Spiritualist Church. The medium came to me. "I have Scottish John with me. He has black hair, not a grey hair in his head, even though he's in his mid-fifties. He wants to say hello to you and tell you that life on the other side is even better than you told him."

The message puzzled me. The only John I could think of was Norman's friend in South Africa. Surely, he couldn't have died as we were traveling home. The next day at work, my secretary Barbara followed me into my office and shut the door. "Pauline, have you heard about John?"

"Oh, don't say he's been in trouble while I've been away!"

"No, not that. John died three days ago from an asthma attack."

I plunked down. So that was what the message in the church was about! I would miss him. I'd been supervising John for almost four years, and he'd been doing so well.

I smiled. "The good news is . . . he's gone to heaven, Barbara."

Another longtime client was a rapist. I wrote several reports on Roy for rape offences, for which he was imprisoned three times. The final time was for life. Through regular visits I made during his two previous prison sentences, I came to know Roy well. I was the only person interested in him, and he knew it. His family had disowned him. Society detested him. People who knew him wanted him dead. And I did not want him to be released when his second term of imprisonment came to an end, because he would certainly rape again.

Roy's emotions and desires were damaged when, twenty-four years earlier, as a nine-year-old boy, he watched a video of a man chasing a frightened woman through the woods. When he caught her, he raped her. The scene was seared into Roy's brain. One psychological theory is that we behave in the way that will fulfill fantasies that meet our subconscious needs. That goes for offenders too. Change the fantasies and you change the behavior. Using visualization during prison visits to Roy, I tried retraining his fantasies away from raping women, a method that had had some success in stopping sexual predators from reoffending. A prison visiting room is not the ideal place to do therapy, but I was so desperate to help Roy in order to protect women, I was willing to try. Roy said he wanted to stop raping. However, he could not let go of his fantasy. It was too much a part of him. With his second prison term's release date fast approaching, I tried every avenue to keep Roy in prison. And failed. The only way would be to have him declared insane, and he wasn't. He was released without parole supervision.

Two months after his release, Roy held a woman against her will at knife point in her apartment and raped her. Roy pleaded not guilty. I worried the jury would get the verdict wrong. In British courts, the jury is not informed of the defendant's prior convictions until sentencing. Watching the trial in crown court, I closely monitored the jurors' reactions as the lawyers lunged, parried, counterattacked and rebuffed one another's cross examinations.

After four days, the jury went out to deliberate, and the court adjourned. Expecting the jury to quickly reach a decision, most people remained in court. I rolled my neck and shrugged my shoulders, open and closed my mouth trying to release muscles tight from the strain of attending the trial. I was writing notes for my files when I became aware of the lawyers discussing how it was nearly impossible to rape a woman who did not want to be raped.

The defense lawyer waved his arm airily. "It's too difficult to penetrate when the woman is twisting and struggling to get away."

The prosecutor approached the defense lawyer, got in his face, and held a pen to his throat. In a quiet, menacing voice, he said, "If you struggle, I'll kill you. If you resist, I'll kill your kids sleeping in the next room. Now get on your knees and give me a blow job."

With a fear-filled face, the shaken defense lawyer nodded. The prosecutor's role play had been so impressive, I was scared too.

The verdict was guilty. Hallelujah! Jurors gasped in surprise and murmured Thank Gods to one another when the judge read out

Roy's previous offences. Energized, they filed from the jury box. Tensions had fallen away to be replaced by satisfied expressions at a job well done in this he said/she said case.

The judge sentenced Roy to life in prison.

Two months after this, Betty Gunn, who was studying for a Bachelor of Arts Degree in Social Work Administration, came to work with me as an observation student as part of her course. She was also a medium and president of the spiritualist church. I had butterflies in my stomach, I was so excited. I had strong intuition, and with her psychic gifts, she would be able to tell me how accurate my intuition had been. I had one young probationer going to court charged with theft. I felt he was not telling me the whole truth about the situation. With Betty beside me in court, I learned not only was my client not telling the whole truth, the police officer involved was lying too. How did Betty know this?

"His aura is orange. A dead giveaway," she said.

I took Betty to see Roy in Wakefield prison. He was interested in numerology and seemed to have some talent with it. He told us that numerology had indicated he would never see the outside of prison again. We discussed how he could adapt to the lack of a future outside of prison walls. Could he be helpful in teaching someone to read? He said he had people go to him for numerology readings.

"I wish a medium would come and visit me," he said.

"What would you ask the medium if one came?" Betty asked.

He reeled off areas of concern. Would his family ever accept him back after disowning him? Would his life be short or long? Would he ever be released from prison?

Betty Gunn told him she had a bit of ability as a medium and that she didn't see him being in prison in twelve to eighteen months.

The next time I visited Roy, he told me, "I'm not impressed with that so-called medium that came with you on your last visit. Everyone knows I'll never see the light of day again."

THIRTEEN

A bulky letter arrived from Peter's sister in Michigan. Jean did not write letters. She didn't even send Christmas cards. Jean and her husband John had emigrated from England to Canada twenty-five years previously when in their twenties. From there they had moved to Michigan, owing to John's pattern-maker skills being in demand in Detroit's booming auto industry.

I had first met Jean ten years earlier when we went to visit her after Peter and I had been married one year, hoping it would help alleviate Peter's depression at being unemployed. She had asked us to bring our birth and marriage certificates in case we liked America. If we did, she would petition for us to immigrate. She was hoping we would, because she and John had been much more successful in creating an affluent lifestyle than her brothers who still lived in England. As none of her six brothers had followed her to the States, her three children had grown up without extended family around them. She hoped we could fill that gap in their lives.

Now here was her letter, apologizing for misplacing the letter she had received eight years before, the letter from the American government saying we had been accepted to apply for immigration. She had found it when she and John were preparing their house for a remodeling project. I contacted the American Embassy in London. We were still in their computer. The woman I spoke to said they had sent us a parcel, but had received no response from us.

"We never received any parcel," I said.

She would send us another package with papers to fill in.

Pondering over why we were to immigrate at forty-four years of age rather than eight years earlier, I reviewed what had happened during those eight years. The main things I could think of were that we had started attending the Greater World Christian Spiritualist Church on Gresham Road. From this we had gained a greater understanding of spiritual matters. We had also become certified spiritual healers after taking most of the courses offered by the National Federation of Spiritual Healers. I was convinced we were being given the opportunity to immigrate to advance our healing work. Despite the heartache involved in having to leave my family, especially my two granddaughters and my daughter who was pregnant with her third child, I felt it was our destiny to move to America. Besides, we did not want to reach old age and say if only (we had immigrated). Better to try than live a life of regret.

Once we mailed our immigration forms to the American Embassy, I began to feel ill. My doctor tested my liver, checked for gallstones, ulcers, etc. Every test came back negative. Having ruled out a physical condition, I realized these organs are influenced by the solar plexus energy center, which is the chakra concerned with issues of personal power such as control, ambition, success, achievement, or the opposite of these attributes—having no control over your life, feeling you are a victim, feeling inferior. My feeling ill was directing me to take charge and make choices to break me free of stagnation and misery regarding Joanne's adoption.

At this point, we phoned our friend Vicky Kingsley and asked if we could take her out for lunch. An excellent psychic and medium, Vicky was called in by police on occasion to help solve difficult cases. We had known her for many years through the Spiritualist Church.

Vicky greeted us with, "What are you up to?"

"Before we tell you that, we'd like you to give us a reading," I said.

"That sounds exciting. Can I eat my chicken biriyani first?"

Son-in-law Gordon, Daughter Jackie, me and Vicky (right) 2003

We ate the aromatic Indian food and talked about family and the spiritual awareness classes she was teaching. Then she said, "What's going on? I'm seeing an American parade, marching bands, people cheering . . . oh, and it's all for you. A big celebration. Feels good."

I said, "We're immigrating to America, Vicky. We want to be sure we're doing the right thing. It feels right to me, but we'll be leaving family and my job . . ."

"The universe is applauding your decision," she said. "It's the right one. Go. Everything will work out fine. You think you're well prepared, but you'll be going on a wing and a prayer. But you have two unresolved matters to clear up. They're making you feel ill."

Wow! I hadn't mentioned I was feeling unwell.

"I know you were raped," she said. "You only need to remember that your greatest enemy is your greatest teacher and come to an understanding of what that means, then you will be free of it. You also have another matter to work on before leaving the country. Remember, all will be well."

It turned out Vicky was right.

We traveled to London for our immigration interviews at the American Embassy, on January 16, 1991, the day the First Gulf War broke out. First port of call for our medicals was in what used to be a mansion house in its glory days, now divided into various offices. The waiting room was full of silently waiting hopefuls. The sour-puss receptionist had filled the space with her sour-puss negativity.

With no greeting, she glanced through our paperwork. "I'd like ninety pounds—per person—in cash. No checks or credit cards," she said, her voice bored. That was the first we'd heard of having to pay the medical fee in cash, which, of course, we didn't have.

Peter responded, "So would I."

Titters erupted around the waiting room. We lost our place in line while we went in search of a bank to withdraw one hundred and eighty pounds, cash. Returning to the mansion, a technician, who at least was professional, took chest x-rays. The conveyor belt system moved us on to the nurse who took our blood. She made such a hash of taking Peter's blood he jokingly asked where she'd been trained.

"I'm not really a nurse," she said. "I came for a receptionist's job."

"Don't let my wife know," Peter said. "She's terrified of needles. She once punched her dentist in the face because he forgot and came at her with a needle."

Blood drained from the receptionist/so-called nurse's face. Peter patted her arm to reassure her. "You'll be all right as long as you do a good job. She can be quite disciplined when you don't upset her."

Next came the farce of a medical. "Open wide," the doctor said, shining a light down Peter's throat. "Say aaah," he continued, as the light reached Peter's ear. And so it continued in similar vein until we were declared fit enough to go on to the next part of the process.

The embassy was besieged by demonstrators. I hoped this was not an omen against our immigrating. We could make no headway in forging a path through the mass of people surrounding the embassy. We waved the large brown envelopes, containing our x-rays, high above our heads. That caught the attention of security guards who pushed their way through the crowd to escort us to the safety of the embassy. A woman behind a counter checked our paperwork and passport-style photographs.

"Oh, these won't do," she said. "You'll have to have them retaken."

"Why's that?" Peter asked.

"Your ears, we can't see your ears."

"What do you think those things are sticking out the side of my head?" Peter asked.

But she would not be swayed. Off we trotted to a nearby photographer's seedy studio for Peter's new photographs to be taken. The photographer took a comb and gently combed back the one eighth of an inch of hair touching Peter's ear.

"You've got to be kidding!" Peter said.

"Nope," the photographer said, putting the comb to one side and moving to his camera.

We returned to the embassy after lunch and again pressed through the crowds. After the excitement outside, the immigration interview was so laid back it was an anticlimax. We didn't realize it was the interview, until the interviewer congratulated us on being allowed into the United States.

St Catherine's House was the central registry for all births, deaths, marriages, and adoptions in Great Britain. And it was only a short walk from the American Embassy. We headed there to do something I had promised myself I would never do, and that was impose myself on the daughter I gave away. I had always felt it was Joanne's prerogative to seek me out if she wanted to. However, with our departure fast approaching, I couldn't leave without finding out if she'd had a happy life.

We arrived one hour before closing and quickly checked the adoption records then the death records in case Joanne had already died. I found no one with her name. From her sixteenth birthday, I searched through all the wedding lists of women bearing her adopted name. I found her name and jubilantly hurried to a clerk to fill out the forms with barely a minute to spare.

St. Catherine's House had a procedure to follow in order to make contact with a child given away for adoption. I gladly paid the fee, delighted to know I would soon meet my long lost daughter. I stepped outside into the darkness of the late-winter afternoon. The need to make contact with Joanne, however brief it might be, was overpowering. I was satisfied knowing it would happen soon.

We continued taking courses while we waited. One was a four-day spiritual development "Second Aid" course with Judy Fraser, an internationally known alternative psychotherapist and spiritual teacher. On the third morning of the course, I woke up crying, unhappy from the loss of Joanne. We were the first attendees to arrive at the course room and found Judy there. Usually, it would have been full of people by this time.

"Why are you crying, Pauline?" she asked.

After listening to my woeful tale, Judy said, "Before you were born, you made a contract with spirit to provide Owen and Sheila with a child as part of your spiritual growth. You're to be congratulated for carrying through your part of the contract despite the huge emotional cost to you. Now, you have to complete the part of the contract that involves emotionally letting go of your daughter by trusting that what happened was all part of God's plan. Understand and trust that everything is unfolding in the best possible way for all concerned."

Then Judy, who was adopted as a baby, said she had searched for and found her original parents with whom she had maintained contact. I needed to believe if it was meant to happen, my daughter would contact me. But, alternately, Joanne could be so content and secure, she had no need for exploration or adding meaning to her life.

Judy's words helped, but I had a long way to go.

Another course I went on was a gestalt therapy course. One of the issues I wanted to work on was healing my broken heart at giving Joanne away for adoption. It turned out that Tom, the facilitator, was adopted. Were the powers above reassuring me that adopted children come through just fine?

FOURTEEN

After twelve years as a probation officer, I was moving on to the next stage in my life. I had one week left to wrap up loose ends for my successor. Word was out, and many ex-clients came by to wish me luck and bid me farewell. The first surprise was a young man I had supervised when he was fifteen years old. His mother told him I was emigrating, and he traveled all the way from the Liverpool area, on the other side of the country, to tell me how my supervising him under the court order had changed his life. Dumbfounded, my mouth hung open. I thought I'd achieved nothing with this young man, that I had not been able to reach him at all, and here he was telling me I had changed his life.

"When I left school, I went across country to find work," he said. "I was lucky. I found a job, nothing great, just flipping burgers. But I live independently. I'm clean of drugs, thanks to you, Mrs. Hayton. Every time someone tried to persuade me to try them, I remembered your words and all the talks we had. It gave me the strength to say no, to not be influenced, and be myself. Thanks."

"Hey, it's your strength. It was there all along. I just helped you find it within yourself. You can go on to do good things with your life. You're still young. You'll do well." I wished I could remember what I'd said to him that had such an impact.

Another client, a struggling alcoholic whom I had helped to stand up to his brutal bully of an ex-con brother, turned up at the office drunk, so my secretary told me. He didn't wait to see me but left me a very expensive bouquet of two dozen velvety red roses. Now, this client could not possibly have had the money to buy them. I was perturbed and hoped he hadn't stolen them from a florist shop. Then I noticed they were not as fresh as they could be and suspected he had taken them from a grave. I chose not to tackle him about my suspicions, but left a note in his file for my successor to deal with the matter.

My biggest surprise came from an ex-client called Mike. Shortly after 9:30 a.m., my secretary came into my office.

"I've just had a phone call from one of your old clients. You're under strict orders not to leave until Mike arrives," Barbara said.

"Mike? Which Mike?"

"Mike with the gravelly voice, broken nose, and tattoos. He heard you were emigrating and is on his way here now to take you out for lunch."

Wow! Mike who tried to hang himself in shame! I sat down slowly, trying to take in that one of my ex-clients wanted to take me out for lunch.

"He set off at six this morning, so I don't know where he's driving from," Barbara said.

Another amazed "Wow!" was all I could muster.

Around midday, Mike arrived, beaming. "I just had to see you before you disappeared. Where shall we go for lunch?"

He took my arm and led me outside to a shiny, red Ford Capri convertible sports car.

"Is this *yours*?" I asked.

"Yeh. Isn't she lovely?" he said. His chest puffed out, he patted his car fondly.

"Mike, you must be doing well! I can't wait to hear what you've been up to."

"Where would you like to go for lunch?"

I chose a pleasant pub ten minutes away. With a meal ordered, I was impatient to hear Mike's tale.

"After my probation ended, I saw an advert in the *Evening Gazette*, asking for people to train as nurses down south. So I applied, and they took me on."

Really! His tattoos and broken nose didn't deter them?

"I finished my training, and now I'm doing really well. I manage three nursing homes for people with dementia and Alzheimer's. I have a nice flat. I have a steady girlfriend, and I've bought myself a nice car and, Mrs. Hayton, it's all because of you. I wouldn't have done this without your help. I couldn't let you emigrate without telling you. That's why I drove up from Surrey this morning."

"Whoa! Just a minute, Mike! All I did was hold a mirror up so you could see what I saw in you. *You* did it. *You* passed your tests. *You* took the initiative, not me. And my God! You drove over three hundred miles to tell me how well you're doing? You deserve all the success you have." I paused, choked up. "Thank you, Mike, for showing me I did some good in my probation work."

I almost regretted leaving my job. I had helped more people than I realized. I felt humble and honored to have had this opportunity to be of service.

Peter and I had one more matter to organize. We had a busy schedule doing healing work in our spare time. Wanting to ensure our clients continued to receive healing after we emigrated, we asked Bob to take over those people who were too sick to attend healing services in the church. Bob accompanied us to see Paul and his wife Doreen so that we could introduce them.

Peter and I had been working with Paul and his wife for seven months, but Paul, who had lung cancer, was not improving. Sometimes, healing isn't about a cure, but a way to make a person's passing less distressing. I intuitively felt that Paul was extremely disappointed in what he had achieved in his life, but he refused to open up about his feelings. Cancer was an acceptable way out for him. We also gave healing to Doreen. The strain of caring for her husband and facing his death was taking its toll on her health. She actually needed more healing energy than Paul.

Bob began channeling healing energy to Paul. In no time at all, we could see Bob's multi-colored aura expanding to fill the room. It was beautiful and perfect, exactly as illustrated in Barbara Brennan's book *Hands of Light*. What a wonderful sight, the rainbow-colored energy bands, the trumpet-shaped vortices of the chakras. Amazing!

As we left the house, Bob said, "He won't last long. He doesn't want to live."

Thus Bob validated my feelings about Paul's situation.

We had failed to sell our house. The day after we put the house up for sale, the market crashed thanks to a steep rise in interest rates to slow the runaway housing bubble. We spent the last two weeks in England saying goodbye to friends and family. It was particularly hard saying goodbye to Jackie and our now three granddaughters. But Jackie and Gordon were happy, and my parents were still around for family support. As always, my parents did not believe we were emigrating until we sold our furniture.

One worry was finding a home for our calico cat called Bru, short for Bruiser. Bru had been a stray kitten, given to us by a friend. We named her Bru because once she realized she had a place to call home and humans to protect, she defended them against anyone and everyone. An aging Labrador used to pass by on the footpath, carrying his owner's newspaper in its mouth. If Bru was outside, she would charge the poor dog and hit him with her paw to move him on his way. We advertized in the newspaper for a new owner for her. With only days to spare, a woman came to see Bru and instantly fell in love with her. Bru's future was assured.

Less than a week before leaving, we received a low-ball offer on the house. I was indignant, feeling the buyer was taking advantage of us in our situation of pending departure from England. How foolish could I have been? As foolish as my stupid ego would let me. I failed to see that God was again taking care of us and was probably taking care of the buyer, who could only buy the house at a low price. If we had accepted the buyer's offer, we would have been free and clear of the responsibility of the house, and we would have had sixty thousand dollars in the bank to support us in building a new life in a new country.

Our two oldest granddaughters' birthdays were in May. Jackie held a birthday party combined with a farewell party for us at her local community center. Sarah was born two years after Donna. Prior to that, my mother had doted on Donna. Then, when Sarah was born, it was as if Mum put Donna aside to focus solely on Sarah. I did my best to become more involved with Donna to redress the balance, but Donna, at two years of age, had been damaged and confused by the switch of interest. And here was I, abandoning her to go to America. I felt guilty and sad, and worried about Sarah now that she had a new baby sister, Rebecca. Would she grow up with an abandonment issue dogging her life too?

Sarah (4), Donna (6) and Rebecca 4 months.
The granddaughters we left behind when we emigrated to Florida

For Peter's large family, Peter's brother, Richard, and his wife Chris hosted a farewell barbecue. It was a chilly May day. We were in the garden, trying to keep warm wrapped up in down jackets and wooly hats. We didn't feel sad at the barbecue. We had bought a return ticket in order to attend Richard's daughter's September wedding. Once upon a time, emigrants were more or less saying farewell forever when they moved to another country. But with the expansion of inexpensive air travel, family could be reached in a few hours. My heavy heart was still wrestling with unfinished business. I'd received a letter informing me that the Joanne I had found at St. Catherine's House was not *my* daughter Joanne. I would have to leave for America without finding her. The best I could do was write a letter explaining the story behind her adoption, including her sister's and father's information, which would be kept with her birth certificate.

With belongings given away or sold and the items we wanted to keep placed in storage, we took our leave. Tears were many as we said our farewells to Jackie, Gordon, and our granddaughters. I felt as if we were abandoning them, but we had to go to America. It was the right thing to do. Exciting? Not sure. Scary? You bet! Exhilarating? Absolutely!

Our plans on arriving in America were fluid. Jean was disappointed that we did not want to live in Michigan. "Too cold in the winter," we told her. "We want to live somewhere warm." To us that meant Florida, California, or Arizona. Peter ruled out California because of earthquakes. Florida had its hurricanes, but at least you were warned well in advance of impending storms. There were also inexpensive, vacation charter flights from England to Florida, making it easy for family to visit. Our first port of call would be the "Sunshine State."

FIFTEEN

May 8th, 1991, we stepped from the plane at Miami, Florida. It was hot and muggy. Peter and I flashed wide grins to one another.

"Yes!" I said, lifting my fist in the air in an excited winner's salute. I couldn't stop smiling at the warmth after our shivering barbecue in England.

Passing through immigration took hours. We'd certainly arrived in a cosmopolitan country. Our fellow immigrants were Chinese, South American, and Vietnamese. We were the only English-speaking immigrants being processed. Eventually, we made it to American soil. All we knew of Florida, we learned from watching the television programs *Flipper* and *Miami Vice*. First, we explored the east coast of the state. It was busy, built up, and full of traffic.

"If this is Florida," I said, "we're going to Arizona."

Giving up on the east coast as a place to live, we traveled west to Naples, on the Gulf of Mexico. It was quieter, less developed, and still had small town charm with its brightly painted cottages in downtown. Medians were landscaped with tropical plants and palm trees, and snowy egrets glided across the roads in front of us. We fell in love with the beauty around us. Naples would be our home. The deal was clinched when we drove north on the Tamiami Trail, our thoughts on finding a place to stay and searching for work.

We were jolted into the present moment by a deputy sheriff's car traveling on the other side of the median going in the opposite direction with its siren blaring and lights flashing. He swerved across the median to block our way. Traffic stopped. Unable to see what was happening until we started moving again, we discovered the deputy sheriff had stopped traffic to allow a mother duck and her eight ducklings to cross the road without mishap. Naples put the well-being of ducks before traffic flow! Definitely our kind of town. Only one problem—the season was over. No work to be found anywhere. Not having enough money to last us six months until the season started again, we went to stay with Peter's sister Jean in Michigan.

Jean and her husband John took us in. They lived in a big house, on five lake-front acres. Even with three children, they had room for us. To earn our keep, we cleaned house, worked in the garden, demolished an old boathouse, and generally did whatever we could to help. That included helping oldest daughter Angela choose a different direction for her life. I found her in the kitchen early one afternoon.

Frustrated, she shook the letter she had just opened. "All my attempts to get on the right courses so I can study for a marine biology degree are hitting snags."

"Maybe you're meant to be doing something else with your life," I said.

"You think so, Aunty Pauline?"

"You've been trying to go the marine biology route for months, and all you are coming across are barriers. You may need to rethink your path."

That night she went out with her friends. Next morning, she found me in the kitchen, brewing coffee. Taking my hands, she waltzed me round the island, happily singing, "I know what I am going to do. I'm going to be a chiropractor."

"That was sudden. What made you decide that?"

She set me down on a chair.

"I met a chiropractor last night while I was out. He was telling me about it. Made it sound very interesting. You know, if you hadn't helped me open my mind, Aunty Pauline, I might have missed it."

While at Jean's, I received a letter from Barbara, my former secretary. It contained a newspaper clipping informing me that my client Roy, serving life for rape, was dead, stabbed to death by another inmate. So, Betty Gunn had been right in her reading. She told Roy he would be out of prison in twelve to eighteen months, and he was. I felt I had to pray for him. And so I did, every day. And every day I was taken to a very dark place in the afterlife. It was like walking into a bar in a dangerous part of town, the type of place where you stood with your back to the wall, where you did not wear expensive jewelry or pull out a wallet showing all your money. It was a horrible place to go, but go I did. I prayed fervently for Roy to be guided to a place of light and love. I prayed this way for several months until I felt he had no further need of my prayers.

After attending our niece's September wedding and spending time with family in England, we returned to Michigan to say farewell to Jean and family before returning to Naples. We drove a snowbird's car fourteen hundred miles from Michigan to Delray Beach. After delivering the car to its owner, in Florida for the winter, we rented a car to travel to a healing conference in Ashville, North Carolina, where the National Federation of Spiritual Healers was attempting to start an American branch. It was exciting to be at the forefront of helping spiritual healing become accepted in America. At the conference, Peter and I met Tony Leggett, a British spiritual healer, who had lived in America for many years. His friendly, humorous, and knowledgeable presentation at the conference drew us to him.

"I was going to do great things with my healing work," Tony told us. "But no matter what I tried, I couldn't earn a living doing healing work. Mind you, I never lost money either. Then I was offered the job of Agony Aunt, or in my case Agony Uncle, for the problem page at the *National Examiner*. Of course, I turned it down. I was going to be a healer. It took a while before I understood that answering people's problems was healing work. Not only that, I could reach four million people every week. I took the job and have been doing it ever since."

We had that conversation twenty-four years ago, and Tony is still taking care of the *National Examiner's* readers' problems.

In Naples, we took up residence in the inexpensive Trail's End Motel and took stock of our situation. We only had a few hundred dollars left, and our rental car was due to be returned. With no money to rent another car, top priority was to buy transport. Our great credit record in England meant nothing in America. We were starting from scratch. No credit history. A motel resident directed us to a "buy here, pay here" place. The only car we could afford was a gigantic, V8, gas-guzzling Buick. The car had several dents in its bodywork, some of them more like craters. We took it for a test drive.

"It's old. What if it gives out on us before we've finished paying for it?" Peter said. He sounded trapped, close to tears. He didn't want to be in this situation. Neither did I, but we were.

Our choices were limited. With no public transport system in Naples, we had to be realistic. "Right now, we have to get around somehow. It's this or bicycles. What do you want it to be?" I said.

With huge misgivings, we bought the Buick and for seven months paid fifty dollars a week for the privilege of owning it. Despite its battered appearance, it turned out to be a gem. Next, we had to search for jobs and more permanent accommodation than Trail's End. With money running low, that was going to be difficult. We had no money for a down payment or first and last months' rent. In fact, we were just about out of money. Period. We asked the motel receptionist if she knew of an efficiency we could rent.

"You don't want to live in an efficiency," she said. "There's a new rental complex, outside Naples, on the way to Marco, trying to attract renters. You only need a ninety-nine-dollar deposit and first month's rent."

We raced to the apartment complex and rented a clean, new, one-bedroom place. At this time, we still weren't panicking. We still felt that moving to America had been the right thing to do. Vicky had warned us we would be creating a new life for ourselves on a shoestring. At least we were living in clean, pleasant surroundings. I could feel the hand of God guiding events.

The day we moved in, we arranged for phone service so we could be reached by prospective employers. Moving in was easy. We each had a suitcase and a travel bag. Nothing else. We went on a spending spree for the basics we needed—a shower curtain, paper plates, plastic cutlery borrowed from Wendy's, a small saucepan, two pillows, and a thin blanket. We slept and sat on the carpet for nine months until we could afford to send for the few bits of furniture and personal belongings in storage in England. Still paying the mortgage on our house in England, we were strapped for cash. Vicky was definitely right. We really were starting from scratch.

Over the following weeks, neighbors, seeing our plight, brought us a chair, a television, a twin bed, and later an old sofa. We found Americans' kindness to complete strangers awesome.

Peter found work as an electrician. With his tools in storage in England, we had to scrape enough together to buy a few basic tools for him to work with until he received his wages, but he was laughed at by his workmates, who had a hard time believing he was a master electrician with no tools.

Looking through job vacancies in the Sunday newspaper, an advertisement for a Unity Church service caught my eye. The sermon was to be: "The Universe Will Provide."

"Peter, look at this. We must go," I said, hoping it would be a sign for us.

We were sitting on the carpet, our backs resting against the wall, going through a fear crisis. We had hit rock bottom. What the hell have we done? Giving up our comfortable professional lifestyle in England to sit in an empty apartment in Naples, Florida, and trying to start a new life at forty-four years of age was not working. Or maybe it was. We were at the crossroads of a new life, starting a new cycle of change where we were being forced to confront and heal our fears in order to release ourselves from restricting patterns of belief, attitude and emotion. Going through this, I often recalled Vicky's words: "You have exactly what you need in your life, right now."

Off we trotted to discover how the universe would provide. We enjoyed the service in the welcoming church even when the pastor gave his sermon and fearful tears rolled down our cheeks as we held each other's trembling hands. Filled with desperation, too emotional to mingle, we returned to our apartment to spend the evening sitting on the floor.

Then Jean phoned. "How are you two doing?"

"We're doing well. We have a car and our apartment is really nice!" I told her.

"How are you managing for money?" she asked.

I choked up, couldn't speak, and handed Peter the phone.

"Okay, what's up? You took too long to answer." she said.

Peter told her we were fine. Doing great! She didn't believe him, thank goodness. Four days later, six hundred dollars arrived in the mail. We wept with relief. As well as being placed in situations to face and heal our fears, we were also being taught to learn to accept help. In England, we were financially sound, and *we* were the people who did the giving. Now the tables were turned. We had to learn to receive gratefully and joyfully. The universe certainly provided and saved our bacon. I could have stopped paying the mortgage for the house in England. That would have solved a lot of problems. But I wasn't one to renege on my financial obligations.

Then Jackie, who was overseeing the house for us and keeping the garden tidy, went to check it was secure. She called us in tears. "Mum, your house has been vandalized. Someone broke in and stole copper piping, the boiler, the light fittings, and carpets. It's been flooded."

She felt responsible, even though she wasn't.

"It's not your fault, Jackie. Now, I want you to forget it. It was too big a responsibility. I shouldn't have asked you to do it. We'll hand the house over to the bank, and that will be the end of it."

And we did. The vandalism released me from my overly strong sense of responsibility that was preventing us from rebuilding our lives in America. I again berated myself for not taking the low-ball offer on the house prior to leaving the UK. Now we had nothing. There was only one way to go and that was up. We girded our loins and got on with it.

Peter relaxing with Joe Sweiger

The apartment complex's management supplied food and drink for a monthly social for residents. That's where Joe Sweiger came into our lives. Joe, fifty-five, divorced, and living alone except for when he had a roommate, had lived, according to him, quite a life with lots of business successes and failures under his belt from when he lived in New York state. He was self-employed in his radon mitigation business, checking houses for cancer-causing radon gas. If it was present, he would build a venting system so the gas was diverted harmlessly to the outside. As radon mitigation had not really caught on as a necessary part of house buying, the call for his services was limited. Joe was always short of cash and scrambling for money, but his being broke didn't match our being broke. He could afford to go out for breakfast! No such luxuries for us. And he always kept his refrigerator well-stocked with beer. Anyway, Joe, a man with an upbeat, aging-hippie-attitude, took us under his wing and taught us about American customs such as Thanksgiving, health insurance, and to always make sure we had uninsured driver insurance on our auto insurance policy. He showed us how to have lots of laughs, with a few drinks, in the most unlikely places, such as the afternoon we spent at the car wash with a few friends. The happy glow stayed with us for days. Fun with Joe was therapeutic and free of charge, the perfect antidote for the skepticism and insults Peter faced every day at work.

I found a job cleaning hotel rooms. A few weeks later, I changed jobs to become a housekeeper in a luxury high rise in Pelican Bay. The job provided health insurance. My parents thought it hilarious that their undomesticated daughter was actually cleaning condominiums for a living. In England, my mother used to nag me to clean my windows. I always replied that Jackie would remember and value the time I spent with her and not how clean our windows were. Now, here I was, cleaning eight hours a day five days a week. I duly noted the irony of the situation with a smile.

We lived frugally and saved our money. Jackie had unexpectedly become pregnant soon after giving birth to Rebecca. It should never have happened. Jackie was taking the birth control pill. The shock of it all had Gordon running for a vasectomy. They were struggling financially as it was with three children. However would they cope with four?

"This baby must really want you as its parents," I told Jackie. "I'll book a ticket to try and arrive around your due date."

I flew to England in June 1992. My sister met me at Middlesbrough coach station. "Jackie's in the maternity hospital, but nothing's happening yet."

"Let's go there anyway," I said.

Feeling a sense of urgency, I ran through the corridors to arrive out of breath at maternity reception and blurted, "I've just arrived from America and want to see my daughter."

"Of course, you can," the nurse said, smiling at my desperation. She pointed me in the right direction.

Gordon floated from the maternity ward, wearing a euphoric grin and dazed as if he had won the lottery. "Mum, I've got a son, at last."

I gave him a hug and ran to Jackie's room and stuck my head round the door. "How's this for timing?"

They named my grandson Christopher. His development was slow. As he grew, it became obvious that he was developmentally disabled. Gene testing, along with numerous other tests, could not explain his difficulties. It was hard for Gordon to accept that his long-awaited son was not the child Gordon wanted him to be. But as the years passed and Gordon's spiritual knowledge grew, he realized what a wonderful gift God had given him and his family in Christopher—a lesson in unconditional love. Now Christopher is a six-foot-plus strapping young man, with the mind of a young child. He is the gentlest spirit I've ever come across and does not have a mean cell in his body.

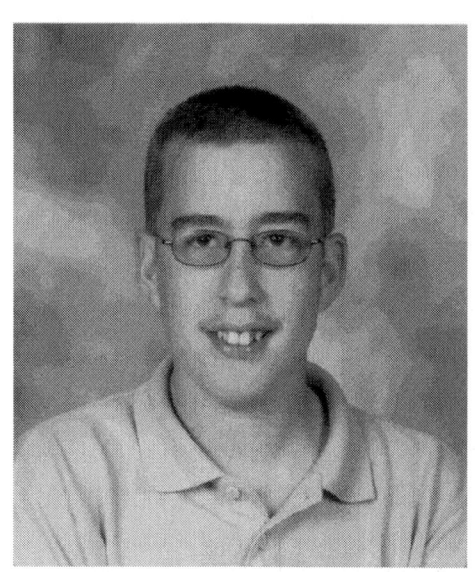

Grandson Christopher

When I returned to Florida, our belongings in storage in England arrived soon after. We'd no sooner set up the wall units and bedroom furniture than monster Hurricane Andrew was bearing down on us. My whole being screamed to get the hell out of there.

With ATMs empty, no gas in the car, and no money to buy gas, we were stuck. We would have to ride out the hurricane in our apartment. Having seen on television the devastation Andrew inflicted on Homestead, we piled what we could on top of shelves, the washing machine and dryer, the kitchen counters, and the breakfast bar in case we were flooded.

Wind and rain swooped in. We huddled in the living room, listening to the wind battering the building. Rain pelted down, obscuring the view. We lost electric power. With no television to watch, we were in the dark about the storm's progress. Then the phone rang. It was family in England wanting to know if we had survived Andrew safely.

"We'll let you know when it's over," Peter said.

From then on, only family's phone calls from England kept us informed. "What's it like?" they wanted to know.

I said, "Well, we can see the flat roof on the outlet mall billowing up as if someone were laying a tablecloth, and the dumpster's heavy steel lids are flapping in the wind like pages in an open book."

Gradually, wind and rain eased. Our apartment buildings that to me appeared badly constructed and just thrown together had survived with little damage. People began to emerge from their homes, happy to have escaped so lightly. Joe wandered over, bringing a can of celebratory beer for Peter.

"Cheers, Peter. We came through it okay."

"It wasn't as bad as we thought it would be."

"Don't be fooled. At the last minute it veered thirty miles south going over Marco Island rather than us."

We had experienced our first hurricane and escaped lightly. Lesson learned? Next time no pushing our luck. We'll evacuate.

SIXTEEN

Peter's sister Jean was our first visitor in Florida. As our guest, she slept in the twin bed someone had given us, while I grabbed a blanket and lay down on the carpet behind the sofa. I was glad she saw no cockroaches during her stay. A week earlier a large one had scurried across my face as I slept on the floor—a revolting experience. Jean returned to Michigan happy that we were surviving. Even though we still had no furniture, our spirits were high.

Peter had had enough of being the butt of his work-mates' jokes. After thirty years working as an electrician, it was time for a change. He applied for a job as a maintenance man at a surveying and civil engineering company. He personally delivered his resumé to the receptionist and left. Two minutes later, realizing he'd given her his master copy, he returned to collect it so he could make more copies. When Peter entered the foyer, Marty, the human resources manager, was gathering the resumés to read. She offered to make some copies for him, and while she did so, Peter charmed her with his dry wit and personality. She ended up giving him the job, later telling us that if she had not met Peter, she would not have read his resumé. Her assistant felt he was over qualified and his resumé was already on the unsuitable pile. But by meeting him, Marty realized he had the sense of humor and general disposition to cope with working alongside demanding engineers.

Another instance of God at work?

Peter stayed with the company for ten years, and we became firm friends with Marty and her family.

My parents arranged to visit, bringing with them our granddaughters Donna aged six and Sarah four. That meant we needed to move to a bigger, second-floor apartment on the complex. Not too much of a tragedy. The apartment walls were thin. We were tired of being awakened early by the girl upstairs having sex with her new boyfriend whom we called "10 to 5." I leave you to figure out why. Then there was a police raid in the apartment next door, searching for drugs. Of course, I had my ear pressed to the adjoining wall to listen to what was going on. A police officer ordered, "Put the gun down, lady! Put the gun down!"

Yikes!

Because I couldn't expect my parents to sit on the floor at their age, we needed to buy seating. We scoured garage sales and thrift stores. I even placed a notice on the Pelican Bay condo's notice board. A resident in the penthouse had a sectional she wanted to get rid of. She would sell it to me for five hundred dollars. I told her I'd discuss it with my husband, thinking where on earth was I going to get five hundred dollars? Over lunch, I vented my frustration to Kevin, the maintenance man, and Eileen, the other housekeeper. Jim, a man doing painting work in the building, was taking a break too. I was sitting on my chair, balancing on the two rear legs.

"I'll lend you five hundred dollars," said Jim.

I set the chair down onto its four legs with a thud. "But you don't know me from Adam! How do you know I'll pay you back?"

"You can pay me when you get your Christmas bonus. I know you won't let me down."

His generosity left me speechless.

Peter and I found a table and chairs being sold by a couple who were moving to Colorado. We're still using them to this day.

Such situations made me aware of the help and guidance we were receiving. Our fearfulness frequently raised its head. Each time we questioned and doubted, we would be reassured in some way.

Occasionally, I would become belligerent. "You know, God, I'm sick and tired of not really knowing why I'm here. If we're in America for healing-work purposes then I want to know. If we aren't, then I want to know that too so I can just forget my frustration at not doing healing work and get on with my life!"

Of course, I didn't need a lesson in patience and faith, did I?

People in need of healing did occasionally come our way—a woman with a badly burned leg and no medical insurance, a man with a heart condition, a woman who came for healing for her arthritic hands who experienced a dramatic drop in her cholesterol levels and there were others. We loved the fact that all we had to do was open up to channel the energy then get out of its way so it could go where it was needed. God knew that better than we did.

My parents' visit put their fears for us to rest. We had fun in Disney World. It was hard to recognize who were the biggest children there, my parents or my grandchildren. My heart warmed seeing them enjoying their first visit to America.

At the airport, as they were about to leave, I asked the grandkids, "What did you like the most about coming to Florida?"

I was expecting them to say the beach, Disney World, Busch Gardens. But what excited them the most were the myriad ways they discovered of turning on the faucets and hand dryers.

Eight months later, during a phone call to Jackie, she asked if I had space on my credit card to buy her a ticket so she could come to Florida. Gordon had lost his job and could look after the children while she was with me. When she arrived, any concerns she had about our new way of life were put to rest. She saw that it was good, even though Peter and I had had a rough start. So good, in fact, it created a spark in Jackie to move to America.

There followed lots more family visits over the years. Gordon confided that he knew Jackie wanted to move to Florida to be near me, but he didn't want to immigrate. When Jackie tried to pressure him, I advised against it. "Florida has lots to offer," I said. "Let

Gordon discover that for himself. The more you push, the more he'll dig in his heels."

Our emigration from England was an inspiration to some family members. My nephew Steve had been dreaming of immigrating to Australia for some time, but with a wife and children to support, he was afraid of failing.

"I'm not going to improve my situation in the steelworks, Aunty Pauline, even though I got an engineering degree at night school to improve my career prospects. I've been waiting and hoping I'll be made redundant. With redundancy pay providing a cushion, I'd go in a shot."

"Listen, don't let fear hold you back," I told Steve and Judy. "Every day you wait is a day lost in your new life. Every day you wait is a miserable day longer in your present situation. And so what if you go to Australia and fail! You can always return home. The important thing is to have a go. Set the process in motion. You won't regret it."

I did regret that Naples was devoid of spiritualist churches. In fact, when we arrived in 1991, there appeared to be a dearth of matters psychic and spiritual, except for what was offered at the Unity Church. Peter and I put some courses together—Psychic Development, Heal Yourself, Can You be a Healer? We held them at the Aquarian Center near Pelican Bay, and they were successful and well received.

Learning that British healer Malcom Southwood was offering an Integrated Healing course in West Palm Beach, Peter and I attended. I was still struggling to cope with Peter's negativity. I normally had no trouble cutting detrimental issues from my life, so I couldn't understand why I was still with Peter, unless it was a karmic matter. Maybe I owed him from a previous existence.

During the course, Malcom used me as a subject to demonstrate how to regress someone to a previous life in order to heal them. I was taken back to a time when I was an ancient Egyptian princess, whose brother was the pharaoh. My husband was Imhotep, the same soul who was my husband in this lifetime. Even in trance, I cringed saying the name Imhotep. When people claimed to be well-known important people in previous lives, I found it hard to believe them. Why weren't they ever Jack Smith the plumber? Anyway, in my regression, Imhotep was a highly spiritual, wise man, a genius, who was skilled in architecture and medicine. He was my pharaoh brother's right-hand man. Imhotep was fully embroiled in his works, especially the building of a pyramid, and he neglected me. As well as being an Egyptian princess, I was also a jealous schemer, who tried to take the throne from my brother Djoser. Caught in the act, I was walled up alive in a room containing a throne (as I had wanted one so badly) and numerous oil lamps. When I was on the verge of death from lack of air, my dead father came to comfort and guide me into the next world. My father in ancient Egypt was my same father in this lifetime. Having made my passing, I felt totally desolate, sobbing about the way I had squandered my life on feelings of jealousy, pettiness, and resentment.

Researching this period later, I was amazed to discover that Djoser had a sister whose name had been purged from almost every record. Could that have been me?

The regression showed me why I was so strongly bonded to Peter, despite my unhappiness with his negativity. Spiritually, I had made a commitment to ensure that when he made his transition, he would not feel the despair I had felt through wasting my potential. I renewed my determination to help him overcome his negativity and lack of self-belief, which was holding him back. His negative attitude was preventing him from using his high intelligence and spiritual knowledge to make his life fulfilling. That was quite a challenge as his fears and lack of belief ran deep, stemming from destructive experiences in his childhood. My job was to help Peter become more aware of and give expression to the wonderful person he is, to strengthen his gentle nature and shrink his fears. Peter's work with me was to give me the opportunity rise to a higher spiritual level to develop unconditional love.

We continued our healing work by removing a spirit attachment from a friend's energy field. The female spirit was afraid to go into the realm of spirit and was clinging tightly to our friend's energy. This resulted in our friend, an executive by profession, having difficulty making decisions. During the healing, we pried the spirit loose (it was like removing gum from the sole of your shoe) and sent her toward the light. Our healing work made life worthwhile.

We spent our spare time looking for a property to buy. I wanted a condo for a simple life and few chores. Peter wanted a house with land. One day, I was vacuuming a large area in the Pelican Bay high rise, when a voice told me not to do anything about finding a house until after the middle of August. Of course, true to form, I ignored the voice and kept looking. Then we arranged for a realtor to show us some lots in Golden Gate Estates, an area classed as semi-rural, where the smallest lots were just over an acre. One Saturday morning, we arrived at the realtor's office. He was talking on the phone and motioned for us to sit down. The date on his desk calendar—August 15th.

He replaced the receiver and after introductions said, "I've selected five lots to show you in your price range. However, last night I received a phone call about a close-in lot that might be of interest. It's already cleared. I'd like to show you that one first."

The lot was beautiful with majestic pine trees, but five thousand dollars more than we had budgeted. We checked out the others on the list before returning to the first lot again. This was the one we wanted. How we were going to make a five thousand dollar adjustment, I did not know. But we knew this was the lot that spirit wanted us to buy, so all would be well. In the end, we saved five thousand dollars from the construction price of the house by chopping off two feet all along one side of the house I had designed and allocating that to buying the land.

It was around this time Peter had a falling out with Joe. I still continued my friendship with Joe, after all, I hadn't had cross words with him, and I enjoyed his company. He was light-hearted and made me laugh, and I occasionally met him for lunch. Then one day he phoned when I wasn't at home, and Peter answered. As Peter was putting the phone down, he heard Joe telling him to fuck off. Peter told me about it when I returned home.

"Do you think you should remain friends with someone who talks to me like that?"

No, I didn't.

Joe's stupidity had knocked the stuffing out of me. I valued Joe's company. He cheered me up, added lightness to my life, and by trying to score points over Peter, he'd destroyed it all.

I braced myself to phone my friend. "Hi Joe, Peter tells me you told him to fuck off when you phoned earlier."

Joe paused. "Yeah, I guess I did."

"I wish you hadn't because now I can't see you again. It would be too disloyal to Peter to remain friends with someone who doesn't show him respect. Really, Joe, I'm so mad at you for this. Goodbye."

Ending this friendship left a hole in my life.

We moved into our custom home. Then reality struck. We had no money for drapes. It had completely slipped my mind. We taped newspaper to the windows for privacy. At work, I told my friends I needed drapes, and I had no money. "I'll have to pray hard," I said.

One week later, Kevin, the condo maintenance man, came looking for me. "Been praying?"

"Of course."

"You must have a special connection to the Lord, Pauline. Come with me."

Kevin led the way to the back wall of the trash room where he had piled six black plastic sacks full of bundles of sheers and beautiful designer drapes, enough to cover every window in my house.

"Mrs. G. is redecorating," Kevin said. "She's throwing these out. If you want them, they're yours."

I grabbed Kevin and danced for joy round the trash room. I was quickly learning to live a life of gratitude.

It wasn't all sweetness and light at the condominium. Receptionist, Angela, thought she was superior to us to the extent she would not even sign a co-worker's birthday card. She tried playing power games with us, but we just laughed at her attempts. Angela wanted to fight, but really the fighting was going on inside herself. She tried to monitor our every move on the cameras dotted about the building so she could complain to the manager if she thought we were slacking. She didn't realize we knew where all the cameras were and could move about the building without being seen on the monitors.

Angela liked to play nasty tricks on Eileen, who had low self-esteem and lacked self-confidence. Eileen was going on vacation and needed her pay check to arrive on time so she could cash it during her lunch break. Angela kept telling Eileen the check hadn't arrived, and Eileen kept getting more upset and worried. I didn't believe Angela, and when she left the office for a minute, I peeped in her drawer. There was Eileen's check. Livid, I dusted and tidied until Angela returned.

In a low, menacing voice, I said, "You're a mean, nasty, spiteful woman. I know you have Eileen's check in the drawer. Give it to her right now. And if you ever try any more dirty tricks on Eileen, I'll wring your fucking neck."

At lunchtime, our manager Gene came to the break room. Kevin and Eileen looked on as, Gene, took a final nervous drag of his cigarette then deep in thought stubbed it out in the ash tray. He looked at me, trying to appear stern and not smile. "Pauline, I know Angela's a pain in the neck, but you can't swear and threaten her like that."

"She's nasty, and she's brought a dark cloud to this place. But you're right. I shouldn't have spoken to her that way, but I'm glad I did, even though it's not very spiritual of me. Don't ask me to apologize because I won't. But we need to pray for her to be moved on out of our space."

So we prayed and only two weeks later, Angela handed in her notice. Nobody cried!

Not long after this I noticed the new condominium board was giving Gene a hard time. They felt he wasn't working hard enough for them. Were they aware his son was dying? I watched him sag, not only from grief, but the frequent criticisms and unrelenting pressure being put on him to perform better. I'd had enough, and handed in my notice.

The president of the board hurried to see me. "Pauline, we're very happy with your work. You're the one person we don't want to leave. Will you reconsider?'

"No. I don't like what you're doing to Gene. It's horrible to watch. You realize his son is dying, don't you? I really don't want to work for you anymore."

And with that, I left. I didn't give a thought to not having a job to go to. But all was in hand. Two days later, the phone started ringing. Residents at the high rise, having heard that I'd stopped working for the condo association, wanted me to work for them as their personal housekeeper. I thanked God and started a new career as a self-employed housekeeper for two years, until fate stepped in.

February 1996, I made arrangements to meet a friend for lunch.

"Could we call into the Florida Massage Academy on the way to the restaurant?" she asked. "I have an interview there." She waved the massage school folder at me. "I'm ready to try something new."

At the Massage Academy, I was ushered into the interview with my friend. The interviewer kept including me in the discussion and her pitch for the school.

"Don't talk to me. It's my friend who's interested," I said.

Nevertheless, the interviewer gave me a folder to take home. After studying it, I was the one who trained as a massage therapist and not my friend. Classes were held four hours a night, five nights a week for six months. I signed up. That would fit in well with my housekeeping work, which was seasonal, as most occupations were in

Naples. Winter was the busiest time, summer the quietest. I would have plenty of time to study.

By now, my nephew Steve was living with his family in Australia. After visiting him where he lived near Perth, Joan and Herby, almost sixty years old, decided to immigrate to Australia too. They had tried to emigrate when in their twenties at a time the Australian government was encouraging people to go there by offering a ten pound fare. But when Herby's mother became ill, they opted not to go. Now their latest application was fraught with hold ups and other annoyances.

"I'm ready to give up trying to get to Australia," Joan confided during a phone conversation.

"There must be a reason for the delays. Just be patient," I kept telling her.

As for us, we had been in America five years. Time to apply for our American citizenship. Gordon had come to like America and wanted to live here. As soon as we had our citizenship, we would petition for Jackie and the family to join us in America. We had to hand in our permanent resident green cards with our applications for citizenship, which meant we would be unable to leave the country until everything was settled. Correction. We could leave the country, but we would be unable to re-enter.

Then my mother was taken into hospital. The family doctor said it was gallstones. The hospital said not. In the meantime, she deteriorated while Joan frantically kept phoning me saying the doctors thought she had cancer then something else, and then they didn't know. Mum was rushed into intensive care. Finally, they discovered she had a large abscess where a gallstone was stuck in her bile duct. And I was unable to leave the country to see her. All I could do was rant and rave, swear at imbecile doctors, and try to reassure my sister.

Peter comforted me, saying, "Stay calm. You've been steered into training as a massage therapist, as well as becoming a U.S. citizen. Surely, you don't believe that God will sink your boat by allowing your mother's condition to deteriorate to the point that you would need to return to England and miss your massage exam and chance for citizenship."

At least I was able to tell Joan that was why she had not been allowed to leave for Australia. One of us had to be with Mum and look after Dad while she was in the hospital. Joan phoned daily. It helped that she promised to let me know if I needed to return in a hurry.

Joan and Herby outside Middlesbrough Football Club

Soon after mailing off our applications for citizenship, I received a phone call. The woman introduced herself as Mary X, immigration officer from the Department of U.S. Immigration.

"Oh, good!" I said.

Silence.

"Hello? Are you still there?"

"You surprised me," she said. "Most people are scared or worried when I phone, but you're not."

"No, I'm not worried. I'm happy."

"Could you come to a naturalization ceremony next week, on Monday?" she asked. "If you want to do that, it will mean missing the grand swearing-in ceremony, which takes place six weeks later."

"Absolutely. The sooner the better. I'm not concerned about the grand ceremony. My mother's seriously ill in intensive care in England. I need to go see her as soon as I can."

"I'd like to talk with you before the ceremony, "she said, "I've been reading your application forms. I'm fascinated regarding what you said about being members of the National Federation of Spiritual Healers. When you arrive, ask security to bring you to my office."

I was so excited I couldn't sit still while waiting for Peter to arrive home from work. I booked airline tickets to England, as we still had our British passports, and after the swearing in, we would have dual citizenships. I also planned a celebration trip.

Peter had barely walked through the door before I was talking. "Guess what, Peter! We're going to be sworn in as citizens on Monday. You'll have to arrange time off work. Also, because I'm getting my certificate on Thursday for passing my massage exam, we could have a long weekend at Key West and call in at Miami to be sworn in on the way home."

Used to my craziness, Peter said, "Mind if I put my car keys down first? Now, tell me again, what have you planned for us?"

We drove to Key West. I was happy. I'd passed my exams as valedictorian. No worries there. I'd studied hard enough. That evening, weary from the five-hour drive, we mingled with the swell of tourists in Duval Street, heading west toward Mallory Square to watch the sunset. The numerous restaurants and bars lining the street spewed out mouth-watering odors of food cooking, triggering pangs of hunger. Next stop after Mallory Square would be an eatery. Ahead of us, we could see a middle-aged, drunken man stumbling along the sidewalk. He created a parting of the ways by hurling curses and diatribes at passers-by who veered left and right of him like drivers avoiding a car wreck.

I recognized the situation. He was another Scottish John, drinking to numb his emotional pain.

"Let's send him love and light," I said to Peter.

We opened our hearts and focused on sending him peace and love. When we reached him, his glad-to-see-us-friendly-word-slurring greeting poured over us like chocolate sauce on soft ice cream. Then in no time at all, he was weeping and telling us his sad tale. Years before, he had been training to be a priest but was expelled from the seminary because he was homosexual. His parents too had disowned him because of his sexuality. Drinking was his way of dulling the pain of that rejection. We surrounded him with loving energy and found positive things in his present life he could be happy about—his friends in Key West, for example.

"My friends in the amateur dramatic society," he added. When we started to walk on, he called, "Look me up next time you're in Key West!" He was smiling.

First thing Monday morning, we arrived at the Immigration and Naturalization Office in Miami. Such a drab, dark place. We were ushered into an office, where a Haitian officer greeted us warmly. Introductions over, with no preamble, she asked us about our spiritual healing. Her interest stemmed from her Haitian heritage. She had been brought up Catholic in Miami, but had recently visited her grandmother in Haiti, who turned out to be a voodoo priestess. Her grandmother's powers had a big impact, mainly because Mary knew she had such powers herself. This had sparked a need in Mary to know more about her Haitian background, and she was struggling to blend the two aspects of her life into an understandable whole. Mary had few people she could talk to about such matters, and some people she had approached thought she was becoming unbalanced and dealing with the devil.

Assistants kept tapping on her door then sticking their heads round to remind Mary the ceremony was waiting for her. "I'll be there soon," she kept saying, still picking our brains on matters of healing.

We reassured her she was doing nothing wrong in exploring her spirituality and her grandmother's legacy. She had nothing to hide, no need to feel uncomfortable, only the necessity of realizing that not everyone is aware enough for her to be sharing her thoughts and feelings about her spiritual searching.

At last, she was ready. Twenty-four people waited to be sworn in. I choked up as I swore allegiance to the flag. I was now an American citizen, but glad that with dual citizenship, I could also remain British.

True to her word, Mary expedited the processing of our American passports, which arrived three days before we left for England. We had hesitated to say we were spiritual healers on the citizenship application form, yet the fact that we did had sparked Mary's interest, which allowed us to become citizens weeks earlier than if we had not.

Being true to who we were paid off.

SEVENTEEN

Still in the hospital, Mum was weak. After nine weeks in intensive care, she was expected to make a full recovery. My heart filled with gratitude as I soaked up the sight of her looking so well after coming close to dying. I asked her if she had ever felt my presence. I mentioned a time I had been sending her distant healing. I'd had such a strong vision of being beside her as she lay in intensive care that I felt sure she had to have known I was with her. Joan, who was visiting Mum with me, told me that she had given her healing at that exact time. She was about to tell me how she had done it when I held up my hand. "Don't tell me! You held your left hand over her forehead and your right hand over her stomach, didn't you?"

Joan gasped. "Yes, that's exactly how I did it."

"I guess we were working together then, don't you think? Mum couldn't help but get better."

Approval to emigrate to Australia was finally bestowed on Joan and Herby, but they felt unable to leave England, because no one had shown an interest in buying their house.

"Book your ticket, Joan. Show the universe you're committed to going. Then tell God you're ready to go, and that you need to sell your house. You'll get an offer. Take it. Don't make the same mistake I did," I said. "I know you're going to get to Australia because my intuition is telling me we're going to visit you there."

A month later, I began to have doubts about my advice to Joan. Had I been overly confident? I was so relieved when only four weeks before Joan and Herby were due to leave the country, a young couple appeared. It was frantic, but all the paperwork was signed, sealed, and delivered just days before Joan and Herby flew out to start their new life. It sure would be less nerve-wracking if God didn't wait until the last minute, wouldn't it?

Pauline visits Joan in Australia 1998

On this visit to England, I finally plucked up the courage to see the house we'd left behind. I'd been too apprehensive to check on the house during earlier visits, anxious that the home we had loved, and the garden we had planted and tended, would be neglected. Peter parked the car a short distance from the house. We caught one another's eyes. Were we ready for this? With tense shoulders and stomach muscles, we reluctantly walked hand in hand toward the house. Drawing closer, we smiled. Fear dissipated. The new owner was continuing the care we had lavished on the house and garden. Peter lifted me up so I could see over the rear garden wall.

I wriggled with delight. "It's just as we left it, Peter!"

Almost skipping with joy, I grabbed Peter's hand and pulled him to the other side of the house where the owner had built a greenhouse in the place we had set aside for one. "Look! It's still lovely! He just continued where we left off!"

Any concerns we had about the house melted away. I was as happy as a bear with a honey pot.

Returning to Naples, I was kept busy building my therapeutic massage practice. I *loved* helping people to stop hurting. To have clients walk into the office, grimacing in pain, and then walk out, smiling and saying, "I don't know what you did, but I feel so much better now." Life doesn't get better than that.

As my business grew, I jettisoned my housekeeping jobs one at a time, until I was earning a living purely from massage. It was an ideal situation, except that some massage clients thought a massage came with sexual activity. When a new client phoned to make an appointment, it was demeaning to have to say, "I don't provide sexual services. I apologize for being blunt, but I don't want to waste your time or mine."

Once we moved into our new house in Naples, our spiritual healing work gradually faded away, and we ceased to teach any more courses. Feeling lost and once again asking God for guidance, Peter and I were despondent. Then, at the end of 1996, we received a letter out of the blue from a lovely lady called Pat, who was also at this time asking for guidance in her quest to become a spiritual healer. In her letter, she explained she had been told in a dream to contact us, and we would show her how to grow as a healer. She was surprised because she had only met us once, several years earlier.

Pat's dream occurred three days before her husband, Mac, was diagnosed with advanced stomach cancer.

And so began months of healing work on both Pat, who was recovering from Lyme's disease, and Mac, who, despite his grim prognosis, never lost his sense of humor. Pat told us she felt the hand of God bringing us together, because she desperately felt in need of comfort, having lost her first husband to stomach cancer.

Hearing Pat tell us this, Mac quipped, "You really must learn to cook, Pat." which had us curling up with laughter.

Intuition told me Mac had personal issues to resolve, particularly with his family, and I encouraged him to open up about the emotional pain he had experienced growing up. To help him move toward a healing and forgiving of the people who had hurt him, I shared my story of how I had been raped and the many years it took for me to heal.

"Healing came when I grew to understand spiritual law. It's so easy. What you give out is what you get back tenfold. For every action there is a reaction. No one can escape this law. Understanding this, I lost my hate and anger and desire for revenge. All I had to do to deal with my attackers was swat them away as if they were flies being a nuisance, knowing that God's law would scoop them up and deal with them. I didn't have to do a thing. It was impossible for my attackers to escape their actions."

I told Mac how my friend Vicky had told me more than once, "Your greatest enemy is your greatest teacher," which led to me being able to relate to my attackers without anger or bitterness.

"In fact, Mac, I can now think of them with gratitude. Their actions moved me along a path to becoming a probation officer. I loved my job for all of the twelve years I worked in the probation service. And the psychotherapy I had gave me the opportunity to know myself well and understand my relationship with my mother."

If I were able to forgive my attackers, Mac felt he could do the same with the people who had hurt him.

Another time we discussed that he could do much of this forgiving without actually having to make contact with the people involved. I told him the story of a counselor who was helping an angry, bitter woman who had been divorced seventeen years. She could not forgive her husband for being such a bad marriage partner, even though she hadn't had any contact with him for many years because he lived in Australia. With counseling, she was able to heal the hurts. As she let go of her pain, her ex wrote a letter to their daughter in which he enclosed a letter for his ex-wife, asking that it be given to her.

The letter stated that in recent weeks, he'd been thinking of her a great deal. He felt the need to tell her how sorry he was that he had been such a poor excuse for a husband. The breakup of their marriage was his fault because he had behaved so badly. He just felt it was important to write and say sorry after all this time.

How did this response come about?

One spiritual teacher explained it to me this way: We're all part of a giant web of connection. If someone tweaks the web on one side, the vibrations caused will flow throughout the web. Each thought and feeling you have toward yourself or another tweaks the web. (Remember thoughts are living things.) Different vibrations are created depending on the type of thoughts and feelings you're having. As the counselor's client began to let go of her hatred and pain, she created new vibrations, which when they reached her ex-husband, allowed him to lower his defenses (or justification as to why he could not be anything but a bad husband to such a horrible wife), enabling him to reach out and complete the healing process between them.

Mac was fading fast. He had avoided exploring some of the more painful episodes in his life, but at least he would die with some of his least-threatening emotional issues healed. One morning, Pat woke up to discover Mac had disconnected his IV and left the house. He returned an hour later having been to Dunkin Donuts for coffee. Later that day, he took a turn for the worst. "So much for Dunkin's coffee," he joked.

Toward the end, he told us he could hear angelic music and see people on the far side of his room, playing cards while they waited for him to make his passing. They didn't have long to wait. He died the following day.

One difficult lesson for healers to learn is that we can identify issues within the client and encourage the process of healing, but ultimately, the client is free to choose to become well or not, deal with issues or not, and his decision must be respected.

After Mac's death, we continued giving healing to Pat, who was also attending healing courses to expand her knowledge. Peter had been despondent since Mac died and had lost faith in his work. I was filled with sadness and grief, not because of Mac's passing, but because I'd reached fifty years of age and Joanne, the daughter given away for adoption, had not re-entered my life. It seemed that all the talk shows were covering emotional reunions of adopted adult children being reunited with their birth mothers. I would watch with tears streaming down my face and a lump in my throat. At one point, I even went so far as to obtain the address of the *Montel Williams Show* in order to ask for help in finding my daughter. Instead, I turned to Pat for help.

Pat had been training as a hypnotherapist. I asked her to stabilize my roller-coaster emotions. The long session certainly helped, but I still carried a lot of grief. She urged me to take a course run by medical intuitive Patti Conklin, who was teaching a weekend workshop in our locale.

I enrolled. I had been on many courses. Most I found disappointing for one reason or another. Some were too basic in their content, others focused on technique, while I was searching for guidance to move to a higher spiritual awareness.

Patti, a woman of exceptional spiritual power, could see the blockages in me that needed healing. "I'll keep coming to you throughout the weekend to give you small zaps of healing energy," she said.

The first day of the course was full and interesting, but I didn't feel any difference within myself. However, when I awakened for the second day, I could not stop crying. Blinded by tears, I don't know how I drove safely to the course. Patti duly noted the goose bumps on my arms from my saturated T-shirt turning cold in the air conditioning. Nothing was said, nothing explained, just an allowing of things to flow. And again, throughout the day, Patti sent zaps of healing energy until my body told her I had had enough.

Within three days of taking the course, I felt lighter, freer. I was so impressed with Patti, I planned to attend another one of her courses in Georgia and persuaded Peter to attend with me. Apart from being dejected about Mac, Peter was also frustrated in his work environment. He had dreamed of climbing the ladder at work, but he was beginning to realize that option was not available. Patti could surely help him overcome whatever blockages were holding him back.

We drove the seven hundred and fifty miles to Hartwell, Georgia. I was looking forward to learning how to become a medical intuitive, a skill I hoped to incorporate into my massage practice.

The weekend did not unfold as expected. Friday evening was an introductory session, where Patti explained what we would be doing. On returning to our hotel room, I began to feel ill. By Saturday morning, I felt ghastly. My joints were painful. Every part of my body hurt. I was vomiting and had diarrhea. Had I been poisoned? I was determined to attend the class even though all I could do was curl up in a blanket at the back of the room. I hadn't traveled all that way to spend the weekend feeling ill in our hotel room.

Throughout the day, Patti checked on me. Why did I feel so ill? Patti explained that I was completing the releasing and cleansing process that started when I attended her course in SW Florida ten weeks earlier. My will was focused on learning to be a medical intuitive. My inner wisdom was taking the opportunity to free me of the dense, dark grief energy I was holding in my body.

Patti also used her abilities to loosen the blockages in Peter's energy. He had made some progress since the early days of our marriage. His protective wall had shrunk and flexed more often. His immediate response of "no" because of fear, eventually gave way to "well, maybe" or "okay, we'll do it." But he still had much work to do.

EIGHTEEN

Almost two years after Joan and Herby immigrated to Australia, the Asian crisis occurred in September 1998. Airfares fell drastically. Although we didn't have much money, we couldn't ignore the opportunity to save over a thousand dollars each on air fares to Australia. Peter and I took a two week vacation to visit our family in the Perth area. One of the first things we did there was visit a nearby spiritualist church.

After the hymns and the address, the medium stood on the podium. "Does anyone here know someone who was stabbed to death?"

Six people raised their hands, including me.

"This man was killed in prison."

Some hands disappeared.

Further questions eliminated the other hands, until only mine was raised.

"I have Roy here. He wants to thank you for your prayers. Your prayers helped him into the light. Your prayers helped him to understand spiritual law. He says he is grateful you did not ever give up on him. He is in a much better place and is a much better being. Thank you."

Although I had been given much proof of life everlasting over the years and had learnt a lot about spiritual truths, I was shocked. Nobody in Australia knew me, and here was Roy taking this opportunity to get things off his chest. I was so pleased he had made good use of my prayers. The message also helped strengthen my belief in the power of prayer.

Joan and Herby drove us around, showing us the beauty of the area where they lived thirty miles south of Perth. For me it was a fascinating mix. Traveling along narrow winding roads amid views of rolling hills, quilted by fields of colorful crops separated by dark green hedgerows, the landscape reminded me of England, dotted here and there with brick-built homes, shops and farmhouses. Then we would reach an area of town where the landscape was more Australian with cacti, palm trees and jarrah and karri trees lining the road. Many plants duplicated those found in Florida. Was it really surprising that Joan and Herby liked their new country? It helped that their oldest son Stephen and his family lived nearby.

Of course, they took us to the beach. It was still chilly in September, and we had to borrow jackets to keep warm against the fresh sea breezes that nipped noses and tousled our hair. We strolled along a crescent of golden sand lapped by a teal and turquoise sea, teeming with dolphins that entertained us close to shore, and amazingly, this beautiful beach remained unsullied by development.

Kings Park in Perth, bigger than New York's Central Park, touched my heart. We meandered along curving paths in the botanical garden area, crossing arched bridges that took us over fountain-filled lakes. We soaked up the natural beauty of thousands of species of plants from delicate flowers to majestic trees. Strolling past swathes of pink, white and yellow flowers, passing ponds bordered with boulders and crossed by stepping stones, we reached a vantage point to look down on Perth on the far side of the bay, its skyline dominated by commerce's bold, grey skyscrapers glinting in the sun. But the highlight of the park was walking along avenues lined on both sides by hundreds of tall eucalyptus trees. A placard in the ground in front of each tree was dedicated to a soldier, sailor or airman who died in action in the world wars, the tall, sturdy trees symbolic of the promise of strapping young men whose lives were nipped in the bud.

Being sensitive to the energy vibration of sacrifice, I choked up and said silent prayers beside several dozen plaques, so much more evocative than being included in a list on a memorial.

Another park Joan and Herby took us to was full of aviaries containing parrots. In one walk-in aviary, Peter, who was wearing a pink shirt, attracted the interest of a pink Galah parrot. We laughed at Peter's effect on the bird. He would not leave Peter alone, trying to mate with him as he strolled round. Peter was always a big hit with old ladies and young children, but parrots?

After enjoying many barbecues with family, and satisfied that Joan and Herby were settled in their new life, Peter and I made the long journey home. Some weeks later, Vicky telephoned. She was miserable, having lost out yet again in love. It was difficult to comprehend how someone so successful professionally could be so calamitous in her love life.

"Come and visit us," I said. "You won't stay down long in Florida's sunshine."

Our friends loved Vicky. She gave readings, demonstrated mediumship, and held some classes. When the time came for her to return to England, we didn't want her to leave.

I left Peter in Florida and flew to England on New Year's Eve 1998 to look after my father for three weeks, while Mum was in the hospital having a knee replacement.

While toasting our toes in front of the fire one frosty January night, I asked my father to tell me about his childhood in order to write a family memoir. Jackie and family would eventually move to America. It was just a question of time, and when my grandchildren grew up, they would probably want to know about their roots in the North East of England.

He started by telling me how he delivered milk before going to school then switched to describing his adventures as a Royal Engineer in the British Army during WWII. I found his adventures so fascinating, I mentally tossed the memoir to one side to record and write down his war stories for my grandchildren. They had only ever known him as a doddering, old man. I wanted them to know the handsome, dashing, brave man he had been in his younger days. The project took on a life of its own. I took it as a sign that I was on the right path when, back in America, the history channel aired non-stop documentaries about Dunkirk and the war in Burma. I found writing groups that helped me hone my writing skills, and before I realized it, I had written a book *A Corporal's War*.

Being a writer was never on my bucket list, yet here I was, writing. I felt guardian angels were leading me along a new path. Writing was fulfilling a need in me, bringing me satisfaction and a sense of purpose. I forged new friendships with other writers who saved me from the loneliness I felt living with Peter. Unable to interact with his negativity, I had closed off from him emotionally, and until I started writing, it was mainly the relationships with my massage clients that sustained me.

I researched details for *A Corporal's War* by going to the Public Records office at Kew or the Imperial War Museum in London every time we returned to England to visit family. It was in the Imperial War Museum that I stumbled across another true story of a British woman's remarkable feats in India during WWII. I knew instantly that Ursula Graham Bower would be the subject of my next book. The research was stimulating, and reading of soldiers' bravery and sacrifice in battle touched me deeply. Most people I spoke to had little or no knowledge of the China/Burma/India Theater of war. I vowed to write more books to inform people of that time and place. Surrendering to the great adventure that life was offering, I would go wherever I was led.

In the middle of writing my father's story, I was shocked to be diagnosed with vulvar cancer, discovered during a routine visit to my gynecologist. I was one of the healthiest, most dynamic people I knew, and here I was, being diagnosed with cancer. Vulvar cancer is a rare cancer with fewer than 4,000 cases a year in America. My gynecologist arranged for me to see gynecological oncologist Dr. O., a gentle man who liked to believe that he empowered his female patients. His diagnosis confirmed my gynecologist's.

"We'll have to operate on you, perform what is called a vulvectomy which means I will be cutting five centimeters of tissue from around the cancerous lesion. Then you should be fine."

The date of the operation was set.

Stunned, I meekly complied, until the shock wore off a few days later. I was having a cup of coffee when, with growing horror, it dawned on me that the size of the top of the coffee mug was the amount of tissue Dr. O. wanted to remove from my genitals. The thought of such mutilation at first made me nauseated. Then I got mad. I ran to my computer to research vulvar cancer and its treatments. Yup, that was the protocol. Powerless and despairing, I sagged then sat up straight. Not beaten yet, I called the cancer help line and spoke to a wonderfully, kind lady.

"I've been told I need a vulvectomy. I've read about the protocol that will remove five centimeters of tissue around the cancer, and I won't go through such mutilation. I'd rather die first. So, I want to know how they came up with this protocol. What was the baseline before this protocol was decided upon?"

It took a few minutes for her to grasp what I was getting at. "Gottcha," she said. "Hold on a minute while I go into my computer to do a search."

I would have held on forever for a better solution to my disease.

She came back on the line and gave me a reference to check in a computer search.

"Basically, the research says that if the surgeon removes only 0.75 centimeters from around the cancer, it will increase your risk of cancer reoccurring by 0.8 percent."

Unbelievable! I thanked her profusely. "You've possibly saved my life with this information. Thank you." I heaved a sigh of relief. "The removal of tissue the size of a dime is a damned sight better than chopping out a coffee-cup-sized piece of flesh."

How blithely the gynecological oncologist was willing to mutilate me without a second thought! Would he have done the same to a man's cancer-stricken penis? Would he have chopped off four inches when he could have gotten away with half an inch?

It took some time before I calmed down enough to trust myself to phone the hospital and remain civil. I reached Dr. O.'s secretary and asked for him to call me. Three times I called over the next few days and three times, no response. Fourth and final call, I cancelled the operation.

He phoned and asked me to come see him.

I handed him a print-out of the research the cancer helpline had found for me. "I'm not prepared to let you mutilate me with the standard protocol," I said. "I want you to remove no more than 0.75 centimeters of tissue from around the cancer. It only increases my risk of a recurrence by less than one percent, and I'm prepared to take that risk."

At first he was stunned into silence then he agreed.

Then I added, "I'll draw up a contract to that effect, and I want you to sign it. If it turns out I'm worse than first thought, I'm not having you cut away more than I've stipulated without further discussion. Agreed?"

Lost for words, Dr. O. was a caught trout out of his element, gasping for breath on a riverbank. He'd already told me he liked to empower his patients. I figured he never counted on meeting someone like me.

He slowly breathed out, smiled, and agreed.

"You know what, you said it was a slow-growing cancer," I said. "I think I'll try to get rid of it with visualization."

Out of the corner of my eye I could see Peter squirm. Dr. O. saw it too.

"Tell you what," he said, "let me take a picture of your cancer so we have a baseline. Then we can measure it again in four months, when I want you to promise you'll return to see me."

He left the room.

Peter sat as still and grey as stone, studying his hands clasped in his lap.

"What do you think, Peter?"

Slowly, he looked up. "It's your cancer, your decision. I'll support you whatever you decide."

I decided.

We went on a trip to visit family in England. I did visualizations every day along the lines of an early computer game called *Space Invaders* gobbling up the enemy. I also visualized ray guns blasting the cancer and imagined it to be shriveling away. I did this for ten minutes three or four times every day. End of November, I revisited Dr. O. who took another picture.

"How did I do?" I asked.

"I've got to say, I'm surprised to see there's a slight improvement."

"In that case, I'll keep doing what's working for a bit longer."

He finished his examination then left the room while I dressed.

Seeing Peter's ashen face, a surge of compassion filled my heart. I bit my lip in guilt. I was being a selfish jerk with my cavalier attitude. It wasn't only my life but his.

Dr. O. returned.

"Let's set a date for the operation as agreed in our contract," I said.

I'd shocked the pair of them.

The operation took place shortly before Christmas. I asked my closest writer friends in the Inklinks and Scribblers groups to pray for me and send love and light the morning of the operation. After my experience with Roy, I had no doubt that prayers worked. Peter took me to the hospital. Lying in bed surrounded by curtains in the pre-operation area, I began to cry. A nurse heard me sobbing and came to my side. Her crazy Christmas headgear of springy red pom-poms bouncing around did not raise a spark of cheer in me.

"I can't do this. I don't want to do it. Get me out of here!"

When she failed to soothe my fears, she called Peter.

I clutched his hand and begged him, "Get me out of here. I don't want to do this. I want to go."

At that moment, the anesthesiologist arrived and injected me with a sedative. I remembered no more until the operation was over.

Driving away from the hospital, I was in a tirade, swearing at God, demanding, "What the hell are you up to, dammit?" Feeling violated, I raged on for ten minutes or so.

Concerned that he would be included in the thunderbolt he was sure was coming to strike me for cursing God, Peter said, "Hope your aim's good, God. It's not me cursing you out, it's her."

Normally, Peter's wit never failed to make me crack a smile, but I was too upset about the cards I'd been dealt. When I calmed down, he asked, "Straight home?"

"No, I've had no breakfast. I want to go to the English pub for fish and chips."

Peter shook his head. "I don't believe it."

He knew I was always badly affected by a general anesthetic. Even if the operation was minor, it usually took me a week to recover from the anesthetic, and here I was saying I felt great, and I wanted fish and chips.

I even returned to work the following day. Now, I was not in a sedentary job, sitting at a desk all day. I was a self-employed massage therapist who carried her thirty-five pound massage table in and out of client's homes. I felt fabulous, and knew it was the prayer power of my Inklinks and Scribblers writing friends.

The following November, I was given the all clear. I shrugged off the illness as a fluke, finished my father's book, and attempted to find a publisher. Many rejections later and having made a start on my second book, cancer returned four months later in March, 2002. I'd found a lump in my vagina. My doctor thought it was a blocked bartholin gland and prescribed antibiotics. It didn't completely go away, but as I had an appointment with the gynecological oncologist, I waited to see what he had to say.

Dr. O. examined me, vaginally and anally. "I don't like this lump, Pauline."

"What do you think it is?"

"Does it hurt?"

"No."

He listed four health issues that were possibilities, but wanted a gastroenterologist's opinion, only there was a hitch. Despite his staff phoning every gastroenterologist in both Collier and Lee counties, he could not get me an appointment until June 12th, seven weeks later. From Dr. O.'s office, I went straight to the walk-in clinic to see a doctor. As he was examining me, I complained, "Cancer doctors are always looking for cancer. I had cancer two years ago. I sure as hell don't have it now."

The doc removed his latex gloves and threw them in the trash. "Pauline, I have to agree with Dr. O.'s possible diagnosis."

He consulted over my chart with the nurse. Deflated, I sat on the examination table, tears dripping from my cheeks.

The doctor looked up, handed me a box of tissues and said, "I bet you're thinking, why me?"

"No, not that. I'm thinking why didn't I learn what I had to learn the last time I had cancer. Then it wouldn't have come back again."

I left the clinic and sat on the beach to watch the sunset. Peter's brother Richard and his wife Chris were visiting us from England, and Jean was down from Michigan. I wasn't ready to face them.

Researching Dr. O.'s possibilities on the internet, I knew it wasn't good. I obviously had anal cancer, and, as no treatment could be started until confirmed by a gastroenterologist, I was convinced the cancer would become inoperable before a diagnosis was obtained. I could feel the tumor growing rapidly. It wasn't too much of a problem when I was walking, but I couldn't stand for long before needing to sit down.

Believing I was going to die, I left Peter behind in Florida and returned to England to spend time with my family. I was going to say my goodbyes by creating happy memories and taking lots of photographs of us all together with happy smiling faces. I rented a van and drove everyone to the Lake District for a four-day vacation. We had a memorable time, exploring the pencil museum, the Beatrix Potter museum, and enjoying the beauty of the hills and lakes.

On returning to Middlesbrough, I arranged to have dinner with Vicky.

Settled at the table, she asked, "So, how's it going?"

"Very well," I lied, not wanting spoil what would probably be my last time with Vicky with bad news. "Just wanted to see the family."

"No, Pauline, I mean what's happening down there," she said, nodding toward the tumor.

I controlled the urge to sob and said lightly, "Oh, the doctors think I've got anal cancer, but it's not confirmed yet. Let's order."

When the waiter had taken our orders, Vicky said, "You're not going to die, Pauline. You'll be cancer free by September."

Vicky was famous in our area for her psychic abilities. But I didn't believe her, suspecting she was only trying to lift my spirits. After all, I could feel the thing growing like crazy inside me.

I returned to Florida and Peter and mentally readied myself to meet death. After going through the agony of a colonoscopy, the diagnosis was clear, confirmed by a CAT scan—anal cancer. Appointments with an oncologist and Dr. Freeman, the radiation doctor, followed.

Dr. Freeman studied my medical notes and looked up. "We can cure you in five weeks."

My knees almost buckled. "You can *cure* me?"

"Yes, you're fortunate. The tumor has not breached its boundaries. We will treat you daily with radiation, which will kill any cancerous cells you have in your body. The treatment will be aggressive and tough for you. But you will be cured in five weeks."

"Will I suffer radiation burns?" I asked.

"It will be like a bad sunburn," she said.

Even though I was an advocate for alternative therapies and didn't do drugs, not even prescribed medicine, she had said the magic words. She could save my life. As for the treatment being tough to go through, well, I was tough too.

"Let's do it," I said.

As we left the office, Peter said, "I'll help you any way I can."

"You may want to reconsider that offer, because I want a divorce."

As far as I was concerned, we had drifted apart. I was tired of playing second fiddle to Peter putting all his energy into achieving an unrealistic expectation that he would climb the corporate ladder, at least to some extent, from his lowly position in the company. And all such ideas only fueled his dissatisfaction and negativity. He neglected jobs around our house to do for the company, making the building secure just before a hurricane, out there late at night fixing air conditioning units on the roof, along with many other things he did that passed unnoticed. For some time I had been feeling it was time to move on.

"Let's deal with first things first, and we'll deal with the rest later," Peter said.

For the record, later never came. Peter refused to discuss or consider divorce after I recovered.

Eleven days before I was officially diagnosed, Peter started a new job at a private school on June 1, 2002, thanks to Marty, formerly the human resources officer where Peter worked, who had gone to work at the school a year earlier. She had put Peter's name forward when the school was looking for a maintenance manager. Not wanting to jeopardize his new job, and the substantial pay increase that came with it, meant that Peter would not be able to take time off work to be with me during treatments.

I had an operation to insert a port into my chest. The treatment protocol, which had an eighty-five-percent success rate, required chemo for four straight days both at the start and end of the five-week radiation treatment, a total of one hundred and ninety-six hours of chemotherapy, coupled with twenty-five radiation treatments.

I ploughed ahead, thinking I knew what to expect. I had no idea what I was letting myself in for.

NINETEEN

Twenty-five days of treatment—no big deal. I supplemented the chemotherapy and radiation with vitamin IVs twice a week at Dr. Pynckel's office in Fort Myers, a forty minute drive away. Our next door neighbor, Tom, dropped by on day four of my treatment to see how I was doing. Tom had lost his first wife to cancer, and he was concerned and protective.

"Doing fine," I reassured him.

Day five, a Friday, around 3:30 p.m., I felt a prickling in my genital area. The prickling quickly increased in intensity, until it was so painful, I didn't know where to put myself. When Peter came home from work, he insisted I call the doctor's office. I phoned Dr. Freeman and explained the situation to her nurse. Dr. Freeman would not be in the office until Tuesday.

"Just rub corn starch on the area. That will help," said the nurse.

"I need more than corn starch," I said, through gritted teeth.

"Sorry, doctor won't be in the office till Tuesday."

Soon, I was in agony. I couldn't pee without screaming.

"Sit in tepid water," Peter suggested.

It didn't help, and drying myself afterward was torture. I never thought of going to the emergency room. Possibly because of my lack of experience with the American health care system, or the nurse's off-hand response that I only needed to rub cornstarch on the burns. I didn't feel cared for by the medical profession. Treated, yes. Cared for, no. The weekend was horrific. The pain unbearable. Second-degree and third-degree burns covered my genitals and backside. Peter tried to comfort me as I suffered and sobbed like I'd never suffered and sobbed before in my life. I was beyond being comforted. I slept on doggie training pads to protect the mattress from the fluids oozing from the wounds. Crying with pain, I drove to Fort Myers on Monday for a vitamin treatment. Although concerned, Dr. Pynckel felt unable prescribe anything to help. As I was another doctor's patient, it was down to the radiation doctor to treat the burns.

Tuesday, I eventually saw Dr. Freeman. She was shocked that I had burned so early in the treatment. "I wasn't expecting it to happen until the final week," she said.

She wrote a prescription for pain medication and burn cream.

"You lied," I accused her. "You said it would be at worst a bad sunburn. These are second-degree burns."

"You're having an exceptional reaction. This normally doesn't happen until much later in the process."

I was angry, felt misled, didn't take the pain pills. My body was being poisoned enough by the chemo and radiation. The following Friday, day ten, I went for my daily dose of radiation. The technicians tended to keep an emotional distance. I didn't blame them; they probably saw too many of their patients not make it back to health. I hated the treatment. I was powerless to refuse—it was a question of life or death. I felt I was being raped in a particularly cruel way in that I had to agree every day to be treated in this obnoxious manner.

One day towards the end of my five weeks when I arrived for a radiation treatment, blood poured down my legs from burn wounds in the crease where my legs joined my body. I rushed to the rest room and cleansed myself with damp paper towels and washed the blood out of my skirt in the sink. No member of staff showed the least bit of interest in what was going on with me, not even when my skirt dripped water on the floor on my way to the treatment room.

Dr. Freeman's nurse asked me if I was feeling better now that I was taking the pain medication.

"I'm not taking it. I'm being poisoned enough."

I swear, in other circumstances, she would have had me by the throat, up against the wall, bashing my head against it, to get through to me. Instead, in a stern, don't-mess-with-me voice, she said, "Take the pills. It's stupid to be in pain when you don't need to. And don't take one only when you start to feel pain. Take them every four hours. There is absolutely no need for you to be in so much agony."

I took the pills.

Sunday, the start of the third week of treatment, Colleen knocked on my door. She had been a close work colleague of Peter in his previous place of employment. Through the grapevine, possibly Marty, she had heard that Peter was stressed because he couldn't take time off work in his new job to be with me.

"I've come to drive you to your treatments."

I didn't know Colleen well, but I did know she worked full time, and she would have to make up any hours she took off work.

"There's no need for that, Colleen. I'm coping."

"What times are your appointments on Monday?"

"Really, Colleen, there's no need to do this."

"What time do you want me to come?"

We were two bull-headed people, and we could have gone on forever, but mindful that I might have been having this experience to give people the opportunity to be givers and for me to learn to receive help, I stopped arguing. Later, I asked why she came that day.

Being the good person she is, her answer was simple: "It was the right thing to do."

Once she started driving me to the doctor's offices, I marveled at how I'd ever coped on my own. I was becoming extremely weak and fragile. At Dr. Pynckel's one day, I was set up with my vitamin IV. Colleen didn't sit with me until the inserting of the needle was over. Halfway through the treatment, I could feel the life force flowing into me. The mucous membranes in my mouth felt more moist and normal, easing the discomfort of my numerous mouth ulcers.

Colleen lifted her head from her book. "You're feeling better now, aren't you? The energy in the room has changed." Then she went back to her reading.

I certainly wouldn't have survived the chemotherapy and radiation without the vitamin IVs. In fact, after the first ten days of treatment, I was so weak and in agony from the burns, I was ready to quit. The oncologist persuaded me not to, but I didn't feel safe with the man. Every time I went to his office, I had to have blood work done, but he never read the reports before he saw me. After he had persuaded me to continue with the treatment, I asked him if there was anything I could do about my low white blood count. It was then he actually studied my blood work report and saw how anemic I was. He wanted to prescribe Procrit, which required phone calls to my insurance company for permission because one injection cost around $800. The first injection worked a minor miracle. I woke bright and chirpy the following morning and astounded Peter by offering to cook him a bacon sandwich. The effect didn't last long, only a day or two before I weakened again and returned to my bed.

With my burns, I couldn't wear panties, none, in fact, until three months after the treatment ended. I put my T-shirts and shorts to one side and pulled some flared skirts from my closet. I always had to put towels on any seat I used so as not to mark them. When I wasn't going for treatment, I retired to my bed because if I moved around, I dripped bloody fluids from the burns onto the carpet.

I don't consider myself a Christian, but at least a dozen times a day, I repeated the twenty-third psalm: "The Lord is my shepherd, I shall not want . . ." as my mantra. It wasn't that I was afraid of dying. I knew life on the other side was much better than on earth. I was concerned that I had not yet had my dad's book published. He was eighty-three, and I wanted him to hold the book in his hand before he died. Also, I hadn't finished *Naga Queen,* about Ursula Graham Bower.

That my normally sharp mind was lost to brain fog saddened me. I was no longer living each day, I was floating through it. On days I felt well enough, I attended my Inklinks writing group. I needed something normal in my life, and that was writing. With my brain was not functioning properly, I was unable to write much, but I enjoyed the camaraderie of my writer friends. I let it slip that I had not told my daughter what was happening. They were horrified. I figured that because the treatment protocol was eighty-five-percent successful, and as I had been in excellent health, my chances were good. There was no need to tell Jackie and cause her worry or feelings of impotence because she could not be with me to help.

My friends convinced me otherwise.

After mulling it over, I phoned Jackie. "I have something to tell you, and I don't want you panicking or imagining the worst, okay?"

"Okay."

"I have anal cancer. I'm getting chemo and radiation and that seems to be doing the trick, so you're not to worry."

"Did you have it in May when you came to see us?"

Oh-oh, nothing gets by her.

"It hadn't been properly diagnosed. Vicky said I was going to be all right. I don't want you getting a shock when we meet you at the airport when you come for your vacation, so I'm warning you. I'm thinner, weaker, and half my hair has fallen out." I could hear her crying. "I know. It's been a shock. But all is in hand, and there really isn't anything to be concerned about. You don't get rid of me that easily." I waited until the crying stopped. "Don't tell Gran and Granddad. They won't come to live with me when you immigrate if they think I could die, leaving them to Peter's tender mercies."

During the five weeks of my treatment when, as far as I was concerned, I should have been in a burns unit, my focus was solely on doing my best to overcome the disease. "Peter," I said, "you must get on with your life as normally as possible. Find people to support you. There's so little you can do for me. This is my battle, and that's where my attention will be."

Peter pulled up his emotional drawbridge, retiring to the safe place in his mind that he had created as a child, until the all-clear sounded when I was informed I was cancer-free.

On day twenty-one, Peter took me to the doctor's office for my final course of chemotherapy. I was so weak, I could barely stand. When the nurse tried to insert the needle into the port, she missed the mark. I screamed and began sobbing. I could take no more. I was done. Peter rushed in to comfort me. Angry that I'd been subjected to unnecessary pain, he confronted the nurses and demanded better care for me. "Can't you see she's all in?" he shouted.

August 15 was the last day of treatment. Having been told that the patient keeps cooking for two weeks after a radiation treatment, that would bring me to September. Vicky's prediction that I would be cancer free by September could possibly be spot on. That was also the day I lay in bed, resting, when Peter brought in the mail.

"There's a letter from immigration."

I ripped it open. Tears of joy. After six years of waiting, Jackie and Gordon, having been accepted to apply to immigrate, should contact the American embassy in London. They were due to arrive in Florida in ten days. We would keep this good news until then to help offset the shock of finding me a mere shadow of my normally vibrant self.

Nevertheless, Jackie *was* shocked to find me in a wheelchair. Sadly, I was too weak to participate in the usual Disney theme park activities with the family. I left them to it to return home to Naples to rest and rebuild my strength before they came to our house

When they did, we opened a bottle of wine. The family gathered round my bed to celebrate the letter from immigration. Jackie, Gordon, and the grandchildren were all excited smiles. The end was in sight. They had fallen in love with America during their visits to us over the years and were eager to live in Florida.

"If anything like this happens again," Jackie said, nodding toward my shattered body, "at least I'll be here to help."

I shook my head. "Nothing like this *will* happen again."

TWENTY

With the tumor destroyed and me along with it, the doctors patted themselves on the back and gave me a clean bill of health. I cried with relief. The poisoning was over. How was I going to repair the damage? I needed to heal from the torture inflicted upon me both physically and mentally, torture every bit as horrendous as water boarding. I needed to rebuild myself and mourn for the Pauline who had gone. That vibrant, sexual woman was no more. All was lost to burn scars and could not be restored, barring a miracle. I had to adjust to a new image of myself as a fecally incontinent woman with a burned-to-a-crisp useless anus, and a vagina so damaged by burn scars it was preferable to think of myself as asexual.

My Inklinks writer friends encouraged me to write down my experience as a means to healing, but I could find no words to express what I'd been through, at least, not until ten months later, shortly after I brought my parents to Florida. I awoke in the middle of the night with a poem in my head. I'm no poet so I knew this was important. I rushed to scribble it down before it disappeared.

Dark Night of the Soul

A tumor she said, a large one, in the rectum, treatable.
We can radiate and chemo you, cure you in five weeks.

Did she say CURE? Five weeks? That's nothing.
I don't believe in such treatments. They're barbaric, belong in the dark ages.
It will be tough. We can cure you—in five weeks.
I'll think about it, I said.

I sleep, dream of loneliness, a gulag of chill in a-dead-of-night winter in a deserted, snow-hushed Moscow square.
I wake. No morning bird song. No sustenance. I am alone.
In place of the comforting presence that has been with me all my life is a vacuum.
Where is God?
My thoughts launch into the blackness of space
beyond twinkling stars—and reverberate in emptiness.
God is gone, is not there, is not here, gone.
I am alone in my plight, abandoned by God.
Visions wash over me—cold, black, desert night, mournful howls of coyotes.
Scorpions wait for daylight to warm their blood, activate their stings.
The tarantula creeps and crawls, on the prowl for prey.
And I am it. No protection, abandoned by God to my plight.
Where is my safety, sense of connection?
Amputated, bailed out, abandoned by God.
No ministering angels, I'm on my own, alone, face the future with dread.

Let's do it I said.

Did she say tough? Horrific more like, ready to quit after ten days.
My body, a raw, swollen, alien agony, don't recognize it as my own.
I am frail, the bedroom a retreat from living,
the battlefield an opiate-numbed mind on a posturepedic.
Putrefying ooze seeps brown stains into the pad beneath my form,
fills the room with the stench of death.

Which will prevail—death of a carnivorous tumor
or death of the victim chosen at random to face a gladiator in a
Roman arena?
Will the fight lead to death or to life?
Poisoned by the chemo and the rays they say will save me,
my sharp mind deserts me, retreats to another place,
a fetus in trance, floating in amniotic fluid for the duration.
A sob escapes my heart to echo on my lips.

In the bathroom mirror, I see a pain-grimaced face crumple,
accusing, pleading for mercy as I cleanse the raw wounds dripping
bloody fluids.
Trembling fingers rub soap into the creases.
As from a stun gun hit, the sting prickles my eyes, burns my flesh.
I writhe in pain, break out in cold sweat.
Liquid beads form on brow, upper lip and chest.
I gasp, cry out in agony.
And I weep and I weep and I weep.
Exhausted, I stagger to my bed, lie down, rest, regroup,
to go through the ordeal of dressing to face the day
and visit with the power of the rays.

And God is nowhere to be found.

My psyche was starting to heal, but my body was taking forever to clear itself of toxins. I drove to Miami to see Jay Foster, the Body Chemist. Among various nutrients, he prescribed lots of iodine to counteract the effects of the radiation and milk thistle to cleanse my liver. Gradually, I began to feel stronger, although it took three years before I came anywhere near as energetic as I had been pre-treatment. Psychologically, I was, and still am, saddened by the loss of me, but I'm still pedaling thanks to my British working-class stoicism. So much of my persona had been tied to my picture of myself as robust and filled with vitality. I had been strong, invincible. Going through such weakness and frailty as I had during treatment caused my view of myself to crumble, with nothing to replace it. I have post traumatic stress syndrome to some extent. I dislike having anything to do with the medical profession, and I don't trust them.

The realization grew that I had developed cancer because of my unresolved grief at giving away Joanne for adoption. For years I had sustained myself with the belief that she would come back into my life. Once I turned fifty and that had not happened, I began the grieving process that should have happened when I was eighteen. Despite all the healing work I had done, I could not heal the deep wound caused by giving her away. But I had to do something or cancer could strike again.

I wrote her a letter, explaining everything—my love for her, my hopes for her, the spiritual contract to give her away. Then I lit a candle. Speaking aloud, I said, "God, I am handing my daughter to you in the knowledge that the God who loves me, guides me, and protects me is the same God who loves, guides, and protects Joanne."

With overflowing eyes, I dipped the letter in the flame, burned it to a cinder, and let her go.

❖   ❖   ❖

Jackie phoned me for help. My mother refused to discuss what would happen to her and Dad when Jackie left to live in America. Knowing my mother, she was probably in denial and also afraid. Both my parents were legally blind and had no other relatives to help them. I needed to go to England to tell them they were coming to live with us in Florida, no ifs or buts.

Before leaving for England, I made inquiries about how I, a citizen, might bring my elderly parents to live with me in order to look after them. I received little help from the Immigration Service, which staunchly ignored my letters. Fortunately, a friend, well versed in matters to do with immigration, advised me to bring my parents to Florida on tourist visas. As soon as they arrived, we should request permanent residency for them.

Another reason I wanted to go to England was to connect with Ursula Graham Bower's daughter, Trina Child, so I could research her mother's private papers. For my friends Leona, Colleen, and Judy there would be a third reason—they wanted to visit England with me and Peter to show them around. As they were interested in spiritual matters, we booked onto a course at the Sir Arthur Findlay College for the Advancement of Spiritualism based at Stanstead, near London.

Peter and I had attended courses there before. We remembered the mansion-turned-college as being full of ghosts. Our third day on the course, Peter and I were told to leave. Apparently, the tutors felt Peter's negativity was lowering the vibrational energy in the college (of course, it had nothing to do with the head tutor's ego not liking being challenged by Peter). Being Peter's wife, I was kicked out with him. We agreed to collect our friends when they finished the course and went looking for a nearby bed and breakfast. While they enjoyed the course and developed spiritually, Peter and I explored Duxford air museum, Cambridge, and the surrounding area.

Then it was a drive to North Yorkshire, the area where Peter and I grew up. We stayed in the old millhouse home of Sheila, an artist friend of Chris, Peter's sister-in-law, in the North Yorkshire village of Great Ayton. Richard and Chris lived nearby. We took our friends exploring our old stomping grounds of the North Yorkshire Moors National Park, driving over the moors to the quaint fishing port of Whitby nestled at the mouth of the River Esk. They laughed disbelieving when Peter said, "Sheep have right of way on the moors. If they're wandering over the road, you have to stop to let them pass."

"But you won't find any on this busy road," I said. "They fenced it off years ago. Too many sheep being killed."

We wandered along old town Whitby's narrow cobbled streets that wound their way past picturesque white cottages with red, pan tile roofs. Our friends stopped to watch craftsmen at the glass factory, blowing figurines that were sold in the store, where you had to bend down to avoid hitting your head on the door beam as you entered. They bought local candy and typical English seaside mint-flavored sticks of rock. They stocked up on small watercolor paintings of Whitby and the surrounding area, bought mementos such as semi-precious rocks and fossils and old photographs from curio shops and the post office. Coming to the end of a lane, we reached the spot where people could begin the climb up 199 steps to the ruined abbey that overlooked the town.

"Does anyone want to see the abbey?" I said.

The general consensus was, "Pass."

We wandered back to the harbor area, pausing to gaze in a jeweler's shop window filled with beautiful jewelry made from black Whitby jet.

Judy, Peter, Colleen and Leona in an English pub during our 2003 visit

"Listen," I said, "they do great fish and chips here at the Dolphin pub with a lovely view of the sailboats moored in the harbor. However, we want to take you to my most favorite place in all the world, Robin Hood's Bay, and we can have fish and chips there. Okay?"

Our friends were happy to allow us to take them wherever we thought best.

At Robin Hood's Bay, we parked in the upper part of the village, the newer part, then walked down the steep bank, passing an area where, owing to erosion, the previous parking lot had fallen into the sea. At the bottom of the bank, the old village's charm, with its fishermen's cottages, pubs, tea-rooms and stores, captivated our friends. In the Bay Hotel, overlooking the boat launch and rock scars in the bay, we had lunch then meandered among the cottages along the warren of lanes before slowly gasping our way up the bank to the parking lot.

While Peter took care of our friends one day, I went to see my parents. I had things to sort out.

"Hello," I called, entering my parents' tiny bungalow. "Can a tired traveler have a cup of tea?"

Dad jumped up and hugged me.

With my mother being deaf, the television was booming. It hurt my ears. I didn't know how my father could stand it. Thankfully, Mum turned it off.

"You should keep your door locked. You didn't hear me come in," I warned them.

"We're safe enough here," Mum said.

From my years as a probation officer, I knew the area they lived in was high in petty crime, but I let her comment pass. This was not the battle I had come to fight.

Dad put the tray with tea and cookies on the coffee table.

"I've come all the way from Florida to talk to you."

"It's cheaper to use the phone," he said.

"It is, but I can't sort you out over the phone."

"What makes you think we need sorting out?" Mum said.

"Jackie and the family are immigrating, to America, leaving England, and you don't believe her."

"Is she really going then?" Dad asked.

"Yes, and we need to talk about what's going to happen to you two."

"Oh, we'll be fine," Mum said.

"Don't talk rubbish. You're both ninety-percent blind. You, Mum, are as deaf as a post and can hardly walk with your lousy knee replacements. Who will help you pay your bills? See to you when you're ill? There'll be no one to help when Jackie leaves."

Silence.

"The way I see it, you have two options. You can go into a home, or you can come to Florida and live with me."

"We're *not* coming to Florida," Mum said, "and that's the end of the matter."

"In that case, it's a home."

"We're not going into a home either," Mum said.

"Yes you are, because we're not going to be worried sick in America about how you're coping here alone."

"It's not for you to decide."

I opened my mouth to argue with her when Dad said, "We'll come to Florida."

Mum swung round and looked at her husband, her eyebrows straining to meet her hairline. To me she said, "You won't want to look after us. What does Peter say?"

"He's with me on this one. That makes a change, doesn't it?" I said, laughing. "We want you to be safe and looked after by us rather than have you stay in England where there'll be no family to keep an eye on you. So, Mum, are you coming to America?"

"That's what your father says."

You're such a stubborn old coot, Mum.

I took another cookie. "I'm glad one of you has some sense."

"We're still not too old for an adventure, eh, Ivy?" my dad said, with a chuckle.

"What if we get sick?" Mum said. "You don't have good health care in America like we have in England."

"That's true. But with your savings, you'll be able to afford to go to the doctor's office for small things. And if you do need hospital treatment, they have to treat you whether you can pay or not. Hopefully, you should be all right."

"As long as you don't end up putting us in a home," Mum said.

"That's not going to happen. Besides, we can't afford it. Homes are too expensive. You're stuck with us till your dying day. Isn't that a lovely thought?"

"Yes," Dad said.

I bit into my cookie. "Jackie will help you sort out what to take and what to sell. You don't need furniture. I have all you'll need and a big guestroom and bathroom for you."

Mum set her jaw. "I'm not leaving my bedroom suite; it's brand new and so is my three-piece suite."

"There's no room in my house for them. I suppose we could store them in the garage. Jackie and Gordon might be glad to have them when they eventually move out of our house into their own place, although, they do sell furniture in America, you know. Anyway, I'm coming back for you in four weeks. I'll arrange to get your visas for you before I go home. Jackie will help you sort through your stuff. Keep the personal things, and see what else you want to take. I'm really excited you're coming to live with us."

How I admired them, eighty-four years old and ready for an adventure.

My parents' future settled, we drove to London with our friends where we spent four days seeing the sights before returning to the States. One of those days, Peter and I left the gang to their own devices while we traveled to Mayfield, a picturesque village south of London, where Trina was living with her aunt. We spent the morning plowing through all the letters her mother had written home during WWII.

Several hours later, we were taking a break in Middle House, an ancient, oak-beamed Tudor pub dating back to 1575. Over a delicious lunch, Trina told us how she had recently divorced her husband. He had taken all her money and caused her to lose her deceased parents' house and furniture. Thank goodness her aunt had taken her in. All she had left was the box of her mother's papers. I sensed her bitterness. His actions had cost her everything she had.

"Perhaps he's done you a favor," I said. "He's freed you from being the keeper of your mother's legacy, a responsibility you've had all these years. Maybe it's time to build your own legacy."

Trina sucked in a breath, her hand went to her throat and rubbed the collar on her blouse. She stared at me incredulously, her brain cogs turning. In a thoughtful voice, she said, "That's a novel way of looking at it."

Trina must have taken a liking to us because she let me take her mother's precious letters, so I could photocopy them and bring them back when I returned to England a month later to collect my parents.

TWENTY-ONE

In June, 2003, I returned to England alone. I delivered Ursula's letters to Trina, glad to be free of the responsibility of such precious historical and anthropological documents. I then drove six hours to Middlesbrough to collect my parents. They were ready, having sorted through a lifetime's belongings. Jackie, Gordon, and our four grandchildren would follow two months later. It was a long, tiring journey for my parents, but I was delighted to be able to care for them in the last years of their lives. My sister Joan had wanted that joy and privilege. However, it was easier for me to get them into America than it was for Joan to get them into Australia.

Mum and Dad settled into the guest bedroom. They had attended social activities for seniors in England, so I soon found seniors clubs for them in Naples. I drove them to luncheons, talks, and bingo. Seeing how they struggled to see the small bingo cards, I enlarged some for them to use. Years later, when Mum knew the numbers by heart, she didn't need to see them in order to play. Peter and I took them exploring. Their favorite place was people watching on Naples pier. They complained that they wanted to be less dependent on me running them around. Playing chauffeur was no hardship for me, but understanding their need for independence, I arranged for the special bus service for the disabled to transport them. Mum and Dad never looked back. Their first outing on the

Back row: Dad, Pauline, Herby and Joan, Mum in front
Naples Pier 2006

bus, I was on tenterhooks like a mother hen, wanting to round up and protect her chicks.

As my parents adjusted to their new life, rejection letters flowed in from publishers. A friend suggested self-publishing. A warm glow of pleasure enveloped me when, a few months, later I placed a copy of *A Corporal's War*, a memoir about my dad's WWII adventures, in his hand. Whether or not I sold any copies was irrelevant. It had all been worthwhile just to see Dad's delight. My interest in his stories had given him a sense of pride. He walked with his head held high and with a touch more swagger, at least, until Mum's impatience and criticism sapped his joy.

I sent each member of the family a copy of *A Corporal's War*. Joan's three adult sons were filled with newfound pride, soaking up this new portrait of their grandfather, an unassuming hero. These were heartwarming moments, but this was only one man's tale. Thousands of brave young men had made the ultimate sacrifice in

Burma's steamy jungles during WWII, and I planned to write more about that. My book *Naga Queen* was only the start of my mission.

Jackie and family flew into Miami in August. Peter and I left my parents at home while we drove two hours across Alligator Alley in a van we had rented. We sat and waited in the arrivals hall for the five hours it took for immigration to process the family. By the time they reached us, they were already exhausted, but that didn't stop us jumping up and down with excitement and having a group hug at this start of their new life. There followed a two hour drive to Naples. We arrived home after midnight. Mum and Dad were still up, too excited to sleep. Fatigue was put aside to celebrate being together again. For Peter and me, it had been twelve long years of waiting and preparing.

With processing by immigration control finally over, we meet our weary family at Miami airport arrivals, eager to start their new life in America

Our house had three bedrooms and two living rooms, and we were squeezing in eight more people. It was difficult, but temporarily bearable. Mum and Dad had the guest bedroom to retire to for peace and quiet and privacy. Jackie and Gordon and Christopher slept in the den. The three girls slept in the front living room, Donna on a single bed, and Rebecca and Sarah on a sofa bed.

Jackie, who had been a housewife in England, and eighteen-year-old Donna, who had just left school, had a week to get over their travels before starting work for one of my massage clients, who owned a catalogue company. She was difficult to work for, and therefore had a high turnover of staff. That turned out to be a blessing for Jackie and Donna, giving them the opportunity to gain work experience and references. Rebecca and Christopher started school soon after their arrival while Gordon, who had been in retail all his working life, and sixteen-year-old Sarah found work at J. C. Penney. Sarah made a bit of J. C. Penny history when she became a department supervisor at the ripe old age of seventeen.

Life was good for a while. Then Peter started to feel uncomfortable with and resentful toward the hordes in the house. His anger and resentment erupted one day when I was leaving to see a massage client. I had given our ten-year-old Corolla to the girls to enable them to get around town. Therefore, I was maneuvering our new, unfamiliar SUV in a tight corner of the front yard where three other vehicles were parked. I caught a tree, ripping the front bumper from the vehicle.

Peter raced from the house and yelled, "What the fuck do you think you're doing?"

I jumped out, equally angry at his build up of negativity. "What does it look like I'm doing? I'm ripping the bumper off the car," I said, pulling off the remaining hanging bumper.

Jackie appeared. "Are you all right, Mum?"

"Yes. I'm just destroying our new car, and Peter's having a fit."

And I'm done with married life.

With the atmosphere in the house tense, Jackie and family were walking on eggshells. They were also tired of the cramped conditions and lack of privacy. They moved into a rental apartment, ten minutes from our house, shortly before Christmas, even though I would have preferred they wait, in order to build some savings in an emergency fund.

After Jackie and family moved out, Peter and I went to a counselor.

"I'm done," I told Richard, our therapist. "I've no love left."

"And you want to make it work?" Richard asked Peter.

"Yes, I love her."

"Well, I don't love you. How can I love someone who expresses love and concern by saying 'What the fuck do you think you're doing, after I've been in an accident? If that's how you express love, forget it. Jackie came from the house and asked if I was all right, but not you. And you made them feel uncomfortable when we took them in to give them a new start. You just couldn't suck it up for a few months, until they were on their feet, could you? You had to create a bad atmosphere in the home. I'm through."

"You railroaded me into it. I didn't have any say in it."

"What absolute rubbish! I brought up the subject several times. All you had to do was say no. It's not my fault you didn't speak up."

"Why are you here, Pauline, if you're sure it's over?" Richard asked.

"Because I want us to split as cleanly and as fairly and as amicably as possible, and we may need help with that."

Peter must have been devastated by how strongly I felt. Richard arranged for Peter to have some sessions alone. By the time our counseling sessions were coming to an end, I knew I could never leave Peter. Richard reminded me that I had felt many times that I wanted out of the marriage, and I had not ended it. Why not?

"Peter's already been badly hurt. He doesn't remember why or who. Perhaps it's too painful to face. I don't want to add more hurt,"

I said. "Besides, it's karmic. If I don't deal with it now, I'll have to go through it all again. No thanks."

I faced the truth. I would never be able to leave Peter. He had a gentle, caring side to him, was wise giving counsel. It was only that other side of him, the negativity that I had trouble with. I again committed myself to him and vowed to make our marriage work.

❖ ❖ ❖

On a follow up visit to Dr. Freeman, the radiation doctor, she made arrangements for me to go on a clinical trial being held at the Cleveland Clinic to help people with fecal incontinence. To a certain extent, I had learned to cope. I had to be up and about for three hours before daring to leave the house. Any accidents were usually over and done with the first three hours after getting up, so I was more often than not safe for the remainder of the day. Still, anything that would improve my situation would be most welcome

Some weeks later, I arrived at the hospital to participate in the clinical trial. I was tense, gripping the steering wheel, afraid I'd fall apart if I let go. With my post traumatic stress, going to see a doctor was like an unhappy animal being dragged to a veterinarian, only without the mournful howls.

I locked myself in the disabled cubicle in the clinic's bathroom and prepped myself by using the prescribed enema. It took only seconds for my aching guts to explode into the commode. Oh brother! Did I really want to go through with this? I washed my hands and backside.

My neck and shoulders were stiff as I reported to the reception desk.

"Oh, you're here for the trial, aren't you? Take a seat, Mrs. Hayton. Miss Myers will be out shortly."

Mary Myers, researcher, was the recipient of my fecal-accident diary. We had discussed my situation in *great* detail before I was admitted to the trial. The questions I had answered were enough to make anyone blush.

"How have you been affected by your condition?" was Mary's first big question.

"Well actually, it's all so hilarious. I go into hysterics every time I soil my pants," I said.

"Come on, Pauline, be serious."

"Can't. I'll cry," I said, as tears welled-up. "I'm very depressed about the whole thing."

Mary Myers patted my arm. I was sure she'd heard much more horrific stories of fecal incontinence than mine, yet she understood that even in its mildest form, the condition could be devastating.

"Has it affected your sex life?"

"What sex life?"

Mary looked at me expectantly, her pen poised to make a note.

"My sex life is non-existent."

"Because of the incontinence?"

I nodded, couldn't speak.

"If the trial helps you, would you have the sex life you want?"

My face fell. "No. I wouldn't dare risk it. Who wants to make love to someone who leaks shit all over?"

Mary patted my arm again.

After several weeks of questions and diary-keeping, I had been admitted to the trial.

And today was the day. I followed Mary to her office. As a participant in the trial, I didn't know if I would receive the actual treatment or a placebo. Mary explained the procedure again to make sure I understood what was going to happen.

"A bulking agent, miniscule silicone balls, will be injected round the anal sphincter to reinforce it and make the opening smaller. The theory is that the treatment should make it easier to have anal control. Your problem is the scar tissue on part of the sphincter due to radiation burns. It's particularly bad where the tumor was located, but the researchers still want to include you in the trial. There are no guarantees. Do you still want to go ahead today?"

"Yes."

Mary removed her reading glasses, leaving them dangling from the chain round her neck. She studied my face. Terrified of injections, I knew my eyes were wide with fear. I even have fillings at the dentist without Novocain injections.

"Are you all right?"

"I'm fine," I lied, with an exaggerated smile.

She studied me a minute longer, then said, "Good. Doctor will be along shortly. The nurse will ready you for the injections."

I wished she would stop saying that word.

The nurse came in. "Hello, Pauline. We need you to pull down your pants and kneel here on the proctology table while I tape your buttocks apart."

This was too ludicrous for words—as bad as the endless poking and prodding I'd endured before they offered me life. God, I hoped this would be worth it!

"When doctor comes she will give you eight injections around the anus, the first to numb the pain, the rest will be the treatment."

Eight injections! My stomach flip-flopped and tied itself into a pretzel. Dr. Casey was sweet and gentle, but I couldn't shake my dread at what was about to take place.

"I feel like I'm in a torture chamber."

"I'm sure you do. It's not very elegant to kneel here . . ."

"With my bum in the air for the all the world to see."

"Just me and the nurse, Pauline. Ready? I'm going to give you the first Novocain injections now."

The injections were painful, but I kept my derriere still as instructed. With my face buried in the table, I was half crying, half laughing.

"I can't tell if you're laughing or crying," the doctor said.

"Both. It hurts like hell, and I can't help picturing how preposterous this must look."

"I don't understand why it's hurting so much. Oh, yes, of course! You're filled with scar tissue. No wonder I had trouble getting the needle into you. I'm sorry it was so bad. It doesn't normally hurt. In a few minutes I'll inject the silicone beads, and then it will be over. You'll be a little numb for the rest of the day. We'll have to see how this goes. We may have to repeat the procedure in three months."

My heart sank. I didn't think I could go through it again. I felt clammy, nauseated, then hot and cold, and was trembling.

"I need a bowl. I could be sick."

Nurse hurried over with a stainless steel vessel. I took the dish in shaking hands.

"Are you all right?" Dr. Casey asked.

"I'm in shock, that's all. I'll be fine. Give me a few minutes."

Doctor and nurse stayed until I felt better.

"Okay. See you in three months. We'll send you an appointment in the mail." Dr. Casey sailed from the office for her next victim.

The nurse gave me a cup of water. "Holding up? Okay to drive?"

I nodded.

Making my way to the car, I felt shaky. Thank goodness for electronics. A push of a button on my key ring and the car unlocked. I could never have placed the key in the lock with my trembling fingers.

Sweat beading on brow and upper lip, I sat in the car, trying to pull myself together, doubting I would be going through this again in three months.

The two weeks following the treatment, there was no sign of improvement.

I had a further interview with Mary Myers, research coordinator. "I'm depressed. It looks like I got the placebo. I hate to think I went through all that for a placebo."

"I don't know who got what, Pauline. But I do know Dr. Casey prefers to go slowly in administering the dosage. It's not helpful to over bulk. So, if you got the real deal, she'll be adding more bulking agent in three months."

I felt sick. "I'm sure she knows what she's doing." *What if I can't face it again? I'll have to put up with being incontinent for the rest of my life—but I can't, I can't.*

Tears pricked my eyes. "It will be hard going through it all again."

TWENTY-TWO

I was away in Tampa on a massage training course, when it happened, the event I'd been waiting for most of my life. As soon as I returned to Naples and entered the house, Peter said, "Jackie wants you to phone her. She won't tell me what it's about." He seemed annoyed that she was not sharing with him whatever it was she had to tell me.

"I'll see you in ten minutes," Jackie said, when I called.

She was beaming with excitement as she sailed into the house. "While you were away, Mum, Joanne contacted me through the Friends Network, asking if I was her sister. She wants to get to know us."

My knees felt weak. Stunned, I read and re-read the printed emails Jackie handed me. Then I cried with gratitude. So, I was right, she did come back into my life. When Jackie was thirteen, I told her she had a sister, who had been adopted, so for Joanne to come into our lives was as much a joy for Jackie as it was for me.

"Mum," Jackie said, in awe, "the day she contacted me was the last day of my subscription to Friends Network. I was going to let it lapse!"

A wave of gratefulness swept over me. *God taking care of us.*

I had to go to England to do some final research for my book, *Naga Queen*. After some months of exchanging emails, Peter and I arranged to visit Joanne, her husband Colin, and our two grandchildren, Connor and Eva, who were close in age to Christopher and Rebecca.

We stayed in the Middle House pub in Mayfield, which was only five miles from Uckfield, where Joanne and family lived. It was shocking to realize I had been so close to her only eighteen months earlier when I met Trina. Amazingly, when Colin was in the army, they had been stationed at Catterick Camp, only thirty miles from Middlesbrough, my home town. Joanne and I could have passed one another in the street when she came into Middlesbrough to shop. I

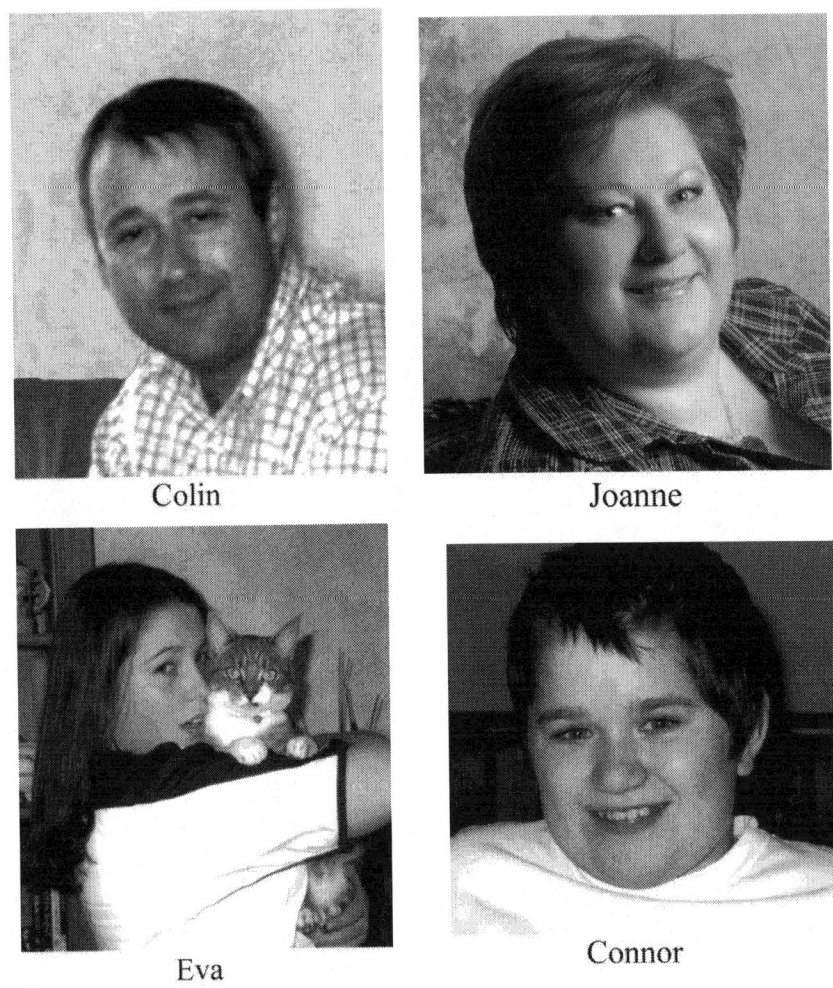

Colin

Joanne

Eva

Connor

couldn't visit Trina while we were in Mayfield. With my encouragement and blessings, she had gone to live in New Delhi, India. She had met someone she liked, and she was busy working for the betterment of the Naga tribes that her mother had lived with as an anthropologist during WWII.

Joanne and Colin joined us for dinner at the Middle House pub, a safe neutral place to meet. Nervousness made Joanne distant but polite. Colin, a friendly, easy-going guy, was tuned in to any distress his wife might feel, his keen senses weighing up every nuance, ready to take action should it be necessary. Joanne's main concern over dinner was why I kept Jackie and gave her away.

"You have to know, it wasn't that I loved you less than Jackie," I said. You were only a few weeks old. It would have been less of a wrench for you to be parted from me than for Jackie. It broke my heart to let you go. I wanted to keep us all together, but didn't have the financial means to do it."

Joanne nodded hesitantly, avoided eye contact. She was holding back, assessing how much she would open up to me. I had failed to convince her of my love. Thank goodness for Colin, who carried the evening with his easy manner and ease of conversation. He smoothed away the tension and fortunately, got on well with Peter. This first meeting passed without catastrophe. They invited us for lunch the following day to meet her parents.

Joanne moved more freely in her own environment. She had shed her heavy-duty protective emotional armor, replacing it with more flexible chain mail. Progress.

Sensing she feared I would be gushing and overly affectionate when really we were strangers, I said, "I know I can never be your mother. That's not what I'm looking for. I just hope we can grow to like one another and be friends. I want to know if you had a happy childhood, a happy life."

"Yes, I've had a happy life. Mum and Dad will arrive soon. They live in Banbury, near Oxford. They're driving down to meet you. It's a two hour drive."

I handed Joanne an envelope. "I brought a photo of your father and his details should you ever want to look him up."

She glanced at the photograph and put the envelope to one side.

Sheila and Owen arrived. They were as pleased as Peter and I that at last we had Joanne in our lives once more.

I hugged Sheila and whispered, "Thank you for being good parents. I'm very grateful."

After a delicious lunch, we poured over photographs. During a conversation, Joanne nodded her head to emphasize her point. Peter and I looked at one another, our mouths hanging open. That was one of my mannerisms. How had Joanne developed it when I'd not been around to influence her? From what we had seen, Joanne's personality was very like mine. She was a go-getter, made things happen, efficient, intelligent, energetic, strong-willed, yet vulnerable. One thing I didn't understand was that both Joanne and Jackie excelled at cooking. Definitely not something they inherited from me.

The visit was a success. I was happy. Joanne and I liked one another. I couldn't ask for more than that. We invited them to visit us in Florida, in order to meet Jackie and family. Her visit came six months later.

Eva and Connor stayed in Jackie's apartment. Joanne and Colin stayed with us. Before they met in person, my grandchildren knew each other well, having communicated via email and Facebook for months. My mother withdrew, became quiet, maybe anxious about the whole thing. Perhaps she felt guilty for forcing me to part with Joanne. I don't know because we never discussed it.

Jackie had her own fears about meeting Joanne. "I've been a single child all my life. I don't know how to be a sister."

"Jackie, all you have to be is your warm and friendly self. Joanne will either love you or not. But I'm sure you've noticed most people like you," I said.

Many times I had to keep reassuring Joanne that my giving her away for adoption did not mean I loved her less. I was despondent thinking that all through her life she had carried the feeling that I valued her less. When Joanne showed no hostility towards her, Mum came out of herself, able to enjoy her new found granddaughter and great grandchildren.

We played miniature golf, enjoyed handsome young men strutting their stuff on South Beach Miami, blocking out derogatory comments from our men folk about the Adonises making us drool.

The visit was a great success. We still liked one another at the end of the two weeks. Jackie and Joanne enjoyed one another's company. All the grandchildren mixed well together. It was the start of a warm connection. The emptiness inside disappeared. I was filled to overflowing. I couldn't have been happier.

A few months after Joanne's visit, I had my fifty-eighth birthday. My energy was as close to normal as it would get after the chemotherapy and radiation, and I wanted to do something big to celebrate being alive. But what? It soon presented itself, my crazy idea of dipping into my retirement savings to go to Myanmar, to follow in my father's WWII footsteps. It would be my sixtieth birthday present to myself.

I spent hours researching and planning. Maybe I should make a video of the trip. If cancer returned, at least my grandchildren would have a film to remember me by. I contacted Miami University, looking for students who were taking an M.A. in filmmaking who might like to go with us, all expenses paid.

No response.

I took that as a sign I was being too ambitious and dropped the idea. But it returned to nag at me. So I contacted Boston University with the same deal. Within the hour, I had half a dozen responses from would-be hopefuls. Peter and I braved the cold October weather and flew to Boston to interview our short list of students. Our final choice for filmmakers was Rohan, a handsome Nepalese with a steady, unruffled manner; German Sarah with her fashion model build, determined, hardworking and conscientious, both in their mid-twenties; and soundman, American,1 eighteen-year-old Dillon, laid-back and curious—all eager for the adventure.

Joan and Herby came from Australia to look after Mum and Dad for the five weeks we would be away. We started filming in Florida to capture the start of the journey with me talking to my father about his wartime exploits, then off we went. I had recently turned fifty-nine. I had meant the trip to be for my sixtieth birthday, but for some reason I felt I had to do it earlier.

We groaned in dismay on learning our connecting flight in London was held up for hours because a bird had flown into one of the plane's engines. Then as we were about to board, luggage on the plane, unaccompanied by a passenger, had to be removed. More delay. Our late arrival at Bangkok had us sprinting through the airport, hand luggage and camera equipment heaving and bouncing. Gasping for breath, we wildly looked for signs directing us to the Yangon flight. We arrived at the gate with barely a minute to spare for the last flight of the night. Thank goodness Jiro, our guide, was still waiting for us at Yangon, having received our email from Heathrow.

Jiro ushered us into a spotless mini-bus, and the driver deposited us outside the four-star Sedona Hotel, a short drive from Yangon city center. We stared up and around the impressive entrance, our jaws hanging. Staff ran to pick up our hand luggage and escort us inside. Two life-sized elephant statues, dominating the spacious, marble-floored lobby, stared down on us as we wiped our hands and face with moist hot towels brought to us by more hotel staff.

"A bit better than the tents we were expecting, isn't it?" I said to the group who were still gawping.

"I thought we were going to be roughing it," Rohan said.

I took the glass of fruit punch offered by a waiter. "So did I."

In WWII, my father had driven from India along the Ledo road to Myitkyina (Mit-cheen-a), Burma, in a truck convoy, as part of the advance party of British 72nd Brigade. He described the drive as a wild ride, not only because of the primitive jungle and precipices, but also because of the frequent landslides. My plan on this trip was to cover the same ground by walking the northernmost section of the Ledo road to the Indian border. Built by American Army engineers between 1943 and 1945, that part of the road was now only a track through mountainous jungle. I also wanted to visit villages where Dad had seen action against the Japanese. Most of our trip was to be off the beaten track, in places few tourists go. We had packed and prepared for the rugged outdoor life and a fifty-mile hike through jungle. And here we were—in the lap of luxury.

Jiro returned from reception and handed us our keys. "Do not worry about your luggage. It is in Bangkok and will come on the morning plane. We have a change of plan, Pauline. The government will not allow you to walk the Ledo road to India. There is unrest in the area, and they are concerned for your safety."

My heart sank. What was I going to do now? Thank God I'd brought lots of information with me. I was going to have to rewrite the film script.

Jiro said, "I go now and return in the morning."

With crew members making noises about going to bed early, Peter and I exchanged conspiratorial glances. "What a shame you're tired. After a quick swill, we're going to Paddy O'Malley's bar," Peter said, nodding to the far corner of the lobby. "Pauline needs to forget her woes."

The crew joined us for a forget-the-day's-tensions-let-your-hair-down night's entertainment with live girl singers from the Philippines and a disco.

The following morning I peeped through the curtains of our hotel room window. The mist was lifting, and in the distance, standing head and shoulders above the surrounding city, gleamed the golden spire of the Shwe Dagon, a most fantastic pagoda that we were going to visit that afternoon. We dressed in clothes that were still damp from washing them the night before. We needed our luggage pronto.

The Shwe Dagon at night from Kandawgyi Lake, Yangon

Jiro came with the bus and driver and whizzed us off to explore. Ancient vehicles, mainly Toyotas, filled the streets. Yangon was a bustling city in a time warp, a city where time had stood still for fifty years. We filmed in and around various temples, capturing the religious flavor of Myanmar before heading to the Shwe Dagon.

We removed our footwear to enter the pagoda. Its beauty took our breath away. There were intricately designed arches and golden Buddhas everywhere; gold leaf covered at least fifty percent of the temples and statues. Heated by the sun, the marble floor was uncomfortably hot on the soles of our feet. The fourteen-acre complex teemed with devoted people there in the late afternoon to light incense and say a prayer on their way home from work. Almost everyone, man, woman and child, wore traditional *lungyis* (wrap-round skirts).

An orange-robed, elderly, monk, his head shaved, grabbed the opportunity to practice his English with me as the crew lined up their shots. "Good afternoon. Are you English? I hope you enjoy your time at our pagoda."

"How could I not enjoy this special place?" Peace enveloped me as I looked into his warm brown eyes and friendly, serene face. "Where did you learn to speak English?"

"At school, many years ago. I enjoy speaking English when I can."

The crew called me for filming. It was difficult to tear myself away.

Two days later, waiting in the airport to fly to Myitkyina, Jiro gave us a pep-talk. "You must be careful when filming in the north. In the tourist areas, it is no problem, but Myanmar has received much bad publicity from foreign writers, and officials in the more remote areas are suspicious of strangers. If I tell you not to film somewhere or to put your camera away, you must do it at once. My job is to give you what you want to make your trip worthwhile, but I must also keep you out of trouble."

We understood. Even though the populace would probably be very nice, they were ruled by a hostile officialdom.

In Myitkyina, we stayed at the Nanthida Riverside Hotel, a hotel Jiro had never used before. Exploring behind the hotel, I found a small temple. Jiro was unaware of its existence. We went to see it together and found a heart-wrenching plaque. In English, it told the sad story of Japanese soldiers, out of food and ammunition, losing the fight against the well-supplied Americans in the WWII battle for Myitkyina. General Mitzukami's superiors had refused permission for him to withdraw and regroup. Instead, he and his men were ordered to fight to the death. Knowing it was a lost cause, he ordered Captain Mutsumi and the troops to disperse and make their escape through the jungles. Then General Mitzukami took his soldiers' shame and dishonor on himself by committing hara-kiri.

Fifty-five years later, Captain Mutsumi returned to Myitkyina and donated this temple, with its enormous, golden, reclining

Temple of the reclining Buddha donated to the town of Myitkyina by Captain Mutsumi

Buddha, to the people of Myitkyina, for helping the Japanese get away by showing them little-known paths in the forest.

We were all touched by the tale and pretty much subdued for the remainder of the evening, thinking about how Captain Mutsumi was still affected by a war that ended over sixty years ago.

The following afternoon, Jiro and the team of guides and a driver he had arranged for this segment of the journey collected us from the hotel. We rode in the back of a pick-up truck to the crossroads in the center of nearby Namkwi Village. All the homes were made of woven bamboo with thatched roofs, except for the white stucco church. I climbed down from the truck, not sure what to do next. I felt a fondness for the village. It was here that my dad had the good fortune to slip in the mud when a Japanese soldier fired at him during a night-time assault. The bullet meant for Dad's heart whizzed by his ear instead.

Villagers stared curiously as we walked along the path to the river where children bathed and women washed clothes. Men, returning home from the fields, drove their bullock carts across the shallow river into the village.

Word of our filming must have spread, because a wandering minstrel, a young man in his mid-twenties and wearing jeans, strummed his guitar and sang for us. Villagers called their children to gather round.

I asked Jiro. "Can you get him to play and persuade the children to sing for us? We want them on film."

Jiro ambled across to the young man and the villagers. They were eager to participate, waving and calling to their children to come close. The ten minutes it took to overcome the children's shyness was rewarded by a self-conscious rendition of "Merry Christmas" sung to the tune of "Happy Birthday to You," resulting in enthusiastic applause and whistles of appreciation from us.

After Namkwi the blue-collar town of Mogaung beckoned. The guides piled our luggage onto the truck and off we went. Jiro had to report our presence there to the authorities. I was in Mogaung to film a report about a famous Chindit battle to capture the town from the Japanese. Also, the villages I wanted to visit and film were only a short drive away. Tourists did not come to this area. That was reflected in the guesthouse, which provided neither towels nor soap. The sheets looked clean, however.

Sarah's room was across the hall. We heard her squeak and call for Dillon, who rushed to her side. We rushed too.

"What is it?" I said, skidding to a halt on seeing a gigantic spider on the wall above her bed. I squeezed back out past Peter. "Can't deal with this."

Dillon efficiently bundled it outside with little drama. Easy-peasy when you're not scared stiff of the monsters.

With filming finished in the Mogaung area, Jiro took us to the Hukawng Valley, also known as the Valley of Death because of the tens of thousands of people who died of starvation or disease while fleeing to India during the 1942 Japanese invasion of Burma. Heads swiveled left and right as we drove along winding un-paved road, at first through orange groves and cultivated gardens, then through more exotic vegetation the farther we traveled. Pampas grass filled fields alongside crystal-clear streams. Hornbills flew overhead. Apart from overloaded trucks with loads tilting perilously to one side, there was little traffic on the road, a couple of cyclists and some people on foot. Once on the plateau, it was a world different to anything I had ever known.

The Ledo road stretched straight ahead. We drove over Bailey bridges built in 1944 by American Army engineers. They were well past their best but still standing and serving the local population. A sign informed us we had entered the Hukawng Valley Tiger Reserve. That night we were going to sleep at the new ranger station at Warazup.

Arriving at the station, Jiro became upset. After a frantic conversation with the station caretaker and shouted instructions to the guides, he lifted his *lungyi*, jumped on the caretaker's moped and raced off.

One of the guides, Thant Zin, spoke English. I went to him. "Where has Jiro gone?"

"The toilets are not finished. He has gone to the next town to find better accommodation."

Jiro returned two hours later looking crestfallen. He had failed us.

"Not to worry, Jiro," I said. "We came prepared to rough it, and so far all you've done is pamper us. We can go behind the bushes."

We erected our tents inside the wooden building. Several times during the night, I needed to go outside into the jungle to pee behind a bush. The next morning at breakfast, sitting round the campfire while Jiro fried eggs and made doughnuts for us, he announced, "The caretaker told me he saw tigers at the riverbank two weeks ago. It caused some excitement."

I bet it did. Was that why the tents were inside the building? To keep us safe from tigers? I almost choked on my doughnut. The riverbank was only a hundred feet away. I'd given no thought to the danger of tigers, poisonous snakes or anything else while I'd been going outside.

We stayed at the ranger station three nights and in-between filming caught up on some much needed rest and relaxation. One afternoon, we were all sitting on the far riverbank, watching a crow enjoying a feast of black tadpoles trapped in a pool. Seeing the driver washing from the platform on the riverbank, we waved. He waved back and splash! He slipped into the river. His slip didn't deter Sarah. She washed in the river later in the day. Peter and I washed with baby wipes, not wanting to risk falling in too, especially after seeing the giant fish the caretaker caught with his net.

I wish I could say that without electricity and the distractions of television or computer, we talked long and meaningfully late into the night, under the starry sky. But it wasn't so. We were all weary from filming and stiff from the bumpy ride in the back of the pick-up truck. Peter and I were eager for some time to ourselves. We retreated to our tent and read by the light of our headlights until we fell asleep.

Having been refused permission to travel beyond Tanai, we had twelve days to fill, which had originally been allocated for our jungle trek along the Ledo road to the Indian border. Instead, we flew to Mandalay to film a segment about British Fourteenth Army's heroic recapture of Mandalay Hill from the Japanese, after which we embarked on a twelve-hour ferry ride down Myanmar's longest river, the Ayeyarwady, from Mandalay to Bagan. Most of the trip we relaxed and snoozed, recovering from tearing around filming in Kachin State. At Bagan, the rewritten script meant filming a segment about Fourteenth Army's river crossing. Getting up at 3:30 a.m. was painful. Peter stayed behind, having caught a stomach bug. The rest of us clambered into a rickety boat, following the beam from Jiro's flashlight. After several turns of the key and some jiggling with the engine, the boat roared into life. It took forty minutes to chug across the river in pitch darkness. Ever resourceful, Jiro took us to a small café for a breakfast of samosas, pastries and tea, while we waited for daylight.

Returning to shore as the eastern horizon offered a glimmer of light, Rohan lined up his shots. Sarah climbed a hill to better film the pagodas glinting on the horizon during sunrise. While Rohan filmed, I related the story of Fourteenth Army's great feat of crossing the Ayeyarwady, a formidable obstacle, particularly when under enemy attack.

When we were done, Rohan asked, "How would you feel if I asked you a few personal questions on film? After all, the film *is* about you."

"Nervous, but you're right."

"We've covered a lot of ground in the past couple of weeks. How do you feel about how things are going?"

"Right now?"

Rohan nodded.

Tears welled in my eyes and my voice was shaky. "Well, right now, I feel tired and depressed. I didn't get to walk the Ledo road to India." I waved my arm at the mist. "The sunrise isn't cooperating this morning, and there's not a pagoda in sight. I really want this film to go well." I paused, couldn't speak for the lump in my throat. When I resumed, my voice was scratchy from emotion. "I might get cancer again, and without this film for my grandkids, their memory of me will fade and eventually disappear like those ancient pagodas over there," I nodded toward the monuments, "crumbled to dust." I sniffed, stared out across the wide river, silent for a moment. "Apart from that, I'm all right."

The highlight of my trip was a visit to the Rangoon Memorial in the Taukkyan War Cemetery outside Yangon, hoping to find the record of the only friend my father lost during the war.

"I'm looking for Corporal Henderson," I told the Indian caretaker. The tall, thin caretaker strode across the records room in his long *lungyi*, returning with a green, leather-bound book marked H-I. He found the page and pointed out Corporal Henderson's entry. I unexpectedly began to cry, possibly because I had come to know Corporal Henderson through writing *A Corporal's War*.

"His name on the memorial," the caretaker said. "Come, I show you."

He led the way to one of the many majestic granite pillars of the memorial, and pointed to Corporal Henderson's name, engraved for posterity, among the names of twenty-seven thousand young men who, like him, died in their prime in Burma's steamy jungles and whose remains were never found. I laid a wreath on behalf of my father in remembrance of his friend. Tears kept falling down my cheeks no matter how often I wiped them away. I felt so connected to these men and their sacrifice, the men called by Tom Brokaw "The Greatest Generation."

After laying the wreath, Peter and I strolled among the more than six thousand well-kept graves in the soft, late-afternoon light,

Taukkyan War Cemetery and the Rangoon Memorial
Yangon, Myanmar (Burma)

the place empty except for our crew and the gardeners. Row after row of gravestones spread across the cemetery, surrounded by the neatly trimmed bushes, colorful flower beds and manicured lawns of this tranquil resting place, a complete contrast to the traumatic, violent, bloody loss of life experienced by most of the graves' occupants. The grave markers provided information—James Adamson, gunner, Royal Artillery, died July 4th, 1945, age twenty; Thomas Young, Reconnaissance Corp R.A.C., died February 4th, 1944, age twenty-four. There were thousands of young men buried here, and I had lived more than thirty years longer than most of them. Uneasy fears that cancer would return to claim me evaporated, disappearing as a choppy sea becomes smooth in a windless sky. Peace filled every cell and fiber of my being. Then the clinking and rumble of tanks and the pounding of hundreds of marching boots disturbed the peace. When I raised my head, British soldiers wearing bush hats were marching in the dust kicked up by tanks traveling alongside them. The soldiers smiled and nodded to me in greeting. They were sending me a message to keep writing my stories about their sacrifices and efforts in fighting the war.

I choked back my tears. I had been thinking of giving up on my writing career. Silently, I renewed my promise to keep on writing about their experiences in the China/Burma/India/ Theatre of War so the world would not forget.

While we were away, we kept in touch with what was happening at home via email at internet cafes. Learning that my father was in the hospital with failing kidneys, I prayed he would be all right. He was home when we returned to Florida, but much frailer than when I left. He enjoyed listening to my tales about the trip. Some of the place names I mentioned were familiar to him. Dad was pleased I'd laid a wreath for his friend, and he laughed, delighted by my story about staying at the Hukaung Tiger Preserve.

Joan and Herby returned to Australia. Joan was sad, realizing this would probably be the last time she would see our eighty-seven-year-old parents alive.

My parents continued their social activities at the senior centers, happily going off on the bus that came to the door to pick them up, but when they were at home, Dad was depressed. I tried talking to him about it, but he wouldn't out of loyalty to my mother. Part of the problem was his confusion, caused by hardening of the arteries in his brain. He was aware he could no longer do things he should be able to such as tie his shoelaces and shave. My mother's constant critical sharpness left him feeling useless, as if he were letting her down as a husband. I felt he couldn't wait to be out of this world and into the next.

Then came the morning Dad claimed a pill I found on the floor as his. Before I could check it, he'd popped it into his mouth and swallowed it down with a mouthful of tea. When my parents left to go to the senior center, I left for my appointment to have Lasik surgery on my eyes. I was at home, resting, when a phone call came from the hospital emergency room. Dad had collapsed while at the senior center. They were admitting him because doctors couldn't figure out why his body chemistry was awry.

I raced to the hospital emergency room. Pulling back the curtain, I found Mum sitting at Dad's bedside, holding his hand. "Oh, Pauline!" she cried. I put my arm round her shoulders and held her tightly.

The doctor followed me in. "We don't understand what is going on with him. Have you any idea?"

The extra tablet! I told the doctor about the blood-pressure tablet I had found on the floor and how Dad had taken it. Maybe it wasn't his, but my mother's. That was the information they needed. They understood the problem and would not discharge him until they had his body chemistry balanced, which could take a few days.

When we visited him the following day, they had tied him to the bed and had inserted a catheter, making it impossible for him to move. Being tied to a bed all day with nothing to do, blind so he couldn't see if anyone was near, was supposed to make him well? As I said about my own medical care, treated not cared for.

I went to the nurses' station. "I'm not having my dad tied to his bed like that. I'm taking him home."

"You said he suffered with confusion. We tie patients to the bed in those situations, to protect them."

Really! I didn't come over on the banana boat, honey!

"I'm taking him home," I said and turned on my heels.

She ran after me.

I started to untie his bindings. "Dad, it's Pauline. I'm taking you home."

"Get your fucking hands off me!" he yelled, struggling to break free.

My hands flew to my mouth. My normally gentle father's swearing and agitation made him unmanageable, and I knew I could not cope with that on my own. The nurse explained it was a symptom of his system being off balance. On our next visit, the doctor said he was fine, and they would be discharging him.

"You've had him tied to a bed for three days. Can he still walk? I need him to walk. I can't push two wheelchairs at the same time," I said, pointing to my mother in her wheelchair.

"Oh, could he walk?" the doctor asked.

"Yes, we'd go for half-mile strolls along the road almost every day."

"I'll arrange for some physical therapy for him."

Two useless sessions with a disinterested physical therapist did nothing to help Dad walk. Leaving the hospital, two male nurses bundled him into the car. How on earth would I get him inside the house by myself? Nobody gave a damn. I took Mum in first in her wheelchair and returned for Dad. Thank goodness he was a small man and not heavy. I had to take his full weight and swing him round into the wheelchair to get him inside. He recovered somewhat once he was home, but a day later, he started to go downhill with serious diarrhea.

I called his family doctor. Because Dad was too ill to go to the office, a nurse came to the house to take a blood sample. It turned out the hospital had infected him with clostridium difficile. His family doctor prescribed a week's antibiotics, and the infection appeared to clear up. I was glad. The virulent diarrhea was burning the skin off my dad's bottom. I still had some burn cream left which I used to cover the sore areas and reduce his pain. I didn't mind the effort and hard work, but Dad was embarrassed and ashamed that I, his daughter, had to clean up his mess and wash his genitals.

"It's a labor of love," I told him. "Little enough for what you've done for me. Just lie back and think of England, and let me take care of you."

Despite Dad wearing diapers, the diarrhea often leaked out, soiling Dad's sheets several times a day. I'd haul him out of bed and drag him to the chair while I changed the sheets. Trying to return him to bed one day, I felt off balance. We were swaying. Terrified we would fall, and that I would not be able to lift him off the floor until Peter returned home from work, I cried, "Dad, help me!"

I don't know what I expected him to do in his condition, but he had the perfect answer. He began to hum the Blue Danube waltz. I started giggling, and as we started to topple, I hurled us both onto his bed with all the strength I could muster, where we lay laughing. But he was weakening. He stopped eating. Even his favorite ice cream couldn't tempt him. I called an ambulance.

I insisted Dad go to the other hospital in town, where he was admitted. His kidneys were failing from the infection, and he slipped into a light coma.

I whispered in his ear, "Dad, if you want to go, go. You don't have to stay here for Mum. I'll take good care of her if you've had enough. I love you. You've been the best father I could ever have had."

The energy in the room changed, and I knew he had decided to take the opportunity to exit this world. He was taken to hospice. I was shocked and angry to discover that hospice care meant drugging him and denying him food and water until he died. I was expecting something totally different for end of life care. It took eight days for

Dad to die. My grandchildren would not leave their beloved great granddad. They brought sleeping bags and stayed with Dad until the last day, when they had to return to school. He died after they left, only five weeks from his mistakenly taking that extra tablet.

I was heartbroken. Still am. My poor mother was numb and in denial. She had lost her husband of seventy years. Full of rage, I wanted to commit murder, especially after the doctor wrote on Dad's death certificate that he died from kidney failure.

I confronted the doctor. "My dad didn't die from kidney failure. He died from being infected with clostridium difficile at the hospital."

"But he actually died of kidney failure."

His words left a bad taste. My lips curled in disgust. "That's like saying someone died from lack of breath when they've been strangled. What are you doing? Protecting the hospital?"

I wrote to the hospital later, pointing out that they had infected my dad with clostridium difficile and needed to improve their procedures for managing the spread of disease. With their biggest concern being to avoid a law-suit rather than preventing infection, they replied, denying all responsibility. That was one statistic that remained unrecorded.

It took a long time before I could step back to see the big picture and accept that the accumulation of medical mistakes, the sequence of events—Dad taking that extra tablet, being infected with clostridium difficile at the hospital, Dad's family doctor prescribing only one week's antibiotics instead of the usual ten-day protocol for treating the infection, the doctors at the second hospital believing that an almost eighty-eight year old man does not require the effort they would put forth for a child, and then the hospice experience—was providing my dad with a pathway to the next world.

TWENTY-THREE

Mum went downhill fast when the loss of her husband finally hit her. She lost her appetite and consequently a lot of weight, eventually sixty-five pounds. Stressed without him, she developed bleeding ulcers that at times required emergency room visits and hospitalization.

Dad, however, was eager to show the family he was still around. When Jackie and Gordon took Rebecca and Christopher to Disney World, my dad's spirit joined them on the rides. Both Rebecca and Christopher saw him sitting on their hotel beds. Developmentally disabled Christopher was incapable of making up such stories, so we knew Dad really was around. Whenever he moved close to either me or Jackie, we would burst into tears, a nervous system reaction to his energy. I often asked Mum if Dad had come to her, but she never let on. I was glad he was around, because six months after his death, his great great grandson was born, and it made us happy, especially Donna, now married, to know her cherished great granddad would be watching her son grow up.

Mum tried to keep up her social life, but with her eyesight deteriorating and being as deaf as a post, she found it hard to be included in any conversations going on around her. She needed me to accompany her to the seniors' luncheons and bingo sessions, which I was happy to do. I wanted her to have a full life. Being self-employed, it was easy to arrange my appointments to suit myself. But in time, Mum gave up on having any sort of life outside her room. Her days consisted of listening to books on tape, until the TIAs (mini strokes) damaged her brain so much she could not figure out how to work the tape player. I got DVDs of television series from the library: *Murder She Wrote* was her favorite. I pushed her in her wheelchair up and down the pier, where she enjoyed the sunshine on her skin. I wished I'd been sensitive enough to realize that my mother, knowing I adored my father and was not emotionally close to her, feared we would become tired of caring for her and put her in a home. This may have caused her to reduce her life to the four walls of her room in an attempt to become invisible and less of a nuisance.

Five generations, left to right: me, Thomas my great grandson, Mum, Jackie and Thomas' mother Donna

Mum's brain was becoming addled from the TIAs. She started to call me Barbara. I'd no idea who Barbara was. As far as I knew, Mum had never known anyone called Barbara. Every fifteen minutes, she called me for one reason or another. It drove me crazy. Have you ever been on the phone for an hour with a computer technician, trying to follow his instructions to put your computer right, while someone else distracts you by calling for your attention every few minutes? I guarantee, by the end of the call, you would be ready to kill whoever was sabotaging your concentration. Eventually, Mum could not be left alone, and I arranged to see my massage clients after Peter arrived home from work. Caring for her was exhausting. Peter and I had no life of our own, and we were becoming angry and resentful.

I called my friend Vicky in England. "I can't take any more. She's driving me crazy, and I'm completely washed out."

"You know your mother is your greatest spiritual teacher, don't you?" Vicky said.

I rolled my eyes. *Don't give me that claptrap.* "It doesn't feel like it. It feels like purgatory. I'm angry all the time. I'm coming to hate her, and I'm at the end of my rope. I don't know how much more I can take, Vicky."

Her voice was soft and kind, like a ministering angel. "You can do it, Pauline. You signed up for this, remember. You're going to be at the top of the class. I love you. Goodnight."

Vicky's words completely changed the way I viewed Mum. If she were my greatest spiritual teacher, then I was being blessed. No need to be angry at being given the opportunity to learn kindness and compassion. I shared Vicky's wisdom with Peter, and he was able to change too.

Mum's health continued to deteriorate. She developed sores on her back. One was the size of a child's fist, but it seemed to be forming a scab and healing. Only it wasn't. One morning, as I was washing her back, the black scab fell into a large hole on her sacrum. I almost fainted in horror. I hurriedly dressed her and took off for the emergency room. Mum's situation was grave.

"She may not survive this," the doctor told me.

I collapsed on a chair, distraught, while arrangements were made for her admittance.

Racked with guilt at my incompetence as a caregiver, I sat by Mum's bed. She was dying, and it was my fault. She lay in bed, pale and motionless. An IV administered heavy doses of antibiotics. I sat for hours, watching over her. Then, that evening, in the corner of her room, I noticed a dozen or so members of her family had gathered, waiting, my maternal grandparents, my aunties and uncles, Mum's brothers and sisters, all dead for many years, ready to guide my mother into the afterlife.

Choked, I ran from the hospital, believing I'd killed her. I was expecting the hospital to call me in the middle of the night with the news that Mum had died. When I didn't receive the call, I returned to the hospital at 8:00 a.m. amazed to find Mum sitting up in bed.

"I'm starving. Where's my breakfast? No one's brought my breakfast," she complained.

I laughed out loud with relief and hugged her. "We can't have you going hungry, can we? I'll find a nurse."

Despite his reluctance, fearing she would die on the operating table, the surgeon operated on Mum to remove the detritus, and I was shown how to treat her wound. I was squeamish, but resolved. My ignorance had caused the wound to develop to a point where it put Mum's life in danger. I would heal it.

I was given advice about providing the right cushions to protect her skin and pressure points—advice I didn't give much credence to. Treating the symptoms not the cause. Mum had been sitting in her chair for over five years without a problem. Something in Mum had changed, not the chair, not her sitting.

Some weeks later, her wound was healing, the hole gradually growing smaller, so her lethargy wasn't due to her wound. But Mum was just sitting in her armchair, zombie-like. I could not persuade her to engage in anything. No life. No energy. No trips to the pier. No social clubs. Nothing. I took her to her family doctor.

"According to her lab results, she's fine," he said.

"But she isn't fine, She sits all day zoned out like a zombie!"

He shrugged. "Well, she *is* getting old, Pauline."

With no indication of problems in her blood work, he was incapable of using his expensively educated brain to figure out what might be going on. Or maybe he did not think his $130 fee was worth the effort. I was so disgusted and frustrated, I could have pinned him against the wall and kneed him where it would hurt most.

I spent hours trolling the Internet, searching for doctors and alternative therapies that could help her. I don't know how or why, intuition maybe, God's guidance maybe, but I took a closer look at Dr. Stein of Hollywood, Florida. One of his specialties was amino acid therapy. I had no idea how that might help Mum, but it felt right to try it. It was a ninety-minute drive to his office, a long way for someone who was not well. Fortunately, Mum slept most of the way.

Dr. Stein, a tall, elderly man with stooped shoulders, asked to see Mum's medical records or blood test results. I didn't have them, had never given a thought about the need for them.

After listening to my information about her health, he said, "We'll use muscle testing to find out what's wrong with her." He turned to my mother. "Climb onto the table and lie down," he said and left the examination room.

Easier said than done. I helped Mum to a standing position, took a deep breath, lifted her in a fireman's lift, and planted her bottom on the table. Dr. Stein returned with his nurse. He examined and palpated Mum, then explained how he was going to muscle test her using the nurse's arm as proxy. He brought out various samples of heavy metals that he laid on Mum's abdomen one at a time. The first one was lead.

The nurse placed her left hand on Mum's shoulder and lifted her right arm into a horizontal position. Dr. Stein explained that the nurse was to resist when he pushed down on her outstretched arm. If the arm was weak, it meant the substance he was placing on Mum's abdomen was harmful to her. Dr. Stein pushed, and the nurse's arm fell down with almost no resistance. He kept adding to the lead, until he knew how badly it was affecting Mum. He repeated the procedure for arsenic, benzene, mercury and numerous other toxic substances, until the testing was done.

He stared at the wall behind the table, arms crossed, thoughtfully rubbing his chin. Then he turned his gaze on me. His forehead creased into lines as he looked over the top of his spectacles and stared at me suspiciously. "I've never seen anyone with so much arsenic in her system and still able to function."

"I haven't been poisoning her!" I protested.

"She's also full of benzene, mercury, lead, cadmium, and other heavy metals. Have you any idea how that happened?"

"All I can think of is she grew up in a town full of pollution from heavy industry."

He studied the floor, pouting his lips. "And you say she has lost a lot of weight recently?"

"Yes, sixty-five pounds since my dad died two-and-a-half-years ago."

"Mmmm. I would say that most of the toxins were being stored in her fat. When she started shedding weight, it released the toxins into her system, and that's why she has been feeling so unwell. The toxins and her lack of nutrition from not eating is probably why she developed bedsores too. I'll prescribe a regime of amino acids for her to take. Boost her nutrition with Ensure. Also, as she has recently received large doses of antibiotics, she needs to take probiotics too. Bring her back in a month so I can assess her progress."

One thousand dollars out of pocket—six hundred for Dr. Stein's fee and four hundred for the supplements—and we were on our way home, clutching a plastic bag filled with bottles of various amino acid capsules and tablets and a large bottle of probiotics. I found the high fee shocking.

I faithfully followed the schedule for giving Mum her tablets, all twenty-five a day. Despite her complaining and her difficulty swallowing tablets, she ploughed her way through the allotted dosage. Until day eight. I entered her room with her breakfast tray—orange juice, scrambled eggs, a slice of whole wheat toast with marmalade and a small dish full of amino acid supplements. I placed the tray on her knee.

She felt around to see what was on the tray, then shoved the small dish of tablets at me. "You can take these away."

"Come on, Mum, get them down you. It's only been eight days. They're helping you feel better."

"I'm not taking any more tablets. I'm sick of them."

Oh, thrill and delight! My cantankerous mother was back.

I persuaded her to continue with fewer tablets, but it was always a battle. Still, I was grateful she had the energy to argue with me. Dr. Stein's fee turned out to be the best thousand dollars I ever spent on medical care for her.

We visited Doctor Stein again, but only twice more. With Mum becoming increasingly more belligerent about taking the amino acids, I was fighting a losing battle. Besides, I was out of energy myself.

Looking ahead to our retirement years, I'd been wondering how Peter and I could live a life with purpose when we retired. We didn't play golf, didn't boat, didn't play tennis. Nothing wrong with enjoying fun pastimes, but I wanted us to have a reason for living.

In 2007, I received a phone call from Trina. As I was asking about her involvement with the Naga tribes, she mentioned that if her mother were alive, she would be upset because Mount Kisha English School, in her mother's favorite Naga village, Magulong, was going to close. Because the village was so remote, most villagers were poor, owing to the difficulty in getting their produce to town to sell in the markets. It had reached the point where parents could no longer afford to pay the thirty cents a week to educate each child, money that paid the teachers' salaries. Because the teachers were not being paid, they left the village. Without teachers, the school would close. Since moving to New Delhi and marrying her Kashmiri husband, Trina, an adopted Naga like her mother, had made it her goal to help the Nagas obtain an education so they could participate in the modern world. Her efforts inspired me.

"We can help with that," I said. "How much do you need to pay the teachers?"

Trina (left) with friends outside the bungalow where her mother lived at Laisong village

And so the purpose I had been searching for was found. We were the proud sponsors of Mount Kisha English School.

Responding to letters from Mt. Kisha English School pupils pleading with us to visit their village, in October 2008, Peter and I made our first trip to India. I was in great need of a break from caring for Mum. Indeed, the dream of a vacation became as water to a woman dying of thirst. I obsessed about going to Magulong to recharge. I had been giving Mum bed baths for some months, because she was too weak to walk or take a shower. After eight months of treatment, the wound in her back was almost healed. Only a quarter-inch-hole was left. Every time I washed her back, which she loved, I told her that we were going on a trip to India, that I needed a break to get some rest so I could continue to take good care of her. Then I began to prepare her for the thing she had always dreaded. She would need to go into a nursing home for two weeks.

My words shocked and distressed her. "You said I'd never go into one of those places. You promised!"

"I know I did, but I need a rest, Mum. I'm worn out. It will only be for two weeks."

"It had better be all right," Mum said, resigned.

I'd done it now. I felt sad for her, but if I were going to survive, I *had* to get away. I took her to see where she would be staying. During her tour of the nursing home, she remained unenthusiastic and apathetic. I told the nursing manager that Mum was ninety-five-percent blind and deaf and could not walk more than a few steps, and that she had a bedsore, which was now less than half an inch long. I didn't want it to get worse after all my hard work helping it to heal.

"Don't worry; we have special cream for that." The nursing manager touched Mum's arm and raised her voice. "We'll take good care of you, Mrs. Wickman. We want you to enjoy your stay with us."

I had thought Mum was taking it well, or, at least, resigned to her fate.

Then everything blew up the night before she was to go to the nursing home. It was like something from Dante's *Inferno*. I put Mum to bed as usual, noting that she was subdued. Then we retired for the night. Peter and I were awakened by Mum calling me in a panic. We hurried to her room to find her upper body hanging out of bed. She was propping herself up by her arms, otherwise, her face would have been on the carpet.

"Mum! What are you doing?" We lifted her back into bed. "Do you want to go to the bathroom?"

"No."

I stayed and stroked her hair. "Are you all right?"

"No."

"What's wrong?"

"I don't want to go in the nursing home!"

"I know you don't, and if there was someone to take care of you while I'm away, you could gladly stay here. But, there isn't anyone. And I have to take a break. It's only for two weeks, Mum. Try to look on it as a holiday for yourself."

She remained quiet and unresponsive. I kissed her good night and followed Peter to bed. Less than an hour later, noises and cries coming from Mum's room had me running through the house. I found her on the floor, having fallen out of bed. She was clutching the curtains, trying to pull herself up off the floor.

"Mum, you've got to stop this."

Her face was flushed. She was hot and sweaty. She didn't respond to me, clearly demented. While I talked soothingly to her, I lifted her into a chair. Peter pulled the mattress off the bed, and laid it on the floor. If she fell off the mattress now, she would not hurt herself.

"Mum, you need to calm down. You'll be fine in the nursing home. You'll meet new people. It won't be bad while I'm away."

I tucked her into bed again and left. We hadn't been in bed more than a few minutes when we heard a crashing sound from Mum's room. We ran in to find Mum struggling underneath the curtains and wooden curtain pole she had pulled down in her attempts to pull herself off the floor. She had a bruise on her forehead. *That's going to look suspicious to the nursing home staff.* Peter picked up the window paraphernalia, hauled it to the spare bedroom, and tossed it inside. With Mum again tucked under the bed covers, I gave her some Aleve, then sat beside her, stroking her hair and humming lullabies. I was numb, my heart in my boots, vacation slipping away. When she finally fell asleep, I dragged myself to bed, hoping to grab a couple of hours sleep.

Next morning, Mum was quiet. She didn't want breakfast, only a cup of tea. She also remembered little of her behavior from the night before and was puzzled as to why she had no curtains in her room.

Around 10:00 a.m., I took Mum to the nursing home and told the nursing manager about her behavior and distress the previous night.

"Your mother may be having a bad reaction to medication," the nursing manager said. "You'll have to take her to the emergency room to be checked before she can stay here."

"What? She's not on any new medication. She's only upset because I'm leaving her here."

"Sorry, but we can't take her without the emergency room giving her the all clear."

Tears welled up in my eyes. My opportunity to take a break was going up in smoke. Angry at the system and at myself for opening my mouth about what had happened the night before, but resigned because I had no choice, I took Mum to the emergency room. Of course, all the tests and examinations revealed no problems. Eight hundred dollars later, and after much checking of the time on the wall clock, fearful we would miss our flight out of Miami, we returned to the nursing home.

I squatted beside her wheelchair. "Mum, try to enjoy yourself. It's only for a short while, and you'll have company here and activities to enjoy."

"All right," Mum said, her voice dull.

I kissed her forehead and left before guilty feelings made me change my mind.

TWENTY-FOUR

We arrived in New Delhi, and Trina met us at the airport. We stayed in New Delhi for two days to spend time with Trina, whom we hadn't seen for five years, and to see some of the sights. It was two days of contrasts. We visited well-tended tourist sites such as Gandhi's tomb, Red Fort, and Chandni Chowk bazaar. And to get there we drove past numerous blue tarpaulin-roofed encampments sprouting higgledy-piggledy like mushrooms under highway overpasses, shelters for the homeless and displaced, looked down upon by residents of nearby modern high-rises. I took it all in my stride, but the twenty-something young man in shorts, showing off his one remaining skinny leg and begging at a road junction where we had stopped, shocked me. Despite Trina's protests not to give to beggars, I found a few rupees and handed them to him.

Trina was happy living in India. She was leading a life of purpose. In her quest to bring education to remote villages, Trina had linked up with Ebamle, described by Trina as "a gutsy lady." Naga women were strong, Trina told us, but Ebamle was exceptionally strong, fighting like a tiger for education for Magulong's children. As per Trina's arrangements for our travels, Ebamle would meet us at Gawahati airport and be our guide on our travels.

We could have flown directly to Dimapur, Nagaland, but I wanted to travel by train from Gawahati to Dimapur to recapture my father's experience during World War II when he was sent, as a corporal in the British Army's Royal Engineers, to build airfields in Assam.

Ebamle in Dimapur, India

On exiting arrivals at Gawahati airport, we found our welcome committee waiting. She was easy to spot, jumping up and down with excitement on recognizing us, the only westerners in the airport. I was surprised to find this strong, gutsy lady was petite, pretty and less than five-feet tall, even shorter than I was.

"Hello, Aunty and Uncle, I am happy to see you. I will take good care of you. Here is my brother. He will take us in his car to the hotel."

We shook hands then tussled with the pair to be allowed to carry our own luggage. They won. We lost.

At the hotel, Ebamle took charge, informing us she would sleep in our room to save money. Needless to say, we were surprised, but Peter had no objection to shapely thirty-six-year-old Ebamle sharing our room.

"Don't worry, Aunty, I will sleep on the floor," she said, my concerns about her comfort dismissed.

With foreheads creased in concentration, we struggled at first to understand Ebamle's thick-accented English. But as the days passed, her English became clearer with practice. I was surprised to discover Nagaland's official language was English, probably left over from the days of British colonialism and also for practical reasons, because each of the seventeen Naga tribes has a different language.

Ebamle commandeered the television remote control, much to Peter's bemusement. For the rest of the afternoon, she was glued to the television, a rare treat for her. We watched several films, drooling over handsome leading men—Ebamle and me—not Peter.

At 6:30, she stood up. "I must go to the railway station to buy our tickets for tomorrow."

"We'll come with you," I said, eager to explore more than the hotel room.

"Oh no, Aunty, it's too dangerous."

"All the more reason for you not to go alone," Peter said.

In the dark evening, we stumbled past small shops and stalls. Apart from the occasional distraction from delicious aromas coming from food stalls that reminded me we had not eaten in a very long time, I was wholly focused was making sure I stepped on secure ground, difficult when the footpath was uneven, full of difficult-to-see holes and mounds of garbage. The last thing I wanted was to sprain or break my ankle. We arrived at the run-down bustling railway station booking hall, the light from fluorescent tubes harsh on our eyes. Several long lines stretched back to the entrance from the counter windows.

"Aunty, this line," Ebamle said, pulling us into line. After speaking to the Indian man behind us, she disappeared to the back of the hall, returning with some forms. "I have to fill in this form, Aunty, to get the tickets." All travelers had to be listed on the form. Peter and I filled in our names while standing in line and handed the form to Ebamle, who wrote down her information. An hour and a half later, we reached the counter. The officious Indian clerk scanned the form and handed it back to Ebamle. He spoke Hindi, which I didn't understand, but his demeanor was clear. He was superior, and Ebamle was a moron.

"What did he say, Ebamle?" I asked.

"Oh, I made a mistake on the form, Aunty. I used a small letter instead of a capital letter for my name. I must fill it out properly. I'll get another form."

She hurried off, and we followed her to the back of the room and once again stood in line. Our feet were aching from standing for hours on the bare concrete floor. Ebamle's tongue protruded as she carefully wrote her name on the new form. Her face was red and sweaty. She unfastened her coat to cool down. Almost two hours later, we arrived at the counter, and the ghastly man again refused to accept the form.

Ebamle shouted at him, shook the form at the window. What could possibly be wrong now? She turned from the counter, panic in her eyes, but her chin set determinedly. She walked round in circles, fists clenched holding the forms to her chest.

"What's going on, Ebamle?"

"I am sorry, Aunty. I am not doing it right." She tossed her head at the clerk. "He says I must write it again."

I studied the line. Other people, Indian people, weren't having trouble. Then it hit me. This was prejudice in action or he wanted a bribe from the westerners. An Indian man, a concerned citizen, tried to help. He was dismayed that our experience at the booking office would mar our impression of India. He spoke to the clerk who refused to listen.

I took hold of Ebamle's arm. "Why won't he serve you?"

She shrugged. "It happens sometimes."

"What happens?"

"Aunty, don't worry. All will be well."

"Ebamle, what happens?"

"Sometimes Indian peoples treat tribal peoples as second class citizens."

Outraged, I shoved my bag at Peter. "Here, take this. I'll sort the jerk out." I tried to snatch the forms off Ebamle. She dodged me. Then I headed for the counter.

Desperate, Ebamle grabbed my sleeve and held me back. She pointed out a policeman standing by the entrance. "I will ask him to help."

She ran over to the tall policeman, who bent low to hear what she was saying. We saw her shaking the forms, the policeman's eyes following her arm as she pointed first to us and then the clerk. He walked with her to counter, went behind it and had words in the high-handed clerk's ear.

Even that did not budge him.

Then the computers crashed.

A groan of despair swept over those waiting in line. The policeman eventually wrung a promise from the clerk that tickets for our reserved seats would be waiting for us at 5:00 the following morning. At that, the policeman was called away to deal with another problem. It had taken three and a half hours to obtain merely the promise of tickets for our five-hour train journey. We waved farewell to our concerned citizen friend.

"Don't worry. All will be well. You will have seats on the Jan Shatabdi Express tomorrow," he reassured us.

We trudged exhausted to the hotel. We were extremely hungry. Not a crumb had passed our lips since breakfast. We were sure the hotel dining room would be closed by the time we reached it, but I couldn't bring myself to try food being sold from a stall. I didn't want to risk getting diarrhea at the start of our journey.

At the Nanden, the receptionist pointed us in the direction of the dining room. "We will take care of your needs."

One table was still occupied. If the weary waiter's heart sank on seeing us walk in, he didn't show it. He led us to a table. We were grateful for his solicitous care after our railway station ordeal. The drably furnished Hotel Nanden went up in our estimation.

Grumpy at being awakened by the shrill alarm clock at some ungodly hour, we returned groggy-eyed to the station. It was so early there wasn't a peep from the sun. The darkness and my cynicism prepared me for the letdown of not having any tickets. But lo and behold, the cheery morning clerk handed Ebamle a bundle of tickets. She gasped with relief, and we were all smiles. Hallelujah! On the platform, we found the concerned citizen with his family. He greeted us like long-lost friends.

A few fluorescent tubes provided dim light on the platform. The only people around were waiting, like us, for the express train. Most women wore colorful saris. Men wore western dress. Families sat on the concrete platform or on their bundles. Some people lay flat out sleeping. Beggars worked their way along the platform, pestering passengers for money. Of course, they made a beeline for us thinking we must have money because we were foreigners. Ebamle completely tuned them out. I was unsympathetic to their plight. They may have had genuine need, but it looked like big business to me as they worked the crowd. Refusals to pay did not deter them. Then a skinny, middle-aged man approached Peter. The man was bare-chested and barefoot. He wore only a *lungyi*. He was blind in one eye, and both his arms had been amputated at the elbow. A plastic carrier bag hung from the longer of his stumps. I wanted to weep at the hardships he was dealing with. Overcome with compassion, Peter's eyes grew moist. He delved into his pockets and stuffed all the rupees he could find into the bag. As the man hobbled away, Peter's eyes followed. Filled with a great sadness, Peter could only shake his head.

The train pulled into the station. Passengers boarded in an orderly manner. There was no need for pushing and shoving. Everyone had a reserved seat on the express. Dawn was breaking as we sped from the station, leaving the grey, litter-ridden built-up area behind. For the next five hours, we would look out of our window and watch rural Assam flash by. At first, I eagerly stared out, nose pressed against the glass to watch alternate splashes of cultivated fields followed by jungle, then, for a change, banana groves, villages of bamboo huts, flooded fields, and swollen rivers from the recent heavy rainfall. After two hours, I was looking for entertainment inside the train. I had gained an impression of what my dad must have experienced, covering this same journey. He had told me that he and 62 Company RE were speculating about where they would end up. It had felt like they were going to the back of beyond. They reached their destination at Dinjan, which was so out in the wilds, they had to create a camp and airfields from virgin jungle.

Throughout our journey, two attendants charged up and down the train with drinks and food, shouting, "Coffee, coffee, coffee," or "Chai, chai, chai." They sold curried chicken samosas, stuffed naan bread and other Indian delights. At first, the only food we dared eat was packets of potato chips. Then we tried the curried chicken samosas. Finding crunchy bits in each mouthful, it felt as if we chewing chicken neck, so it was back to potato chips.

Tired after the previous night's fiasco, we snoozed on and off throughout the trip. Then I asked Ebamle to tell us about herself.

"I have a son, Josiah. He is fourteen. He lost his family, and I adopted him with my sister. He lives mostly in Magulong with my sister and my mother."

"So we will meet him in Magulong," I said.

"Yes."

"What about your family? Do you live in the village?"

"No, but I visit at least four times a year. I must work in the towns to support my family. My father was a headman. He tried to help two villagers come to an agreement over a land dispute. They did not like his decision, so they beat him to death."

"Oh, Ebamle! How old were you when this happened?"

"I was eighteen. I became responsible for supporting the family when I was eighteen. I worked in the fields growing rice. I am also an expert weaver, but now my back aches from the work. At one time, I worked for myself. I would go through the jungle and buy items cheaply, such as cloths, and bring them back to sell at the local market."

"Do you have a boyfriend?" I asked.

"Nooo, Aunty. My chance to marry and have children has gone. I am too old now."

She sounded resigned and sad. But when she began talking about Mount Kisha English School, her eyes sparkled and her voice quickened. "Now I work for the children in the school. They are my life. One time I was headmistress. Educated people in the village take turns being in charge of the school."

At last we arrived in Dimapur. With our restricted area permits checked, stamped, and double checked by the police, we entered Nagaland. Our presence in Dimapur drew curious stares. There probably had not been a sighting of a European since WWII days. A ride in an auto-taxi brought us to the three-star hotel where we were to spend two nights.

The sight of the ensuite bathroom stopped us dead in our tracks. Below faucets and showerhead, orange-brown mineral stains marred the white tile. The turquoise tub was similarly stained. The toilet smelled of stale urine despite the sanitation band across the seat declaring its cleanliness. The three inch wide band of rough caulking around the tub could have been plastered there by a two-year-old with a palette knife. I itched to give the room a good scrub with bleach.

"Pauline, just one time when we go traveling, I would like to stay in some luxury hotels," Peter said.

"Well, this is what you get for coming to the jungle with me," I said with a smile.

Although the bathroom left a lot to be desired, I could cope with its repulsiveness. My ordeal started later that evening. I switched on the bathroom light and pushed the door open just in time to see black cockroaches as big as a man's thumb scuttle across the floor. One hid under the darkness of the door. Its head was in hiding, but its backside stuck out. After seventeen years living in Florida, I was desensitized to large cockroaches, able to take them in my stride.

"Aarrgh!" I yelled and jumped on the bed. "Cockroaches! Cockroaches!"

Ebamle stared at me, her mouth hanging open in amazement.

Peter shouted, "Where?"

Unable to speak, I pointed. He rushed off, shoe in hand. A few thwacks on the floor bashed the cockroach to a pulp. He proudly held it up by its leg and dropped it in the waste basket.

"There were at least two more!" I wailed.

Peter settled back on his bed to continue watching the movie on television. "Didn't see them."

I stood on the bed, agitated, unable to face climbing down in case the deceased roach's friends were waiting for me. Ebamle laughed as I tip-toed into the bathroom in a state of horror.

"It's only a cockroach, Aunty."

Tell it to the marines.

I didn't sleep well that night. Next morning, Ebamle said a cockroach had crawled over her in the middle of the night.

A horrified shiver ran through me. "Didn't it bother you?"

"No. I just brushed it off, Aunty."

Peter was in the bathroom. A few shoe thwacks sounded on the tile floor. He emerged to announce, "Another two bit the dust."

I washed in record time. Forget showering. I wasn't going to be trapped soaking wet and naked in the shower during another roach attack.

The day came to leave Dimapur to travel to Magulong. I couldn't wait. Ebamle spent the night before we left at her cousin's house. She forgot to tell us the Tata Sumo (SUV) taxi would be coming to the hotel at 6:00 a.m. Ebamle's pounding on the door jolted us from sleep. We hurriedly washed, dressed, packed our bags, and rushed to the waiting taxi. The six other passengers in the four-wheel drive vehicle, not understanding a word I was saying, laughed at my profuse apologies, waving their hands as if to say no worries. They cheerfully squished up to make room for us, rare visitors to their area. As we rode along, they quizzed Ebamle about us. Not understanding their language, I could only surmise this from shy glances cast our way followed by torrents of words to Ebamle. But I knew for sure when Ebamle's chest swelled and she drew herself up, she was proudly announcing we were helping her village school. She had status, having been given the important job of caring for Aunty and Uncle.

We jounced and bounced and skidded through the jungle-covered hills, along pot-holed, crumbling, muddy roads. At times, the wheels came so close to the precipice on my side of the vehicle, I gasped in terror. Half the time, I held my breath and closed my eyes in trepidation. White-knuckle driving became the mainstay of our visits to Magulong. One-and-a-half-hour's traveling brought us to the small town of Zalukie, which reminded me of towns in America's Wild West. Here, we would transfer to another Jeep taxi to continue our journey.

We trailed along the high street behind Ebamle in search of town officials to stamp our permits. Failing in that task, she took us to a café where, in the bright sunny morning, we sat outside on the veranda and ordered breakfast of tea and naan bread with a savory stuffing. Two middle-aged men appeared, wearing flip-flops, *lungyis* and padded zipped jackets to keep warm in the cool mountain air. Ebamle went inside the café with them. The men sat at a table with inkpad and official stamp at the ready while they poured over our permits. I watched from the doorway as they shook the permits at Ebamle, and I was troubled by the tone of their voices, first consternation, then warning. Was there a problem? But Ebamle wasn't having any of it. She sweet-talked them into stamping our documents and snatched them up before minds could be changed.

We switched our bags to the Jeep taxi, and off we went. A mile outside of town, the taxi broke down. We all got out and stood around on the road or nipped into the bushes to relieve ourselves. Reggae played on the SUV's radio while the driver raked around in the back of the vehicle. He reemerged with a large rubber band.

My eyes grew wide. My hand covered my mouth. Hardly able to believe what I was seeing, I whispered to Peter, "What's he going to do with that?"

Peter wandered up to the vehicle, had a good look and strolled back. "You'll never guess. He's repairing the gears."

What!

While we waited, Naga passengers laughed and joked together. Ebamle regaled them with such a tale, arms flying in every direction, voice going up and down faster than a trumpeter's valves while her listeners roared with laughter. Some of the Naga women offered us fruit we didn't recognize. They mimed eating, giggled at our tentative tasting of the fruit and beamed, delighted, when we gave the thumbs up.

Repair completed, we piled into the vehicle for the same squashed ride, same terrible roads. I enjoyed listening to the banter between the Nagas, who appeared to have a jovial nature and a great sense of humor. Four hours later, we trundled into Peren and halted at the police post.

The young policeman bent down, looked around the inside of the taxi, singled us out and asked for our papers. "I hope you have not been harassed on your way here."

"No, we've been treated very well," Peter said.

The policeman studied our permits. "Get out, please."

Ebamle said something in Naga, along the lines of "What's the matter? They have permits. What are you doing?"

The policeman asked us to follow him into the police station, and a more senior police officer was called into the room.

He looked at our papers. "Your permit is not in order. You are in Peren district, but Peren is not listed in your permit. Where are you going?"

Ebamle jumped in. "Magulong."

The police chief would not make the decision to give us permission to proceed. We would have to talk to the superintendent of police. The three of us climbed into a jeep with two policemen. As we drove along, Ebamle told them about us sponsoring the school, and that the village had prepared a big feast and was waiting for us. We had to get to Magulong. The policemen were rooting for us to be allowed to continue our journey. Blacktop left behind in Peren, we jolted along a track leading into the hills, bushes and vines closed in on both sides. Were we being taken into the jungle to be shot? Eventually, we arrived at the police superintendent's hilltop office, a single-story, grey, stucco bungalow, perched on the summit of a hill with a commanding view of the surrounding area.

The police officers led us into the police superintendent's office, filing cabinets in the corner, papers stacked on his desk, window overlooking the valley. He was surprisingly tall for a Naga, standing head and shoulders above most Naga men. He was muscular, broad shouldered and oh, so handsome. I was ready to swoon over this gorgeous creature half my age.

He sent for tea, and policemen brought in wooden chairs. We sat and sipped tea while he studied our papers. The police superintendent looked up, flicked our restricted area permits with his fingers, and said in perfect English, "You can go no farther. The papers are incorrect. Peren district is missing from your permits."

Ebamle leapt into action. Determined to get us to the village, she smiled, wheedled, pouted, confronted, demanded and then almost begged. The superintendent winced under her onslaught, but remained firm. "The area is under a security alert. I am sorry, but you can go no farther."

Ebamle was about to launch into further arguments. I touched her firmly on the arm. "Ebamle, this is it. We have to go back."

The superintendent looked down and slowly breathed out. His shoulders visibly relaxed. When he looked up, he was calm but in command. He held out his hand to Peter. "I am very sorry I could not allow you to go on with your journey."

"We understand. Thank you," Peter said.

Ebamle looked at the superintendent, weighing him up. She would not forget this.

Outside, one of the police officers who drove us to the superintendent's office was not impressed with his superior. "Handsome man, chicken heart," was his verdict.

Back at Peren, we removed our backpacks from the roof rack of the taxi where the other passengers had been waiting patiently for us. They were disappointed we were not going with them. Ebamle asked her cousin to phone the village to tell them we would not be coming, and the festivities planned for our arrival needed to be cancelled.

With a sad smile, I waved farewell to our fellow passengers. My body felt heavy with disappointment, as if I were Sisyphus of Greek mythology who was forever compelled to roll a heavy stone up a hill only for it to roll down again before he reached the top. The children had been excited, looking forward to showing us how well they could perform their tribal dances, and we had been looking forward to meeting them. Our journey half way round the world had been for nothing because some bureaucrat had failed to include the new district of Peren on our restricted-area permits. All we could do was promise to return as soon as possible. At sixty-two years of age and

Hanging out in Peren with policemen and their families. This was probably their first experience of meeting a European

growing older by the minute, Peter and I felt we had no time to lose because a trip to Magulong entailed a four-hour hike up a jungle-covered mountain once we reached the end of the road.

A roadside stall, a small shack made of corrugated sheeting, stood next to the police station, its shelves stacked with drinks and snacks, the owner earning a living from travelers in need of refreshment when stopped at the police post. A polite policeman ushered us to plastic chairs in front of the stall and bought us each a soda. He tried, but failed, to find a local official to help us. Apparently, the area was full of security officers, owing to rebel activity and the visit of an important politician. No one dared make a move that would put his job at risk. We sat by the stall for two and a half hours in glorious sunshine, wiling away the time talking to police officers, being plied with drinks from the stallholder, and taking photographs of policemen's and stallholder's children and families.

A young man, Azing, stopped across the road in his SUV. Having seen our European faces, he was curious. On learning we needed a ride back to Dimapur, he jettisoned some of his cargo and offered to take us. Ebamle called ahead to book a hotel room.

"Tell them one without cockroaches," I said.

Another arrival. Another room. Cockroach-free was too much to hope for. Next morning I saw them, two scurrying monsters. Peter was in the shower. I was on my own. Armed with Peter's shoe I chased one down and beat it to death. The other little bugger slunk into an unreachable gap in the woodwork. Still, I had my battered trophy in the corner to show Peter before we left with Ebamle for Dimapur's government offices. Apparently, adding Peren district to our permits could not be done at Dimapur. We would have to go to Kohima, a three-hour drive away. Because we could not reach Kohima before the offices closed, we would leave first thing in the morning. Apparently not. A notice on the wall informed us that government offices do not do interviews on Wednesdays, so it would have to be Thursday; and if we were allowed to add Peren to the permit, it would take at least seven days to receive our papers.

The papers we had only allowed us to remain in Nagaland five more days, not long enough to make the required changes. We had done as much as we could to put things right without success. Dejected in the face of a bureaucratic defeat, it was time to leave Nagaland and return to Gawahati. Ebamle slept in our room on our last night in Dimapur. I woke at 5:00 A.M. Peter snored gently in the twin bed to my left. On my right, Ebamle was lying on the floor beside my bed, awake, staring into space, her eyes despondent, her mouth turned down.

"Good morning, Ebamle."

"Oh, Aunty, I am so sorry. It is my fault it did not work out as you planned."

"It's nobody's fault, Ebamle. If we were meant to go to the village, we would be there. It wasn't meant to be. Why are you awake so early?"

"I am sad that you are leaving."

"I'm sad too. What will you do when we go?"

"There might be work in Haflong, so I will go there."

"What would you like to do with your life, Ebamle?" I asked, thinking she would want Prince Charming to come along on a white charger to rescue her. Her reply surprised me.

"I want to open a hostel, Aunty. Naga children can only be educated to fifth grade in the villages. Parents who want their children to have secondary education must send them to the towns where they stay in hostels. I want a hostel to care for the children, the younger children. The older children can be too much trouble. I have a friend who has a hostel. He tells me to start one, too."

"Does it cost a lot to open a hostel?"

"I have calculated I will need eighty thousand rupees (less than $2,000). I have even found the house I want to rent. The owner wants twenty thousand rupees security deposit and five thousand rupees rent a month. I will get the benches, tables, and beds made in Magulong because that is cheaper than buying them in Dimapur. But it so hard to save the money, Aunty. Nobody helps me. Nobody helps me. It is only a dream."

Ebamle's plaintive words struck a chord in my heart and opened the emotional cesspit left over from those difficult times when I was a poverty-stricken, single parent. I wanted to help her.

"Trina tells me you spend your money on Magulong students."

Ebamle smiled and blushed, giving an embarrassed shrug. "Yes, I do. Too much." Then her face became sad and serious. She looked down at the cloth covering her and picked at its corner. "It's so hard on my own, Aunty."

I squeezed her shoulder and vowed to talk to Peter about lending Ebamle the money to start her hostel.

After breakfast, I phoned the Nanden Hotel to reserve our room.

"You need a room for three nights?" the receptionist asked.

"Yes, possibly longer."

The rustle of pages being turned came across the line.

"You have our key!"

"Yes, we do," I said, laughing at his headmaster's tone. "We'll return it tonight as soon as we arrive."

Both Ebamle and I were in tears at parting. In just a few days, we had forged a deep bond. She had battled for us, boasted about us, done her best to protect us. She loved us for helping her village. We had fallen in love with her courage and her fearless heart.

"We'll return soon, Ebamle," I called, as the train pulled out of the station.

The Nanden Hotel bellboy led the way to a refurbished room that was clean and attractive. We had eight days to fill before our flight to New Delhi but were not sure how many of them would be spent at the Nanden. We discussed the possibility of exploring Shillong or Tezpur or Manas Wildlife Sanctuary but felt it would take too much effort. We were exhausted, had been since long before leaving Florida. Perhaps we should just rest in Gawahati. So we did. For eight days. A luxury. After breakfast, we strolled for at least an hour in the heat and humidity along the busy road outside the hotel where cars, taxis, tuk-tuks, rickshaws, motorcycles and bicycles competed for space. We passed furniture stores, beauty parlors, gas stations, but we made a point of calling into the ice cream shop for a cooling ice cream cone on our return journey. We snoozed, read books, watched movies on TV and news broadcasts on satellite television. The waiter in the bar pampered us. Before we could sit down, he was making his way towards us with a Kingfisher, Peter's favorite Indian beer, and a Bikini Girl for me that resembled the kind of tropical rum and fruit juice punch found in the Caribbean.

On our return to Florida, I emailed Trina to ask her advice about giving Ebamle the money to start the hostel. Trina felt Ebamle was hungry enough to work hard for success. She encouraged us to help. So we did. After eleven days in India and Nagaland, seeing the poverty and hardship, I was filled with gratitude for the life we had. We are not wealthy, not even comfortable by American standards. Basically, we were a couple of paychecks away from financial problems, but with some belt-tightening, we gave Ebamle a new start in life.

TWENTY-FIVE

Unable to bear the thought of Mum's misery, I hurried to collect her from the nursing home as soon as we arrived home. I knew from experience how horrible it was to be in a situation where you felt powerless to change things. I kissed her head. "Hello, Mum. Ready to come home?"

"Oh, am I glad to see you!" she said, clutching my hands as a drowning man would clutch a straw.

"I'm glad to see you too, Mum." To my surprise, I meant it. I hugged her hard. "Let's get you home."

"Oh, yes, please. Take me home. I don't like it here."

I gathered Mum's clothes, thanked the nursing manager and wheeled Mum from the facility.

"Don't worry about it anymore. You'll never come back to a place like this."

A week later, Peter came in from work early. His tight jaw and fearful expression caught my attention.

"Are you all right?" I asked.

"I've been laid off." From the way he said this, you would have thought he's been asked to dig his own grave.

I laughed, delighted. Peter had been the general manager's whipping boy for several years, ever since the man arrived to run the country club. It was a clash of personalities. I'd been telling Peter to quit for months, but fear of not being able to find another job at his age, or how we would cope without his wages, made him stick in his miserable situation. Now it had been taken out of his hands.

Peter flopped down in a chair and stared at me wide-eyed. "What are we going to do?"

"We'll manage."

"I'm sixty-two. I may never work again, not in this economy."

It was the early years of America's Great Recession. My daughter had also fallen on hard times. We were helping her to the tune of $1,500 a month so she wouldn't lose her house.

"Peter, it will work out. We'll have to do some economizing, but we'll be okay," I said, as I quickly calculated that if Peter failed to find another job, we would be down $250,000 in lost income just before our retirement. My dreams of how I wanted our retirement to be floated out the window. Less dining out, fewer treats and trips. So be it.

Peter dismissed my optimism. "What if we lose the house? What will we do?"

"Peter, we've been very careful with our money. We have savings. We won't lose the house, but if we do, you have to remember a house is just a place for shelter. If we lose it, we can move into a tent and still have shelter. It wouldn't bother me."

The first painful task was to tell Jackie we could no longer help her financially. Sadly, this led to bankruptcy proceedings for her. Difficult to go through, but she and Gordon survived, wiser and stronger. We reduced our monthly bills, cutting down on cable television, finding less expensive house and car insurances, and not renewing our cell phone service. We also ate cheaper foods and stayed at home, which all together reduced our monthly outlay by two hundred dollars.

Less than a week after Peter was laid off, a starving, calico cat strolled up our drive. As Peter adores cats, I recognized this as a sign that all would be well. We took her in. Six months later, as homes all around us went into foreclosure, and people left their pets behind when they moved, we were adopted by five more skinny cats. All would definitely be well.

With the economy crumbling, people were cutting back on unnecessary expenses, yet my massage practice unexpectedly grew. Through a word of mouth referral, I received a call from a wealthy, elderly couple who employed me to give them massages three times a week, a definite boost to our income. Joy-filled gratefulness flooded my whole being. My mother could not be left alone. If she felt alone, she started calling for help. I always responded to her calls. I did not want her feeling insecure. With Peter unemployed and willing and able to prepare her meals and change her diapers, I could take on the extra massage work.

We adjusted to our tight budget, and before we knew it, Christmas 2009 was upon us. The care giver for my wealthy, elderly clients took a vacation to see family in the Philippines. Peter stepped in to care for the couple for six weeks. Again, we juggled my massage appointments with Peter's work schedule, so Mum was not left alone.

Another of my massage clients, Jerrie, was the same age as my mother. Because she had been an American Navy nurse during WWII, she had read my book about my father's wartime adventures and had spent time with us during holiday get-togethers. Determined not to spend Christmas alone, Jerrie booked into a nursing home that was offering a four-day Christmas festivities get-away. Learning that Peter would be working as a care giver on Christmas Day, she invited me and Mum to join her for Christmas lunch. Reminiscing about the good old days came to an end when Jerrie indicated she wanted to go and join in the fun and games organized by the nursing home.

I drove Mum home and stopped on the driveway to help her into her wheelchair to take her indoors. I lifted her down from my SUV and tried to guide her to the wheelchair's seat, only I couldn't lift her high enough. Another two inches was all I needed, but I hadn't the strength in my arms.

"Mum, I'm going to have to lower you to the ground until I get some strength back in my arms."

"No! Don't put me on the ground!"

"I've got no choice. I can't hold you up forever. I need to work out how to do this." I lowered Mum gently to the concrete.

All the while she was screeching in my ear, "Help! Get me up! Eek! Eek!"

I sat down next to her to weigh up our situation. The place was deserted. All our neighbors appeared to be elsewhere. I stood up.

"Don't leave me!"

"I'm just going into the garage to see what I can find to help us."

I brought a low stool outside and placed it behind my mother. "Right, Mum, I'm going to lift your bony bottom off this cold concrete and sit you on the stool."

"Thank God for that!"

I pulled her up and deposited her on the stool. After parking the wheelchair behind her, I started swinging my arms to get the circulation going. "Next step is to get you into the wheelchair."

"Come on, hurry up! I'm getting cold!"

"Stop complaining, woman. Okay, I'm ready. Let's do it."

I took a deep breath and lifted her back toward her chair. It was touch and go, but Mum managed to wriggle on once I deposited her on the edge of the seat.

"I never would have thought we'd spend Christmas Day rolling round on the drive," I said, laughing.

"It's not funny!"

"You're right, Mum, but no harm done. We need a glass of sherry to calm our nerves."

"That would be lovely, followed by a cup of tea. You don't get a good cup of tea in America, do you?"

With Mum safely ensconced in her room and the car put away, I handed her a glass of sherry. I sat on Mum's bed and lifted my pretty crystal glass in a toast. "Merry Christmas, Mum."

She lifted her glass. "Merry Christmas."

"Have you seen anything of Dad lately?" I asked.

"No, only children. Spirit children."

"Are they happy or sad?"

"Happy. They come into my room and play games like hop-scotch."

When death draws near, people sometimes see spirit beings. We had been expecting Mum to die for some time, only she kept fooling us. She was afraid to let go of the earthly life she knew and step into the unknown, fearing the loss of control.

"Do you think your dad will be waiting for me when I die?"

"Yes, of course he will."

"I said some harsh things to him when he was alive."

Mum must have been fearful if she was opening up to me like this.

"Mum, I won't beat around the bush. If you had spoken to me like you spoke to Dad in his later years, I wouldn't be at the Pearly Gates to meet you."

She glanced at me and then away. "I was only trying to gee him up. He was in a slump."

"Whatever you were doing, Dad loves you, has for over seventy years. Now he's up there and not restricted by his physical body, he can see the whole picture. He knows you only had his best interests at heart. Never fear, he'll be waiting for you. I'll make that cup of tea now."

It looked like the time for her passing would soon arrive. My load felt a little lighter. I was becoming increasingly concerned about my failing strength and the fact that it looked as if Mum would outlast me. I was running on empty. Sucked dry. What would happen to her if I went first? Who would take care of her?

I needn't have distressed myself. A Higher Power had matters in hand. Three weeks after Christmas, Mum had her final stroke.

The hospital doctor gave me the bad news. Mum's stroke had incapacitated the nerves that helped her to swallow. Consequently, for the rest of her life she would have to be fed by tube. "You need to think about how she is to be cared for, possibly put her in a nursing home."

Filled with horror at the picture that conjured up, I jumped to my feet. "Mum wouldn't want to live like that! What kind of life would it be? She's deaf, blind, can't walk. She'd spend the rest of her days lying in bed, lonely and isolated, being fed through a tube. She would hate that!"

"Does she have a living will?" he asked, kindly.

"Yes, at least, I think so. I'll have to search for it. Probably in the mess of papers on my coffee table."

"Bring it in tomorrow, think about what I've said, then we'll discuss things further."

After he'd gone, I sat by Mum's bed, deep in thought, brushing away unstoppable tears. Did she sign a living will? We talked about it after Dad died. I remember placing the papers in front of her to sign. Did she? She wasn't keen. She either didn't want to think about her death, or she didn't trust me.

The patient sharing the room with my mother, a woman in her early thirties, started crying behind the privacy curtain. She had been talking on the phone for over an hour, trying to find a rehab clinic to accept her. When the phone calls stopped, I assumed she had been successful. Now she was crying. I wiped away my tears. I hesitated, not wanting to intrude, but couldn't ignore her distress.

Putting my head round the curtain, I asked, "Would you like a hug?" and opened my arms.

She fell into them and sobbed on my shoulder.

"Are you all right? Do you have anyone to help you?"

"I'm going to help me. I found a place to take me. I'm waiting to hear from my insurance company to see if they'll pay for my treatment. I've got to get well so I can get my kids back."

We stood close, my arms wrapped round her, until her tears stopped.

"You'll do it," I told her. "You're strong, and you know your children need you. You'll come through this."

She nodded and stepped back. "As soon as I hear from my insurance, I'll be out of here."

I patted her shoulder and made a move to Mum's side of the curtain.

"Wait!" The young woman touched my arm. "Is it your mother in there?"

"Yes, she's had a stroke."

"I heard her talking last night. Not like when she struggles to talk to you, but clear as could be. She said, 'I want to come home, Norman. I don't want to stay here any longer. I want to come home to you.'"

My voice a whisper, my eyes full of tears, I said, "Thank you. You don't know how much I needed to hear that."

I returned to Mum's bedside and sat stroking her hand.

Her first words when she awoke were, "Get me out of here." The distorted words, formed through paralyzed lips, were difficult to understand.

"Sorry, Mum, you're stuck here for now. The stroke has damaged the nerve to your throat. You can't swallow. You'll never be able to eat properly again. You can only be fed through tubes. I've got to figure out how to look after you."

Mum stared at me, struggling to comprehend. She shrank into the covers. Her bottom lip quivered. Her brain may have been wrecked, but her mind was still sharp. With her undamaged hand, she groped for my hand and squeezed hard to make sure she had my full attention. Lifting her head, she pleaded, "Don't put me in a home." Exhausted by the effort to speak, she fell back on her pillow and closed her eyes.

The young woman came from behind the curtain. "My taxi's here." She saw my distress. "Are you all right?"

I shook my head.

She put her arm round my shoulder. "Isn't she going to pull through?'

Again, I shook my head.

"I'm so sorry," she said.

I found my voice. "She's old. I've been expecting her to die for some time, but I hoped it would be peaceful like falling asleep in her chair, not inch by inch like this."

"No, not like this. I'm sorry. Good luck."

"Hey, you too. Get clean for a new life with your kids."

And the young woman left on her way to a new beginning.

I phoned Jackie and told her to come to the hospital when she finished work. Gran was not doing well. I also called Joan in Australia to warn her to expect the inevitable. Then I went for something to eat and a thoughtful walk. Jackie and Gordon were sitting by Mum's bed when I returned to the hospital.

Gordon stood and ushered me to his seat. "You look as if you're taking things hard."

"Her needs have been dominating my life for the past three years, Gordon. There'll be a bloody big hole when she goes."

Jackie began crying. I reached across the bed to hold her hand.

"This is really the end then?" Gordon asked.

"Yes, she can't swallow anymore, and keeping her alive, being fed through a tube into her stomach, isn't the way she would want to end her days."

Jackie pulled her eyes away from her grandmother to stare at me. "She could be kept alive?"

"In a nursing home, yes, feeling alone, isolated, imprisoned by her physical body. Is that what you want for her?" I said, knowing Jackie was having difficulty in letting her grandmother go.

Jackie shook her head and resumed crying.

Mum opened her eyes. Her hand scrambled for Jackie's. "Not in a home," she slurred. "Not in a home."

"You're all right, Gran. We're here," Jackie said, looking to me for help.

"Don't get upset, Mum. I'll take care of you."

Jackie stroked Mum's scrawny hand. "I love you, Gran. The doctors are doing their best. Everything will work out right."

Comforted, Mum closed her eyes.

Next day, sitting by Mum's bedside, as I was thinking how thin she had become in the past few days, her doctor entered the room.

"Good afternoon." He looked at Mum and studied her chart. "Have you given any more thought about what is to happen to your mother?"

"She wouldn't want to be kept alive in a nursing home."

"Did you ever find her living will?"

"Oh, yes! Just this morning!" I pulled it from my purse.

The doctor scanned the document. "Shall I call hospice to come and evaluate her for admittance?"

My hand flew to cover my mouth to stifle my cry of relief. All I could do was nod.

The doctor patted my shoulder. "I'll make the call," he said and left.

Thank you, God, for a wise and compassionate doctor.

I met Jackie, Gordon and the grandkids at hospice. After the staff had Mum drugged and tucked in bed, we went in to see her. This woman, whose inner strength had always made her seem so big despite her small frame, was now so emaciated she barely made a bump under the bedclothes. In the hallway, I asked the nurse if it would be a long wait for Mum to die.

"Looking at her, I would say it won't happen for at least a few days, so don't feel as if you can't leave her bedside," she replied.

I relayed this to the family.

Sarah said, "My boss said I can take whatever time off I need to be here."

Donna said, "Mine did, too."

"It's Gran's birthday on Thursday. Will she still be alive then?" Jackie asked.

"I'm not sure. If she is, we'll have a cake and a party for her. Ninety-one years on the planet is something to celebrate, and knowing your gran, she'll hang around for that."

The next morning, I went to hospice. Knowing that hearing was the last sense to go in end-of-life patients, I talked to Mum, told her not to be afraid. The next world would be a wonderful place. "You'll be free of your damaged body and crippled knees. You'll return to your prime. You'll dance with Dad again, ride your bicycle, go for long walks in the bluebell woods and have all the fun you've been missing. You'll see your parents, your brothers and sisters. You'll no longer feel sad and alone at being the last of your generation left alive. You'll be the newcomer, the baby in the spirit world. And they'll be lined up to welcome you. You'll never feel cold again. You can use your thoughts to create your new world. You can live in a rose-covered cottage if that's what you want. You can travel at the blink of an eye. You'll be able to come back and visit us, watch over us or clear off to do your own thing, whatever you want to do. There's nothing to fear. It will be so good."

I spent the following day the same way, reassuring Mum about the transformation that lay ahead. I felt okay with everything. Mum was not suffering as she awaited her release. I had done her a kindness by choosing hospice death over a nursing home existence.

Jackie and the family met me and Peter Thursday afternoon for Mum's ninety-first birthday party. We arrived with a cake and a pot of hyacinths so Mum could enjoy their fragrance. Peter carried a heavy bag containing Mum's photograph albums.

Sarah said, "I bet you wish you could see your cake, Gran; it's beautiful, decorated with purple violets."

"Because her middle name is Violet," I told Sarah.

Donna said, "Can you smell the flowers, Gran? It smells lovely in here. They're filling the room with their scent."

Subdued, Rebecca sat and stroked her great-grandmother's hand. These were her first experiences with the deaths of people she loved, and she was still grieving from the loss of my father. Grandson, Christopher, understood that his great-grandmother was getting ready to go to heaven to be with Great-Granddad Norman, but apart from that, he was not upset at being part of the family farewell process. Christopher loved Gran. She had always produced candy or cookies for him when he visited her.

Jackie and Gordon kissed Mum's cheek and said hello. After some chitchat, I brought out paper plates and plastic forks and led the family in singing "Happy Birthday." Peter took photographs of Jackie cutting the cake, while I gave a running commentary to Mum.

"I'll blow the candles out for you, Mum. Pity you can't have any cake, you would have liked it. It's red velvet," I told her. "Don't worry, we'll eat your share."

Peter took more photographs to send to Joan. I hesitated to do that. Mum had deteriorated so much, perhaps it was better for Joan to remember Mum as she was four years earlier when Joan had come to Florida.

I spread the photo albums across the bottom of Mum's bed. "Choose which photos you'd like," I told the family. "Don't fight over them. We can always get copies made."

There were three large metal tins and a dozen albums filled with seventy years of Mum and Dad's life together. The family pored over the images while I told the stories behind them. Sarah sat up straight and asked, "Who's Wilhelm? Wilhelm's here, in this room. I don't know who he is. I've never heard the name before."

Peter and I looked at one another.

"Wilhelm was your Swedish great-great-grandfather, my father's father," I said. "I guess he's come to help Gran make her transition. He always had a soft spot for her. Here, let me show you some photos of him." I turned to Mum and raised my voice as she was no longer wearing her hearing aids. "Did you hear that, Mum? Pop's here. He'll be waiting for you when you pluck up the courage to take the plunge."

We poured over photographs of Gran and Granddad smiling and laughing their way across Europe on their vacations—on the beaches in Spain, and in Majorca, and eating and drinking at an open-air restaurant in Brussels. I included Mum in discussions about their fun-filled travels, reminding her of all the good times she and Dad had shared. A lump formed in my throat. *The pair of you certainly knew how to enjoy life.*

When I'd been a working, single mother, Mum and Dad had taken Jackie along on their vacations. Jackie was looking at pictures of herself riding a miniature steam train, riding on a carousel with my dad and eating fish and chips with my parents on the seafront at Whitby. Jackie looked up, caught my eye, and we both burst into tears. Before long, everyone's eyelashes were damp.

As the days passed, Mum was reduced to skin and bone, like a Holocaust concentration-camp prisoner. Nurses came to turn her form.

"How much longer will she last?" I succeeded in keeping my voice on an even keel, even though I wanted to scream.

"I don't see any signs to suggest her time is imminent. Perhaps several more days. It's sometimes hard to say. I feel as if your mother is fighting to stay here."

I felt the blood drain from my face at her words. After the nurses left, I climbed onto the bed, heartbroken. I lay beside my mother, and stroked her hair. I felt sure I had done the right thing by Mum, but what if I was wrong? What if Mum wanted to stay alive? Was it too late to turn things around?

"Mum, don't be afraid to go. I know you are because you can't control it, can you? Dying is a natural process. Everyone must die, just as everyone must be born. Think of life here as being the same as growing in the womb. When you die, instead of being pushed through the birth canal, you will be pulled through a tunnel of light to be born again in heaven. A whole new world will open up for you. It will be wonderful, Mum. No need to cling to this world."

I wept. I'd played God. Made the decision she should die not live. Who was I to do that? Dear God, forgive me.

Saturday and Sunday were family gathering days in Mum's hospice room—and still she clung to life with dogged determination. A day or two the nurses told us. I didn't know how Mum kept going. No water or food for six days and still, she would not let go.

With no middle-of-the-night phone call from hospice, I visited Mum on Monday morning. She was little more than a skeleton covered with skin. How could she keep on breathing? I sat and talked to her, sang songs from her favorite shows, stroked her cheeks and hair, and crying, I begged her, "Let go, Mum. Let go."

I lay beside her, stroking her hair, and humming and singing for hours. When Jackie and family arrived that evening, I was emotionally exhausted. The nurses came to turn Mum.

"Her color is changing. It won't be long," they told us.

Yet we returned home that night with Mum still breathing.

At 2:00 in the morning, hospice phoned. Mum had finally let go. I called Joan and left a message on her answering machine. Then I called Jackie, and everyone went to Mum's room. The nurses had washed and prepared Mum's body, which lay, as asleep, in bed. Classical background music was playing. The lighting was dimmed. A vase of pink and purple tulips interspersed with white lilies stood by her bed. Peter and I were pleased with the nurses' efforts to create a soothing environment for our farewells.

We cried and sobbed our last goodbyes. I was grief-stricken but relieved. It had been a test of endurance, waiting for her to breathe her last. My friends didn't understand why I wasn't happy at being set free from the burden of Mum's care. But I wasn't free. My heart was heavy, weighed down by the feeling I had wounded my soul for deciding to end her life in hospice. If Mum had died within a couple of days of entering hospice, I would have been fine. But to linger . . . for *eight days!* In my head, I still felt I had made the right decision, hospice rather than nursing home, but I found it impossible to reconcile that logic with the feelings in my heart.

Some weeks later, standing at the kitchen sink, absentmindedly washing dishes, looking through the window at the garden, a vision of majestic, snow-covered mountains appeared. Hearing rustling by my feet, I looked down and saw a worm wriggling among dry, autumn leaves. I looked up, bewildered and saw her, my mother, slim, face wrinkle-free, a 1940s hairstyle and dress, a young woman in her prime. She was at the end of the breakfast bar, holding a bicycle. I sensed rather than saw my father behind her. Through the visions, she was showing me she was free of her physical restrictions. All was well.

She communicated telepathically: "Thank you for having the courage to make the decision you did. I know you're upset at how I clung to life in hospice. I was afraid to leave the world I knew. I didn't believe you when you said it would be wonderful when I died. But, you were right. It is wonderful here. I can see. I can hear. I can ride a bicycle and dance with your father."

Tears gushed down my face like waterfalls. Then she asked me to forgive her.

"No, I won't forgive you. There's nothing to forgive. I knew what I was taking on, and I knew you'd be a pain in the neck. You are who you are, and I accept you as you are. Forgiveness is not required."

She paused, hesitating. "Then will you accept an apology?"

I considered, and laughed through my tears. "Yes, because you really were a pain to deal with, Mum. Apology accepted."

"Pauline, I know you are thinking of giving up writing. I won't offer advice—you never listened to me anyway. I'll only tell you that you are like the Little Engine That Could. Once you set your mind to something, you do it. I'm going now. I just wanted you to know I'm alive and well with your father. Don't be upset."

With that, she faded away.

Soon after, I dreamt of a kitten that had been torn to shreds. Bits and pieces, limbs and clumps of bloody flesh, lay around the kitten's head, which was the only part of the animal intact. I was stroking the kitten's head, and all the while, it was purring and looking at me in adoration as if I were its savior. A healing dream. The kitten was me, in bits and pieces, torn to shreds, the message being that as long as I had a head and a heart, loved and cared for myself, I would be all right.

TWENTY-SIX

Peter and I struggled to recover from the stress of caring for Mum. Mentally, physically and emotionally, we were numb, nothing but empty vessels. After five months, we drummed up the energy to sort out her belongings and paint her room, returning it to guest-bedroom status. Four months later, we again rearranged our living conditions when Granddaughter, Donna, with her two-year-old son Thomas, moved in with us after her marriage fell apart. They lived with us for fifteen months, until healed from the hurt of the break-up. We considered ourselves lucky to be able to help and to have such close involvement with a great grandchild. Such an opportunity doesn't happen often.

In their letters, pupils of Mount Kisha English School again begged us to visit so they could perform their tribal dances for us. We felt too exhausted to consider it, and besides, with Peter unemployed, money was tight. Then a year after Mum died, I dreamt we were on our way to Magulong. We were climbing a steep slope. For some reason, I couldn't make my legs work. I was too tired to go on. In the dream, young people from the village came to help us because night was fast approaching, and we needed to get out of the forest and into the village before dark. They pushed my bottom, pulled my arms, lifted my legs over obstacles, and got me to the village gate.

I told Peter about the dream. "I think we're going to Magulong soon."

Ten months later, we traveled to India. Donna, still living with us, took care of the cats, promising to prevent Thomas from teasing them too much while we were away. Ebamle met us at Dimapur airport. We hugged and hugged. It was hard to let go. She wanted us to see her hostel, which was successfully providing her with an income. She had seventeen residents, nine girls and eight boys. After dropping our luggage off at the hotel, a different one to the cockroach-filled hotel of our first trip, thank goodness, we caught a tuk-tuk to Ebamle's hostel. It was in a large four-story building, most of which was divided into apartments. Ebamle's hostel, The Almond Academy, took up a whole wing of the second floor. She proudly showed us round its six rooms and two bathrooms. The boys' room was packed with four bunk beds. The girls' room contained three bunk beds and twin beds. The floors were bare concrete. Ebamle had bought a solar powered battery for the television and lighting she had installed. While we drank tea in the kitchen, the children trickled home from school. They ranged in age from nine to thirteen, except for one youngster of four. Ebamle led us into the living room, full of children watching television.

"Hey, everyone, this is Aunty and Uncle. They have come all the way from America to see us."

I waved. "Hello, everyone."

They were all smiles, even managing to pull themselves away from the television program of NCIS Los Angeles to say hello.

While Ebamle prepared the evening meal, I studied the children's drawings on the wall and the daily timetable.

"Ohmygod! Ebamle, say this isn't so!"

Ebamle came running. "What is it, Aunty?"

"You start your day at 4:30 a.m?" I said incredulously, looking round at the children.

They giggled at my horror.

"Too early for you, Aunty?"

"Much too early."

We dined with the children, a meal of sticky rice, salad, dried fish, and lentil stew.

"Aunty and Uncle have brought a present for you," Ebamle told the children. "Can I give it to them, Aunty?"

"Yes, of course."

She brought Peter's good-as-new Spanish guitar into the room to gasps of surprise from the children and gave it to one of the boys. The children left the kitchen, returning to the television or their rooms to practice playing the guitar.

"Soon, they will put on a show for you," Ebamle said, "and now they are happy. They have another guitar to share."

We wandered into the living room. Ebamle was still in the kitchen.

"Okay," I said, "Ebamle is not here. Is there anything you are not happy with at the hostel?"

A chorus replied, "Oh no, Aunty. We love it here."

I smiled, delighted. Ebamle was doing a good job.

The show began with some heartily sung hymns, all the children being blissful Baptists. Then, while two boys played guitar, another boy showed his prowess at modern dancing using great muscle control. I half expected him to end with a moon walk. Next came country and western songs, very popular with the group. A girl sang a traditional Naga song, another read a poem she had written.

We applauded loudly. They deserved it, having worked hard to welcome and honor us in this way. We took photographs of everyone and then Ebamle shooed them off to bed.

Alone with Ebamle, I said, "The children are very happy here."

"It is hard work, Aunty, but I am very happy, too, even though I have not had any new clothes for four years."

"What's with the little boy?"

"Oh, his parents work away, and he was causing so much trouble and naughtiness at the hostel for younger children, his parents begged me to take him."

"He was fine, tonight," Peter said.

"When he first came, he was a handful, but he is a good boy now," said Ebamle.

"Are all the children paying residents, Ebamle?" I asked.

She looked down, flushed with embarrassment at being caught out.

"Not all, Aunty."

I patted her shoulder and laughed. "That doesn't surprise me. That's why I asked. But you must make sure you get enough paying people to keep the hostel going."

She nodded.

"I also see you don't have a washing machine or refrigerator." I looked at Peter over Ebamle's head. "We'll have to do something about that."

With Ebamle subsidizing half-a-dozen bright children from Magulong, who would otherwise not receive a secondary education because their parents were too poor to pay hostel fees, it didn't surprise me she was doing without essential appliances.

We set out from Dimapur at 4:30 a.m. for the long journey to Magulong. With us in the SUV were Ebamle, Stephen Disuang, a twenty-eight year-old officer on Manipur State's Student Council, Josiah, Ebamle's eighteen-year-old adopted son, and a couple of young Naga men. In a bid to encourage tourism to the area, the government of Nagaland no longer required visitors to have restricted-area permits.

Six hours later, we stopped for lunch in a small village, parking in front of a large wooden house which turned out to be a restaurant called the Rice Hotel. We unfurled from our cramped space and stretched our legs. Looking round the village, I noticed a poster on a clinic wall encouraging parents to vaccinate their children against measles. It was a pretty, rural village, with unpaved roads and colorful flowers tumbling over garden fences. Peter's eye lit up when he saw a small kiosk-style store selling, amongst other things, lots of candy. Trina had suggested we take our own food, such as food bars, nuts and packets of soup-mix, in case we couldn't eat Naga food, which is full of hot chilies. Because we like curry, we figured we would be fine with the food. We'd had no problem eating the food Ebamle prepared for us.

Ebamle went inside to organize our meal. Gentle and solicitous Stephen indicated we should go ahead of him. We sat on benches at tables covered with blue-checked oil cloths.

Ebamle stood up. "Come Aunty, Uncle, get some food."

She led us to a counter holding large aluminum pots containing sticky rice, well-cooked mustard greens, pork stew, a chicken curry, and a dish of hot pickles. A clear plastic jug held water. Stephen, Josiah and the young Naga men traveling with us had already filled their plates and were eating outside on the veranda. Peter and I loaded up our plates and sat down. We studied the food and looked at each other.

"Looks okay," I said.

Peter said, "Of course, it is. Tuck in."

So I tucked into my second Naga meal of sticky rice, mustard greens, a hot pickle, and a pork stew (the pork being more fat and skin attached to miniscule pieces of meat). My lips felt as if I had sucked a hot coal. "Ohmygod!" Tears streamed down my face. I frantically fanned my tingling lips, grabbed my glass of water and gulped it down, trying to put out the fire. Ebamle started laughing so loudly, Stephen looked in. She said something to him in Naga which was met by his raucous laughter. Trying not to laugh, Peter put his pickle to the edge of his plate.

On exiting the restaurant, Peter strode over to the kiosk, eager to see what candy they had for his sweet tooth. He succeeded in stuffing his pockets with goodies before we left.

We continued our journey over more crumbling roads, backsides sliding left then right as we sailed round hairpin bends, wheels almost hanging over the steep precipices. The driver was not engaging lower gears often enough for our comfort. Our clenched jaws felt painful. Our terror-stricken hearts thumped so much when the driver did not have sufficient gear control of the vehicle that we could see our rib cages moving. Peter and I held hands tightly, attempting to reassure one another. After four fearful, exhausting hours, we ran out of road and came to a stop.

Stephen looked around. There was no one to be seen. He spoke in Naga, but we could tell he was angry. He got out of the vehicle and marched off.

"What's going on, Ebamle?"

"There should be bulldozers here, extending the road to the village. We have paid them to do that, yet they are not here."

We waited twenty minutes for Stephen to return, and when he did, his face was tight. A vein pulsed in his neck. He spoke angrily to Ebamle and Josiah, waving his arms, pointing back to where he had come from.

As we unloaded our bags and put them in a pile to be picked up later by youths from Magulong, Ebamle told us, "Stephen is angry. The contractors left our job to work on a side job for nearby villagers."

Just then three young Naga men, wearing jeans and tee-shirts, and one with a red bandana on his head, stepped from the jungle. They carried rifles and a dead wild boar hanging from a pole. Stephen greeted them and walked over. The men lowered the boar to the ground. Ebamle, Josiah and the Naga men who had traveled with us strolled over to see the trophy. Squatting down, Stephen examined the neat red bullet hole on the boar's shoulder. Stephen looked up at them and praised their marksmanship. We couldn't understand the words spoken. We could only guess by tone of voice and gestures. Curiosity got the better of me and Peter, and we wandered over to take a look. It was a clean kill. One neat hole. The first bullet wound I had ever seen. Nodding toward us, one hunter asked who we were. Stephen must have told him we were going up the mountain to Magulong. The man pulled out his machete, and began slashing at a stand of bamboo, returning with bamboo staffs to help us with our climb.

The trail to Magulong

We made our way, slipping and sliding, down a steep, rocky path to a narrow boulder-strewn river where we gingerly inched across a three-bamboos-tied-together bridge with a handrail for balance. We rested at the fishing camp on the far side, used by all passers-by. Sardine-sized fish and a frog were smoking on the fire. The fisherman who had caught them was nowhere in sight. Stephen offered me some dried fish, which I found to be tasty. He pointed out dried fish in baskets tied to the roof, and covered bamboo containers beside the fire, which he said contained intestines. I was relieved he didn't offer me a taste.

From the camp, we climbed a steep, stony path. The walk to Magulong, Stephen told us, should take us three hours. Young Nagas, even carrying heavy loads, could do it in two. After three hours of constantly climbing inclines, most of them gentle, my legs began to weaken. I couldn't make my leg muscles work. My body was screaming for electrolytes, and my salty snacks were in our bag being carried by a young Naga man who had overtaken us an hour before. I had to take frequent rests, which meant we would not arrive at Magulong before nightfall.

Stephen was very patient and encouraging even when I needed to rest yet again. It was just as well. He spotted bloodstains on my jeans and Peter's sock where leeches were feasting on our blood. After relieving us of the leeches, he called the village on his cell phone to explain our situation, telling them to send people to help.

View from the mountain trial on the way to Magulong

Peter, who was recovering from a serious chest infection, kept asking Stephen, "How much longer?"

Stephen always replied, "Only twenty minutes." It became a standing joke during our time in Magulong.

"When will we give out the balloons?"

"Twenty minutes."

"When will the church service start?"

"Twenty minutes."

In the gloom, eight villagers clambered down the slope, male and female, in their twenties, carrying flaming torches and flashlights that cast sinister shadows among the trees.

A young woman pulled me up. "Come Aunty, we help you."

Giggling and laughing, she and a young man pulled and pushed me up the path.

I could hear others trying to help Peter. "I'm fine. I don't need help. I'm not old and decrepit yet."

"Hey!" I called over my shoulder. "Who are you calling old and decrepit?"

Naga laughter filled the air. Eventually, five hours after starting our climb, we staggered, supported by villagers, toward the village entrance and stopped in amazement. Forgetting shaky legs and tiredness, we peered through the darkness at a huge blue banner strung high over the village gate.

It read:

To MR/MRS PETER N PAULINE
WEL-COME
TO MAGULONG

On each side of the gate, looking every inch the warrior, stood a man holding a spear and wearing traditional Naga regalia of hornbill-feather head dress and a black, red, and white woven cloth worn over one shoulder with enough length to cover his black loin cloth. Legs between knees and ankles were painted white. We felt humbled, stunned and speechless by such a welcome. They led the way through the wooden village gate set in a stone wall. We heard singing. Even though we were so late, the children were still waiting to sing to us. They stared at us wide-eyed, possibly the first westerners they had ever seen. Some children were confident, others wary, and some downright sleepy. Behind them, a group of villagers, accompanied by guitar and drum, were singing a welcome. Then it was the children's turn. Wearing school uniforms of light-blue shirts, navy ties and navy skirts or pants, they stood in rows in front of the villagers. The children sang two songs then the adults sang more songs to the beat of a drum and a guitar. Stephen introduced us to the village and school leaders and asked us to give a speech. Peter left that honor to me.

Stephen interpreted as I said, "We are delighted and honored to finally come to Magulong to meet you. You have given us a warm welcome. How could we resist such beautiful letters from the children? We were disappointed three years ago to come so close and yet be sent away because of our permit problem. We were looking forward to the big party you had planned. So here we are, having trotted up the mountain . . ." I paused and looked around, our saviors and others laughing at the joke. "Now we know the way, we will visit you many more times. Thank you."

Ebamle took us to our sleeping quarters in the Baptist Church office. Our makeshift bedroom was cozy with the bed covered in brightly colored, peony-patterned Chinese blankets to keep us warm in the chilly night air. A generator-powered fluorescent light lit the room.

As soon as we had caught our breath, we were shown our bathing facilities, a wooden-framed, corrugated-sheeted cubicle on stilts, with a slatted, wooden floor where water could drain away. A large aluminum container of water awaited us, supplemented with a bucket of warm water Oh, delight and joy! We washed away the journey's grime.

Refreshed, we visited the latrines—up steps cut into the hillside to a corrugated-roofed, concrete building, with "starting blocks" hole-in-the-ground toilets, which we flushed by pouring down a jug of water.

The village elders and officials gathered in our room, sitting on plastic chairs. They wore western dress of shirts, pants or jeans and padded thigh-length jackets. Some wore woolen knitted hats against the cold night air. Around their shoulders, two of the men wore traditional Naga woolen cloths in red, black and white of various designs. We ate sticky rice with our fingers, plates balanced on knees. Women working in the communal room kitchen brought in the food.

Ebamle asked, "Aunty, they killed a bear today. Do you want some?"

Unfortunately, I was not very hungry. To replenish my electrolytes, I had eaten a lot of salted nuts as soon as I found my bag. The Nagas, having hearty appetites, were most concerned at the measly amount of food we were eating. Word must have gotten back to the kitchen.

Ebamle's ebullient sister and her quiet husband, who cooked for communal activities, came to see what the problem was. Neither spoke English. Ebamle's sister launched into a mocking, humorous tirade. With arms waving and gesticulating, she complained to the elders for inviting weakling westerners to Magulong who would never become strong if they didn't eat her food. She flexed her biceps at us, shook her finger, "Eh! Ha!" She mimed eating, pointing to my plate and then mouth. When she had finished, she stood in the center of the room, arms akimbo. The village leaders looked on, wondering what our response would be.

"Nag, nag, nag, nag, nag," Peter said, using his hands to imitate her flapping lips.

Everyone burst out laughing. Ebamle's sister laughed, ruffled his hair and left saying the last word. One elder consulted his notes, and Stephen interpreted the plans laid out for the following day's activities. Ebamle began ushering people from the room, and the elders filed out.

Peter and I smiled at one another and slowly exhaled. We were about to fall into bed and pass out when in trooped Stephen with Ebamle and one of the school teachers intent on massaging our legs so our muscles would not be sore in the morning. When we finally relaxed, the massage was a very pleasant experience. Massage over, we jumped into bed just as the generator switched off, extinguishing the light.

We slept like the dead and woke to a bright, sunny day and a breakfast of boiled eggs and dried bananas in the communal hall next to our room. We spent the morning talking about the needs of the village school with teachers past and present. There were still thirty children in the village who were not being educated because of lack of funds even though the dedicated teachers were more or less volunteers with their low wages. The teachers told us they wanted colorful, educational posters for the classrooms. Stephen, probably to cement his standing with the village council, obtained a concrete promise from us to commit to funding the school for at least another ten years, which was our intention anyway.

We visited Ebamle's home to meet her seventy-eight-year-old mother and Ebamle's sister, who cared for her while Ebamle was in Dimapur running her hostel. Ebamle's mother did not speak English so we had little conversation. But Peter, fascinated by her amazing face with its high cheek bones, weathered skin and eyes that revealed a life of stoicism, courage, strength and sadness from the murder of her husband many years before, could not stop taking photographs of her. Her red cloth draped over her shoulders emphasized her regal bearing. She had an inner grace that commanded respect. We were amazed to learn that this diminutive, barefoot woman had made the strenuous journey to Dimapur six months earlier to visit her daughter. How she climbed back up the mountain, I'll never know. She had been bleeding from the rectum, a symptom of something as simple as hemorrhoids or as dangerous as cancer. We gave her healing, but I knew she needed more. I was so sorry we would soon be leaving.

Other difficulties Magulong villagers faced, apart from the struggle to educate their children, was life without medical care. If someone broke a leg, he would have to be carried down the mountain, across the river, and taken to the nearest medical facility, which was the Assam Rifles barracks where the medical officer offered his services to the Nagas. Only months before our visit, one young woman with three children lost her husband to a simple thing like blood poisoning because medical help and antibiotics could not be obtained in time.

After lunch, we blew up the balloons we had brought and dished them out to the children. We all had a great time playing. Then the children took part in competitive games, such as musical chairs, for

Mt. Kisha English School, Magulong, Manipur State

our entertainment. Peter and I sat in a tarpaulin shelter, protected from the sun during the day and chilly breezes at night, enjoying ourselves as much as the children did.

In the break before the commencement of the evening's entertainment, Peter and I returned to our room. Stephen kept appearing with mothers and grandmothers grateful for our sponsorship that allowed their children and grandchildren to attend school. With Stephen interpreting, they told us they had nothing, yet wanted us to take a small token of their appreciation such as a bag of rice, or chili powder, or dried bananas, or an egg or two.

Peter and I were overcome, often moved to tears, as these people, who had nothing, still found something to give to say "thank you." I had never felt so humble in my life.

That night, the children performed their dances on the earthen-floored school playground, lit by a solar-powered light on top of a tall pole. At the base of the pole, about thirty villagers had gathered to sing and play the drums to accompany the dancers, while saucer-sized, silvery-blue moths fluttered above their heads. Barefoot children lined up on the dance area, wearing their traditional dress—hornbill feather headdress, above-knee-length black cloth wrapped round the boys' waists. The girls wore longer black, red and white woven cloths that covered them from armpits to knees. Stephen announced the "Snake Dance." The drummer began with a strong steady beat. The singers took up the song, and the children began to move. In single file, they moved about the dance area imitating a snake's movements, the line twisting and turning, feet pounding the earth, arms lifting and lowering. More dancing and singing followed, each song ending with a rapid beating of the drum and a crescendo of ululating.

The evening was chilly. Thank goodness I was wearing a fleece Polartec jacket and a warm, traditional woolen *lungyi* (long wrap-round skirt woven in the village and given to me as a gift) over my jeans. Peter jokingly tried to take the hand-knitted muffler we had also been given from around my neck. Needless to say, generous hands knitted another muffler overnight to present to us the next day. The dancers' hands were freezing as they filed past to shake our hands before leaving. Stephen and the elders made more speeches, mainly of gratitude toward us and to encourage parents to send their children to school. I was asked to speak to the villagers.

"We are very happy to be here. It is our pleasure to help." Stephen translated as I spoke. "We consider your children to be also our children, and we are committed to sponsoring the school for at least another ten years." Stephen translated with a satisfied smile like a man who'd won the race. Adults and children alike enthusiastically applauded my speech. A village elder talked to Stephen, who then turned to us.

"Aunty, Uncle, the elders want me to ask about the money you lent Ebamle."

Ebamle was looking at the ground, her hands pressed together and held to her mouth as if in prayer.

"Ah yes, the money." I addressed the elders while Stephen interpreted. "The money we gave to Ebamle . . . was a gift. We don't want it back." The elders nodded their heads and murmured their satisfaction. I turned to Ebamle and smiled. "We only told her it was a loan so she would work hard to make her hostel business a success."

Her relieved smile lit up the night sky.

The pastor said a closing prayer and all dispersed. It had been a most enjoyable day.

Next morning, before breakfast, village leaders streamed into our room. They handed us Magulong's visitors' book and Mount Kisha English School's book.

"Please to write in books and sign," said one man.

Trina had written in the book in March 2000. Even as early as that, she was talking of the road coming to the village, which would surely make life easier. Everything villagers could not make from local jungle resources had to be carried up the mountain—plastic chairs, corrugated sheeting, bags of cement and other supplies. Now it was October 2011, and still the road had not reached the village. North-east tribal regions seemed to me to be neglected by India's central government.

We had been told the Baptist church service would begin at 6:30 a.m. Consequently, Peter and I were up and dressed early. No sign of Ebamle or Stephen. We went for tea in the communal room while we waited. Eventually, Stephen strolled in.

I asked, "What time does the service begin?"

"Twenty minutes," he said, with a grin.

Well, we knew what that meant—two hours. Then Ebamle arrived, and off we went for the service. Peter and I are not particularly religious, but the energy in the little church, packed as it was with a congregation united in a genuine adoration of the Lord, rapt attention to the pastor's words and enthusiastic hymn singing, felt good to us. We joined in as best we could, while the pastor preached partly in English to include us in the service.

After refreshments and a meal of sticky rice for the village children from the communal kitchen, we walked through the village with Stephen. He looked baggy-eyed and tired from all the interpreting he was doing, being a good host to us and catching up with friends and family. Dr. Chandra Disuang Zeme, the Baptist pastor who founded Mount Kisha English School in 1979, accompanied us, while Ebamle spent time with her mother.

We met with the some of the oldest villagers, two eighty-plus ladies, who were such close friends, they were practically joined at the hip, even when, amazingly, they squatted down on their haunches. Some homes we entered were made of stucco. But to meet the oldest man in the village, we went into a house constructed from bamboo. It was dark inside, with a floor of hardened earth. In the center of the living room, a wood-fire burned on top of a concrete hearth. Smoke escaped through a hole in the roof. Baskets were stashed above the rafters. Bunches of corn were hanging up to dry. Gleaming aluminum pots of various sizes lined shelves.

The oldest inhabitant came in, leaning on his staff and guided by his granddaughter. He was ninety-six, blind and wore a long-sleeved black fleece, a traditional woolen *lungyi* and flip-flops. Even if his back were not bent, he would have barely scraped four-foot ten inches.

He strongly grasped Peter's hand. "I am honored to meet you. We are all honored that you come to our village." Through Stephen and Dr. Chandra we asked questions about his life. Becoming weary, he brought our meeting to a polite end. "I am happy you are helping our school," he said and firmly shook our hands.

Outside again, we looked out over dense jungle-covered valleys and mountain ridges as far as the eye could see. In peaceful, beautiful Magulong, we felt as if we were at the top of the world. On the far side of the valley, brown patches on the hillsides indicated slash and burn agriculture was in use. As Stephen and Dr. Chandra told us about the village, we strolled along wide paths to arrive at an engraved stone marking both the silver jubilee and the 2009 golden jubilee of Magulong's youth club. The motto inscribed on the stone said: "We love and serve our people." It reflected what I'd seen in the village. Some of the elders may have been illiterate, but they were wise. In his soft-spoken voice, dignified Dr. Chandra explained, "The whole leadership of the village is intent on helping Magulong's children become educated and capable of fitting and excelling in the modern world."

"With your help, we will achieve this," Stephen said.

Magulong Village, NE India, overlooking mountain ridges

More strolling past the volley ball area brought us to Dr. Chandra's house. Built of stucco with wooden floors, this was the home of a middle-class Naga. We sat on chairs not benches, and Dr. Chandra's wife brought us tea not in bamboo cups but pottery cups. She served dried bananas and nuts. Dr. Chandra proudly told us, "My wife has a PhD, and all our four children have gone to college."

"That's quite a feat, Dr. Chandra. Have any gone into the church?" I asked.

"My youngest son, Raitu, is still studying. He wants to be a Baptist missionary."

Mrs. Chandra changed the subject. "Did the muffler I knit for you keep you warm?" she asked me.

"Oh, it was you who knit it! It's lovely. I didn't think it would get so cold at night. I really appreciated having it to keep me warm. Thank you."

As we were leaving, she showed me her vegetable garden full of the healthy green leaves of chilies, peppers, tomatoes, mustard and potatoes. She touched and stroked the plants like a woman in love.

We took our leave of Dr. and Mrs. Chandra, and Stephen took us to the morung, the bachelor dormitory system that was once an essential part of Naga life and culture, a symbol of pride for the village. Some villagers gathered to see us enter. It was a large wooden building with a high corrugated roof. The village's large drum was safely parked in the rafters. A bamboo frame hanging from the roof and holding six mithan horns dominated the interior space in keeping with the tradition of embellishing the morung with hunting trophies. After Stephen explained this to us, I spotted two women's breasts carved onto two posts and painted yellow.

"Hunting trophies?" I asked, laughing.

That brought forth a few embarrassed grins and laughs.

Our last visit before lunch was to the school. Adah, the headmaster, led the way to the oblong-shaped building with a very rusty metal roof that housed four classrooms and a teachers' room. The walls were part stucco, part corrugated panels and part woven bamboo. Each classroom contained benches for the pupils to sit on and a white wipe board. No wonder the teachers wanted colorful posters for the classrooms.

"We need art materials. We must make school interesting and attractive to persuade all the children in the village to attend," said Adah.

"We'll send money for that, Adah," Peter said.

It was time for lunch, and again we were not very hungry owing to the snacks we had eaten.

"Watch out, Peter. Ebamle's sister will scold us," I said.

Food was served buffet style. We put a few spoonfuls of food on our plates. Hands on hips, Ebamle's sister watched us with eagle eyes through the hatch from the kitchen. She turned to her husband behind her and said something that sounded like, "What is it with these westerners? They don't eat!"

Peter's fingers again imitated flapping lips. "Nag, nag, nag, nag, nag."

Her raucous laughter ricocheted round the room.

Stephen arranged demonstrations of basket making. Trina wanted us to record these skills, concerned they would soon disappear from the Naga way of life. Four village men, including the deacon, sat amicably in a group to show us their skills. While bantering with one another, they used sharp knives to split and shave bamboo to make various baskets. One man whipped together a loosely woven basket with a hole at one end. Explaining everything in Naga, he put his puppy inside so its head went through the hole. Through Stephen he explained he would then weave bamboo across the bottom and that's how they would transport a chicken to market. The weaver gently removed the trapped yelping pup from the carrier to sympathetic "aws" from watching villagers. Another man's deft fingers wove contrasting colored bands into his zigzag design for a square basket. Loosely woven baskets were used to carry produce. Closely woven baskets were used for sturdy tasks, even for sitting on. The rest of the afternoon was devoted to handing out pens and notebooks to the children and watching them play more games. That evening, the Women's Village Council danced for us. They invited us to join in the dance. I followed their steps quite well. Peter was doing his own thing, of course, but his antics made the villagers laugh. The children recited poetry and sang songs in a talent competition. The village had brought in a professional local comedian, and even though he spoke only in Naga, his voice inflections and body language had us rolling around laughing and gasping for breath. More speeches by the elders urging parents to send their children to school and prayers from the deacon, brought our final night in Magulong to an end.

I sat on the bed, knees bent to my chin. "I wish we'd planned to stay longer. It's so beautiful here. No traffic, the air is clean, the view fantastic. The people are wonderful. I don't want to go. No wonder Ebamle comes here four or five times a year."

"I've enjoyed it, too," Peter said, kicking off his shoes.

"But I don't want to leave!"

"We'll come back, Pauline, many times, until we're too old to climb that bloody mountain."

I laughed at my struggle to get here. "I'm already planning our next trip."

Villagers still brought gifts up to the moment we left. A spear and shield and baskets had to be hastily packed to keep them safe. The villagers lined up outside the church to bid us farewell. We walked along the line, shaking hands, cracking jokes through mime about Peter's dancing, getting another scolding from Ebamle's sister who told me I would not get down the mountain because I ate so little. I stopped her in mid–sentence and mimed how vigorous I was, pumping my arms as if I were speed walking, which made her and her friends laugh.

Villagers walked with us to the village gate, singing and playing their drums. They had composed a song for our departure, the gist being why did we come only to go, leaving them feeling so sad. But no tears, because Aunty and Uncle would soon return and bring their great grandson Thomas. (Ebamle had shown them his Facebook pictures on her I-phone.)

We had been in Magulong only two days and three nights, living in a warm cocoon of affection. It felt like home. Never in our lives had we felt so much love and welcoming.

Although the walk downhill was much easier than climbing up, it was not without incident. We had to pass a nest of dangerous, giant bees. Fortunately, the path was wide at that point, and we were able to keep our distance.

We reached a resting place, but rest would have to wait. Ebamle shoved Peter and me up a tree where someone had placed logs in the branches for people to sit on and enjoy the view from this vantage point. Ebamle sat beside me and pointed out her family's fields in the valley below. Scrub-covered hills rose up sharply in a semi-circle round the cultivated patch.

"It takes two hours to reach the fields from the village and then, after a hard day's work, it is another two-hour walk home, carrying our produce." Ebamle told us.

Next, Stephen spotted a small snake lurking by the path. Using a long twig, he pulled it into the open and squashed the red and yellow striped reptile underfoot, twisting and rubbing his sports shoe into the dirt until the snake was dead. Then he kicked it over the precipice. He saw my enquiring look.

"It was dangerous, a krait. One bite and you die in less than a minute" he said.

Oh boy!

Forty minutes later, as we trekked single file down the path, I lost my footing on dry soil like marbles that propelled me on my back towards the edge of the one thousand-foot precipice. I felt no panic. I was right in the moment, my mind dead calm. Nothing else existed. *I'm going over the edge.* I cast about for some way to save myself and saw the bamboo staff in my hand, cut for me by the young Naga man we met at the foot of the mountain. *That's all I've got. How can I use it?* Hearing alarmed cries from our Naga friends behind me, Peter, in the lead, looked back to see me going over the side of the mountain.

Horrified, he screamed, "Pauline!" and ran back up the path.

At least I'm going to my death knowing how much he loves me. Then over I went. I rolled my body to ram the bamboo staff into the mountainside, where it held firm on a sapling root. Feeling around with my feet, I found a tiny toe-hold. As I shifted my weight to precarious toe-hold from the staff before it gave way, animated Naga voices saying something akin to "Holy Shit!" penetrated my concentration. Hands reached down into my armpits and yanked me back onto the path. From start to finish, the whole episode took only ten seconds.

Peter reached me.

"From the way you called my name I could almost believe you love me," I said.

He hugged me so tightly I could hardly breathe. "Don't be daft, you've got the cash and passports in your fanny pack."

I gave his arm a playful slap.

Our Naga guides were fussing and checking me out for injury. After all, I was an old woman to them and on top of that, we'd just promised to support the school for a minimum of another ten years.

Not to be outdone, an hour or so later, Peter wrenched his knee and could barely walk. So we ended our journey ignominiously, being lifted, pulled and pushed up steep slippery paths, over a wet, slick bamboo bridge and down deep treacherous slopes like the old fogies that we were, stripped of our illusions that we were intrepid adventurers.

But one advantage of age is poor memory, and it wasn't long before we were planning our next trip to Magulong.

TWENTY-SEVEN

Over the next couple of years, Peter and I rebuilt our health, seriously compromised by the unrelenting stress of dealing with cancer followed by the demands made upon us during our stint of elder care and Peter losing his job in the recession. Donna and Thomas, emotionally healed from the divorce and ready to move on with their lives, left us to move into their own accommodation. Exhaustion be damned, we forced ourselves to catch up on home maintenance and painting after twelve years of neglect.

My hair stylist, Phyllis, and a few of my friends contributed money to add to our donations to the school, which allowed every child in Magulong to be educated. Things were looking up. Without health insurance for three years after Peter was laid off, we finally qualified for Medicare. First thing I did was make an appointment for a colonoscopy. It wasn't that I was worried that cancer had returned, but as a practical person, it was a wise thing to do.

Even ten years after the cancer treatments, I still exhibited signs of post traumatic stress and was bawling my eyes out when the doctor came into his office.

"Do you want to tell me about it?" he asked.

"You need to know I don't want to be here. I hate doctors, but it's better that I'm crying than filled with rage." I told him of my horrific experiences during cancer treatments and the aftermath of them. "I didn't think I'd be farting my way across a room at only fifty-five years of age."

I think I surprised him with my frankness, and he surprised me by listening. Anyway, the colonoscopy revealed healthy insides. No worries.

We planned a trip to England. John, Peter's brother-in-law, had died of lung cancer, and Peter's sister Jean wanted to scatter John's ashes on the North Yorkshire Moors, where he had loved to hike as a young man. The occasion turned into a multi-generational family reunion. Before leaving America, Trina told me Ebamle's mother was dying of colon cancer. I was distraught. I didn't know why. I had only met with her for two hours in her house in Magulong, yet somehow she had made a strong impact on me. I sent her distant healing and continued the practice while I was with Joanne in Uckfield. I tried sending Ebamle's mother healing on the Monday we drove north on Britain's M1 motorway, only Ebamle's mother came to me and told me, "No more." I knew then that she had died, which was confirmed by an email I received from Trina three days later.

Returning to Florida, I felt Ebamle's mother nagging me to do something. I phoned Ebamle and together we wept. I put down the phone, turned to Peter and said, "I have to go to Ebamle. I know we're broke after our trip, but I have to go and see her."

He nodded. "That's what credit cards are for. Go for it."

Ebamle was amazed and flattered that I was prepared to travel half way around the world to see her. At first, I didn't know why I was there in Dimapur. I arrived in the middle of a curfew after one Naga tribesman had been beaten to death by different Naga tribesmen for stealing a motorcycle. The area was in an uproar. The following day, after the elders had a pow-wow and sorted the matter out, the curfew was lifted.

I stayed in the cheapest hotel room possible. It was excessively hot and the room lacked air conditioning. Even the fan on highest speed could not help sweat-soaked me get even a few hours sleep while I was there. Ebamle was busy with her hostel duties, but we grabbed some time together, sharing crying sessions about losing our mothers.

"Was it bad for your mother at the end, Ebamle?"

"No, Aunty. She was up and moving about with no pain right up until the day before she died. Then she took to her bed and died in her sleep."

I offered a silent prayer. I was so choked at that point I couldn't speak. She had died without pain. The healing had helped her. Thank you God!

I pulled myself together, blinking back the tears pooling in my eyes.

"Ebamle," I said, "I know why I'm here. Now that your mother has died, she wants me to be your mother. So, from now on you have Peter and me as your parents to watch over you. You are our daughter."

Ebamle's stricken expression vanished like trapped frantic butterflies released from a jar. She lifted her head, straightened her hunched shoulders, the yoke of grief lifted. Ebamle had been lost without an elder to watch out for her. Now she had two. An added bonus, I found out when she proudly introduced me to her neighbor as her American mother, was the status she thought such an arrangement offered her.

A year later, in October 2013, Peter and I returned to Dimapur, where we met up with Ebamle and our fellow travelers to Magulong—Lucy, Trina's cousin; American Michael Heneise, studying for his PhD in anthropology and living in nearby Kohima, with his Naga wife; and our friend Trina, who was going to be interviewed by journalist Esha Roy for an article in the *Indian Express* newspaper. Phyllis, my hairstylist, should have been with us, but a family emergency caused her to back out the day before we left Naples.

Recent, prolonged, heavy rains had washed away roads and left others in desperate need of repair. We lurched along, in and out of potholes, feeling sick with tension. I grabbed what reassurance I could from the driver being steady and careful, but at the worst places, all eyes were on the road, willing us a safe passage, accompanied by occasional gasps and muffled screams. Conversation dried up. With the bottom of the SUV scraping along the road at times, we held our breath, fearing the oil sump would be ripped off, leaving us stranded out in the wilds. The journey to Katang took three hours longer than usual, and we were concerned nightfall would soon be upon us.

In 2011, when we traveled to Magulong, the road ended at Katang, and then we hiked five hours up the mountain. But we understood a new road had been built. Because the villagers were excited about the new road from Katang to Magulong, we were too, until we saw a large truck, big enough to carry a dozen sheep in the back. It may have been in its prime fifty years ago but didn't look so good now. The young Naga driver told us the rains had made it impossible for the jeep taxi to reach the village. Therefore, we would travel by truck.

Disbelieving stares. Nobody was happy. We were exhausted, behind schedule and eager to reach Magulong, but not this way.

Anxiety knots played havoc with our intestines. Me most of all. I was intimately acquainted with the steep precipice that ran alongside the new road. I'd been lucky to escape with my life. If the road was too difficult for the four-wheel-drive Jeep, I had no confidence in truck travel, especially this decrepit wreck. I was ready to go on strike.

Night fell. I sat up front with Lucy and the young driver. The short drive from Katang to the bottom of the mountain was along a narrow muddy road to the new cement river bridge that replaced the bamboo poles we used to edge across. The next part of the journey had been an extremely steep path. Now it was an extremely steep road. My heart was in my mouth, my fists clenched as the truck skidded and struggled, bouncing like a kangaroo on a leash to ascend. Petrified, I clenched my jaw to stop from screaming. It was getting late, and the school children would be waiting to welcome us. After numerous skids in the mud brought us too close to the precipice, Lucy could take it no longer. "Let me out! Stop this truck and let me out!" she demanded. "I'll walk to the village." I joined her, slipping from the seat faster than leaping from a sinking ship into a lifeboat. Even though it would take us at least four hours walking, joy welled up inside. I had escaped what I perceived to be great danger.

The truck drove on without us. Minutes later we heard it revving, struggling to get out of another tight spot. Thank God Lucy and I were walking, but would the others be safe? Forty minutes later, we met up with everyone at the road-construction-workers' camp, where Indian laborers provided hot, sweet tea to calm our frazzled nerves. With our truck driver finally conceding he could not get us to the village, the work-crew boss offered to take us in a vehicle called a gypsy, similar to a four-wheel-drive pick-up truck with a canopy. We piled in with our mud-covered bags and crossed our fingers. The gypsy safely transported us to the village gate, a gap in a dry-stone, six-foot wall that protected the southern side of the village.

The Naga custom is to carry honored guests into the village. Trina was *the* honored guest as both she and her mother were adopted Nagas, and Magulong had hosted her parents' Naga wedding in the 1940s. But because there were so many of us, the villagers tied ropes to the gypsy instead and pulled us into the village, all the while singing a welcome accompanied by drums.

The Baptist church's office had again been converted to sleeping quarters for us. Five twin beds and a double for me and Peter were squeezed in. We were all going to sleep together. Cozy. Following food and refreshments, we met with the available villagers. Many others were disappointed we were visiting in October when they were away, harvesting in the fields. We struggled to keep our eyes open while the village council outlined the program they had planned for our stay. Then, exhausted, we stumbled to our beds and collapsed.

Peter and I woke early, eager to look around Magulong, the place we called paradise. We had little choice really, the cockerels started crowing at 3:00 a.m., although nobody else stirred. We quietly slipped on some clothes, grabbed our cameras and left the room.

We looked down at the carpet of mist covering the valley and the sun creeping above the horizon, sluggish as if suffering from a hangover in the cold November sky. Peter and I strode out. Soon we were face to face with mithans (mit-hans), big, black beasts with buffalo horns. We weren't sure how tame they were. It was the first time we had come across these semi-domesticated cattle in the village. Thankfully, the wide, unpaved path allowed us to skirt past them without incident. The village spread out on a small plateau of land. To the west, higher hills, covered in jungle, curved around the settlement. To the south, we looked out at ridges of purple hills as far as the horizon. So peaceful. So clean. As we ambled along, grunting pigs and clucking hens announced their desire for breakfast. People were stirring in their homes.

Stephen found us. "Come. Breakfast is ready." We followed him to the communal room.

Later that day, while the children were participating in a drawing competition, a jolt of electricity hit me on recognizing one villager, a grandmother we met the last time we were in Magulong. She had been on our minds because she had looked so ill, and we had not expected to find her alive for this second visit. Yet here she was, alive and well. Filled with joy, I rushed to her and gave her a quick hug.

Words tumbled from my lips. "Oh, I'm so happy to see you! You looked so ill the last time we were here! Look at you now! You look great!"

She didn't understand English. I looked round for help. Adah was approaching. I explained my happiness at seeing her. I could hardly stand still, a dog wagging its tail. "Adah, please tell her how delighted we are that she is looking so well."

She took my hand and spoke. Adah interpreted "She was very sick for a while, but she got medicine, and now she is well."

The next few days were a blur of activities. Trina, Michael, Lucy and Esha went on an eight-hour expedition to climb Mt. Kisha, accompanied, encouraged and supported by young men and women thrilled to be showing visitors their sacred place. Peter did not feel well enough to make the climb in the heat and humidity, so we stayed in the village. We strolled around taking photographs. One of his jobs later in the day would be to take a portrait photograph of every child in the school for the parents.

We stopped at a gravestone near the school. A village elder dressed in western-style pants and a tank top approached us. He was a former headmaster of the school and spoke English. He drew himself up, puffed out his chest and pointed to the gravestone.

"This is my grandfather. He was the first Naga in the area to become Baptist."

Moving on, we found beautiful bushes of blue flowers to photograph and played peek-a-boo with young children to capture their happiness. Later that afternoon, as we rested outside the communal meeting room, the intrepid explorers returned. The

Nagas almost bounced into the village. Michael strode in, tired, hot and sticky.

He excitedly told us, "It was an amazing climb. I took risks I normally wouldn't, but it was so exhilarating. I've got to persuade some of my climbing buddies to come with me so I can climb it again."

Esha, Lucy and Trina arrived drenched in sweat with overheated red faces. A village girl served cooling drinks before our friends took to the wash-house for cool, refreshing washes. Peter and I were glad we hadn't gone. Listening to Michael, it sounded as if you had to be sure-footed to safely make the climb.

Recovered from the day's exertions, we sat beneath the tarpaulin shelter erected for our visit. While we waited for the entertainment to begin, Michael played guitar and amused the children. I envied him. He was a natural who could play many songs and draw the children in to participate. The favorite game of the night was "Bang the Drum," the Naga version of "Pin the Tail on the Donkey." Most children took part.

Then two children pulled my arms. "Come play, Aunty."

Wanting to make the children laugh, I did my Charlie Chaplin act. My heart filled with joy when they laughed even harder when I tried to bang the drum at the opposite side of the tent to where it was situated. Many pairs of feet shuffled into place as teachers lined up the school choir. I noticed they enjoyed singing so much, they burst into song at any opportunity. Despite the youngest being four, not one child sang out of tune. As on our first visit, adults frantically blew up balloons and attached string to them, gifts the children received as enthusiastically as they had previously. A short break, then the traditional dance shows began. All visitors joined in. Peter, as always, cheered the villagers with his own version of the dances.

The night ended in speeches. Grateful parents stood in turn to thank us for making it possible for their children to attend school. All one hundred and five children in the village were being educated to fifth-grade level. Our new goal is to ensure that every child in

Magulong who wants it will receive a secondary education. We gave speeches to encourage parents to send their children to school and to

Pauline dancing with the villagers

listen to the advice of their village elders. Though most of the elders were illiterate, they were wise and knew that education was needed in the modern world.

Next day, checking out school supplies and equipment with headmaster Adah Newme, we were appalled at how bad things were. The cupboard contained the few books we had sent. The ancient, battered typewriter had died. Embarrassed, Adah pressed a few keys and shrugged. No response from the typewriter. Poor Adah was reduced to writing out hundreds of exam papers by hand. When Peter and I were sponsoring on our own, all we could afford to cover were teachers' salaries. Now, with our friends' involvement, more assistance was available.

"Adah," I told him, "you'll have the money for a computer and printer and art materials before we leave the village, and we'll send tons more reference and reading books."

His face lit up like sunshine bursting through a cloud. He took us to the staff room. With a big grin, he pointed to the wall above the door. We were surprised and flattered to see a framed photograph of me and Peter hanging there.

"To honor you, Aunty and Uncle."

We handed over to Adah the gifts we brought for the children—notebooks and pens, and remembering what he had said during our last visit about making school attractive enough so that the children will want to come, we gave him basketballs, volleyballs, and soccer balls. He was delighted. So was Baptist minister Dr. Chandra Disuang-Zeme, founder of Mt. Kisha English School. Thanks to our friends' involvement, the school's bookshelves held increasing numbers of books, the children had uniforms, art materials, and soon a computer and printer—even if it could only be used when the generator was running in electricity-lacking Magulong.

Our last night in the village, Peter and I watched the sunset over the mountains, wanting to soak in every drop of beauty before the heaviness of leaving made us withdraw inside ourselves. Next morning, we set off early, preferring to walk down the mountain for three hours rather than risk making the descent in a vehicle. Some of the ruts in the muddy road were eighteen inches deep. The young college-educated school teachers accompanied us. They had previously worked in Delhi, mainly in call centers, but because they were tribal people, they met with much prejudice and were treated as second-class citizens in India. Our donations allowed them to earn a living in Magulong, without having to leave village life and their unique culture, which kept the village alive and vibrant.

Our invigorating walk brought us to the bottom of the mountain. We rested and ate boiled eggs, crackers, oranges and bananas while waiting for stragglers to catch up.

A JCB backhoe loader arrived with the rest of our group, the driver having given them a ride down the mountain.

He waved us over. "Come, I take you to Katang."

My immediate thought was "Hell, no!" The man was crazy, wanting to squeeze all fourteen of us into a small backhoe! Then I looked at the quagmire on the far side of the bridge. The thought of putting my feet in ankle-deep liquid mud and ruining my new sports shoes made me cringe. I promptly changed my mind.

With tires barely staying on the edge of the narrow buffalo-wallow-road to Katang, I said silent thankful prayers for the driver's meticulous, cautious driving. He knew his vehicle. At times, when we were dangerously close to falling down the cliff into the river, he would stop and lower the bucket to push us back onto firmer footing on the slick road. The silence of dread or smothered squeaks of terror from those of us, including me, squished in the cab, accompanied his efforts. Ebamle and five Naga villagers rode up front in the bucket; others clung like limpets to the outside of the JCB. Most of the time, I watched them closely for a change in expression that would signal our demise. The rest of the time, I closed my eyes and prayed for safe passage and that my terror-driven nausea would not erupt over my fellow passengers. Once past the most precarious section of the road, the driver rumbled on at walking pace to the waiting jeep taxi.

Exultant in his triumph for delivering us safely, the driver was busy shaking hands with his passengers descending from his vehicle with nervous shaky laughter. I stumbled from the JCB on wobbly legs and rummaged in my fanny-pack.

"Here, take this," I said to the driver, thrusting a few hundred rupees into his hand. "Thank you so much for getting us here safely." I felt almost drunk with relief.

He tried to refuse. Peter approached and put his hand on the driver's shoulder. "Take it. It's a small reward for what you did."

The next day, back in Dimapur, we spent time at Ebamle's hostel, recognizing many of the children from earlier visits. The children played guitar and sang for us. Half of them, bright but poor, stayed at the hostel for free, subsidized by Ebamle. She also employed two Magulong girls to help her care for the children and the hostel.

Sharing good fortune, that's all it took to make life better for a village. So far we have made two visits to Magulong, and each time Peter and I were overwhelmed by the villagers' expressions of appreciation. They couldn't believe that people so far away would help their children. We had not yet left Nagaland, but were already looking forward to our next visit to the people we considered extended family. Hopefully, Phyllis and our great grandson Thomas would be with us.

TWENTY-EIGHT

I was feeling pleased with myself for writing another two books and had my next one planned, so when I went to my ophthalmologist, his words stunned me as much as if he had bludgeoned me over the head with a huge club. "You have dry macular degeneration. It's reached intermediate stage. With your family history, we'd better test you for a gene that hastens the condition along." (It turned out I did have the gene.)

"Is there any treatment?" I asked. "Stem-cell treatment?"

"No, not yet. We *are* moving towards treatment, but none is available now."

I was pensive driving home. I'd witnessed firsthand how blindness can detract from your quality of life when I took care of my elderly parents. Only two years earlier the disease was barely a blip in my eyes. Now, it had reached the intermediate stage. What would it be like in five years? Would I be blind then?

"No treatment," my ophthalmologist had said.

And I was supposed to accept that?

Hell no!

I emailed Don Margolis, chairman of the world's only stem-cell patient advocacy organization, The Repair Stem Cell Institute. I had been corresponding with Don on an annual basis, seeking stem-cell treatment for the internal scar tissue I had as a result of the severe radiation burns during my cancer treatments in 2002. I trusted this man to point me in the right direction. "I'll go anywhere in the world for treatment," I had written. "I do not want to go blind."

A few hours later, he phoned me. "I know of three doctors who can treat you. I'll talk to them and get back to you within a week."

A week later, having robbed my retirement account to make a down payment to the hospital, I had my doctor and plane tickets. Accompanied by Peter, I was going to Bangkok for stem-cell treatment offered by Dr. Torsak of Better Being Hospital. Don had told me the treatment involved injecting stem cells into my eyes. The thought of it almost made me pass out in fright. Peter, being Peter, was filled with misgivings in case the whole setup was a con.

A Better Being representative met us at Bangkok airport. He expedited our immigration processing and drove us to the hospital. Peter wanted to check it out before going to our hotel. "If I don't like it, we're outta here," he said.

Gentle, smiling staff greeted us and happily showed us round the facilities. In the physical therapy room, our hearts were captured by a distressed ten-month-old boy. We later learned his central-nervous-system condition developed after having vaccinations. His parents brought him to the hospital from Malawi, Central Africa.

Dr. Torsak spoke with us, telling us what to expect and no, he would not be injecting stem cells into my eyes. Stem cells would be injected behind my eyeballs as well as into my spinal cord. The stem cells came from umbilical cords and were processed in China. That was good to know because I'd heard that embryonic stem cells could cause tumors to develop in the recipient.

"The success rate is fifty percent," Dr. Torsak said. "You probably will not notice any benefit for three to six months. However, if we are not successful this time, you can return after six months and try again."

Wanting me to receive every benefit the hospital could offer, he asked more questions and discovered I had a whiplash injury and soft-tissue damage to my leg from two separate car accidents thirteen years earlier. He promised I would receive other treatments, such as hyperbaric oxygen treatments, physical and aqua therapies, acupuncture, and nutritional counseling. With its holistic approach, the hospital provided all my meals, healthy food full of protein, vegetables, fruit and some yogurt.

We were taken to our nearby hotel. Patients with serious mobility limitations stayed in resident suites at the hospital. Peter and I heaved a sigh of relief. The energy and atmosphere in the hospital felt warm and comforting. I liked their all-encompassing approach to health. We were happy with our choice.

Next day, I received my treatment timetable. The program would keep me busy five hours a day for two weeks. The rest of the time I mostly slept, my reaction to assimilating the stem cells. I received four stem-cell injections, each four days apart. Dr. Kiti, as I called him, unable to remember, never mind pronounce, his name properly, kept reassuring me the treatment would not hurt. The first injection was into my arm, the second into my spinal cord. The third, the one that terrified me the most, was going to be behind my right eye. Knowing how fearful I was, the staff tranquilized me before the procedure. It didn't hurt, not one bit. Gentle Dr. Kiti was the doctor responsible for giving the injections and acupuncture treatments. When it was time for my final eye injection, I turned down tranquilizing help.

"I'm embarrassed for being such a baby. You're so good, I don't feel a thing" I told him.

"I try to treat each patient as if I were treating my five-year-old daughter," Dr. Kiti said.

During one acupuncture treatment, Dr. Kiti told me he had studied in Texas and was certified by the American Academy of Anti-aging Medicine. Peter usually accompanied me to my sessions, and Dr. Kiti enjoyed Peter's wit. So when I asked Dr. Kiti if his acupuncture treatments would reduce my wrinkles, Peter quipped, "He doesn't have enough needles." Despite doing his best to maintain his professional demeanor, Dr. Kiti couldn't stop giggling.

Going to Better Being Hospital was a highlight in our lives. Something special happened there. To experience the camaraderie with the other people in treatment was inspiring and heartwarming. Staff and patients alike rooted for one another—the Italian father attempting to heal multiple sclerosis, there with his wife and young son; the woman from Eastern Europe, with Lou Gehrig's disease, accompanied by her sister; the man from California, paralyzed from the chest down after a car accident, who traveled to Bangkok with his father; me wanting to save my sight; and other people dealing with cerebral palsy and brain damage—people from every continent all fighting for health, alongside one another, within the cocoon called Better Being Hospital.

We only knew these people for one to two weeks, but the improvements we saw in their walking, and in the paralyzed California man who was able to put on his shirt by himself for the first time in years, touched us deeply. Big battles for wholeness were being fought before our eyes with the main weapon being stem cells.

It looks as if I could be one of the lucky fifty percent. At my last eye test, the ophthalmologist told me I only had early stage macular degeneration. That's a step down from the intermediate level I was diagnosed with twelve months earlier.

I feel blessed. And now I search for stem-cell treatments becoming available to repair the damage caused by the radiation burns. It will come, and I will do it, because, folks, I'm still pedaling, and will be until the day I die.

Lessons from my life:

- Fill the day with love.

- Love your neighbor as you would like to be loved.

- Your greatest enemy is your greatest spiritual teacher.

- Before you were born you entered into a contract to do certain things in your earthly life to enhance your spiritual growth.

- I can hand over to God people who have done me wrong. He is bigger and stronger than I'll ever be. Knowing that God is taking care of everything frees me of any negative emotions so I can fill my day with love.

Book Club Questions

1. What was the most devastating experience for Pauline, and how did she cope with it?

2. What signs did Pauline receive that showed God was with her through her most difficult times?

3. What was most influential in changing monstrous child Pauline into sponsor of Mt. Kisha English School?

4. The fact that Pauline's father was in India during WWII led her to Ursula Graham Bower's story and sponsorship of Mt. Kisha English School. Do you believe, as Pauline does, that God was laying out her life's path long before she was born?

5. Did the proofs of an afterlife Pauline received in the spiritualist church help you to believe life exists after death? If yes, why?

Made in the USA
Lexington, KY
31 December 2018